Praise

"This book by the dynamic duo that led NASA's culture transformation is a hands-on guide to building and evolving values, norms and routines. If you're trying to make your team or your organization more effective, innovative, or reliable, there's something to learn in these pages."

Adam Grant | #1 *New York Times* bestselling author of *Think Again* and host of the TED podcast *WorkLife*

"Drs. Meade and Gallaher bring a unique perspective on organizational culture in *The Missing Links*. Their passion and expertise for helping leaders align culture is evident, and I highly recommend this as a valuable read for forward-thinking leaders. Don't miss the chance to learn from the people who helped transform the culture at NASA Kennedy Space Center after tragedy struck."

Dr. Tasha Eurich | Organizational Psychologist and *New York Times* bestselling author of *Insight* and *Bankable Leadership*

"Dr. Meade and Dr. Gallaher have written a truly timely and insightful book for our time. In *The Missing Links*, you can find a wonderfully woven framework and actionable steps for an organization to truly design and elevate organizational culture, leadership development, and employee engagement. Whether the reader is a founder, an HR professional, a passionate contributor, a leader, or someone just curious about organization culture and change, this book is for you. Applying the lessons for all of us in this complex, hyperconnected time from the Space Shuttle disasters to racial injustice to the global pandemic, Drs. Meade and Gallaher apply systems thinking, organizational design, and leadership thinking in a holistic and understandable way."

Dr. Patrick Simpkins | Aerospace and Systems Thinking Consultant, Former Director of Engineering and Technology Development and former Director of Human Resources for NASA's Kennedy Space Center

"This is the best book I've read on creating an effective organizational culture. It presents an easy-to-follow roadmap about the puzzle pieces (missing links) that need to fall into place for an organization to thrive. Phillip Meade and Laura Gallaher share their rich, first-hand experience from helping to reconstruct the culture at the Kennedy Space Center after the *Columbia* Space Shuttle tragedy. They know what they're talking about and they know how to write about it, making this a compelling 'must read' for anyone hoping to create an effective organizational culture."

James Tamm | Co-author of *Radical Collaboration: Five Essential Skills to Overcome Defensiveness and Build Successful Relationships*

"One of the most asked questions in the world today is 'how did we get here?'
That is followed closely by 'how can this be possible?' These two questions speak to culture and accountability and when it comes to these two concepts, a lot of us have wondered about the how without investigating the why. That's exactly what Dr. Laura Gallaher and Dr. Philip Meade set out to do with *The Missing Links*.
The book is written in a way that equips you with the skills needed to deconstruct the culture of whatever institution you participate in while simultaneously providing action items for you to apply.
Their intersectional approach never leaves you thinking that this book is just for the office. You come away with a clear idea of what the big picture of humanity could look like if we work together to fix OUR missing links."

Tayo Rockson | Author, Speaker, Consultant, and Professor

"I'm grateful to work with Dr. Meade and Dr. Gallaher directly, and I can attest to the impact this work has had on the culture of my organization. The approach they describe in this book is just the right balance of the human element and business goals. *The Missing Links* model shows leaders how those things work hand in hand, rather than working against each other, and I highly recommend this read for any purpose-driven leader who genuinely cares about people.

Suneera Madhani | CEO and Founder, Stax by Fattmerchant

"*The Missing Links* is a powerful book to help leaders see the value of self-awareness when it comes to creating effective organizational cultures. As somebody who has worked with organizations for decades, and a Master Licensed Human Element® Practitioner, I love the way the authors have supported their culture model with research while making the ideas accessible to any leader who wants to improve organizational performance."

Ethan Schutz | President and CEO of The Schutz Company

"I've always been proud of the culture at our company, but I know how critical it is to keep evolving. Healthy things grow, growing things change, change challenges us—and it's been very impactful to work with the team at Gallaher Edge. The concepts in this book have been very helpful to take our organization to the next level—I highly recommend this read for any leader who cares about their company's culture."

Heath Ritenour | CEO of Insurance Offices of America

"This book answered a lot of the questions that my team and I had about what our culture will look like once we get back into the office. If you want a fresh start with your team or just want to make some adjustments, check out *The Missing Links*. You won't be disappointed."

Shawn Johal | Business Growth Coach, Elevation Leaders and best-selling author of *The Happy Leader*

"Buy this book for your psychology student or the culture geek at your office now! *The Missing Links* ties together our 'human-ness' with the sometimes-less-than-human aspects of company culture and organization management. I won't be surprised to find myself going back to this book again and again."

Glenn Hopper | CFO, Sandline Discovery

"Who knew the organizational culture of a company could literally save lives? I learned so much from reading *The Missing Links*. If you need a book to help you take action within your own organization, look no further."

Tamara Nall | CEO & Founder, The Leading Niche and *USA Today* bestselling author featured in *Business Success Secrets*

"Fans of the *Challenger* documentary on Netflix will absolutely love this book! This interesting theory on organizational culture is supported by the work done after Drs. Gallaher and Meade at NASA. Come for the fascinating story, stay for the powerful lessons that these authors learned along the way."

Paul Gunn | CEO, KUOG Corporation

The Missing Links:

Launching a High Performing Company Culture

Phillip Meade, PhD
Laura Gallaher, PhD

Leaders
Press

ISBN 978-1-63735-088-1 (pbk)
ISBN 978-1-63735-089-8 (e-book)

SIMON &
SCHUSTER

Print Book Distributed by Simon & Schuster
1230 Avenue of the Americas
New York, NY 10020

Library of Congress Control Number: 2021907344

Dedication

We humbly dedicate this book to the courageous astronauts who risked and lost their lives during STS-107. Their belief in NASA's mission to further our human understanding of ourselves, our world, and our universe is inspiring.

Table of Contents

Foreword

It's rare that you come across a book that is incredibly practical and pure in its scientific basis. This is such a book. Dr. Phillip Meade and Dr. Laura Gallaher know what they're talking about. They are masters at understanding and explaining Organizational Psychology.

This book clearly explains how organizational culture is the vehicle through which leaders can create and guide organizational performance.

It's no secret that organizational culture is the super-power to the well-informed leader. But until this point, no book has been written for the everyday leader by a true Industrial-Organizational Psychologist *and* an Industrial Engineer with education and research experience and who are also out in the trenches as consultants and entrepreneurs.

That's what makes this book different.

It's a book about organizational culture from experts, not just journalists. Dr. Meade and Dr. Gallaher are culture scientists. They've used their training at NASA and other high-stakes organizations and environments.

They have much more than the advised 10,000 hours of expertise. They work with leaders and organizations of varying shapes and sizes every single day.

This book makes organizational culture not only compelling but comprehensible. By the time you're done with this book, and long before, you will know how culture works. You'll also know how to craft, create, and wield culture to create the environments and outcomes you want.

This is a master class in leadership and organizational success. It's also insanely inspiring and practical.

I am an Organizational Psychologist and have spent the past ten years studying behavior change, leadership, and group dynamics. I became connected with Laura when she commented on one of my articles on Medium. She found me because I was the number one writer on Medium at the time, and the content spoke to her. When I saw what she had to say, I immediately wrote back and told her, "We have to connect!"

Within the week, we were on a call, comparing notes and talking about organizational psychology. And then, within one month, we shared a stage at TEDx Orlando.

I was so impressed with Laura's passion for her work and her perspective. And when you combine her experience and passion with Phillip's complementary background in industrial engineering, you create a partnership that brings such uniqueness to organizational culture.

Read this book and be equipped. Read this book and become the leader you truly want to be. This book will give you the inspiration, the tools, and the science.

You'll never see leadership the same way again. You'll know exactly what to do and why.

—Dr. Benjamin Hardy, best-selling author of *Willpower Doesn't Work*, *Personality Isn't Permanent*, and *Who Not How*

Introduction

Who Are We?

SPACE SHUTTLE COLUMBIA DISINTEGRATING OVER TEXAS

The space shuttle *Columbia* was returning home after a successful sixteen-day scientific mission. After orbiting the earth 255 times and traveling 6,600,000 miles, the crew was a mere sixteen minutes from touching down at the Kennedy Space Center's Shuttle Landing Facility. Suddenly, flight controllers lost communications with the crew and vehicle as the orbiter broke apart over Texas and Louisiana. A hole in the leading edge of the wing had allowed superheated gas to penetrate the thermal protection system and melt the internal structure of the spacecraft. This hole was created by a piece of foam that fell off the external tank and hit the wing during launch. *Columbia*, which had made the shuttle program's first flight into space in 1981, was destroyed on re-entry on February 1, 2003. All seven astronauts on board were killed.

The investigation into the accident called into question not only the technical causes but also NASA's organizational culture. Before NASA was allowed to return the shuttle fleet to flight, Congress mandated that they address this finding. To meet this requirement, I (Dr. Phillip Meade) was asked to lead this effort at the Kennedy Space Center (KSC) to ensure that the organizational and cultural issues had been both identified and resolved. Doing so meant working with a complex, highly technical organization composed of over 14,000 contractors and federal workers. Dr. Laura Gallaher and I worked closely together to transform the NASA culture and to sustain those cultural changes over the long term. The synergy created by teaming a PhD in Industrial Engineering (myself) with a PhD in Industrial-Organizational Psychology (Dr. Gallaher) led to incredible breakthroughs in leading culture change.

These experiences and the insights we gained led to the creation of our consulting company, Gallaher Edge. Since helping the KSC transform its culture, we have continued to work with organizations across multiple industries to help them maintain, improve, and transform their culture in a similar manner. By applying the science of human behavior to organizations, we have helped companies get their edge, achieve together, and enjoy the journey. Now, more than fifteen years after helping NASA and many other organizations, we have condensed our understanding into a simple, easy to communicate model that we use successfully with our clients.

You may be asking yourself, "Is this a book about safety culture?" While the concepts in this book can definitely help to create a safe organization, the simple answer is no. Although we draw heavily on the *Columbia* accident and the impact culture had on safety leading up to that accident, this book is about organizational culture. We will show that safety culture doesn't exist in organizations the way that many people think it does.

Why Did We Write This Book?

We wrote this book because we want to evolve humanity. That is the highest purpose that drives us at Gallaher Edge. It is our way of contributing to make the world a better place and investing the talents and gifts we have been given. Organizational culture is incredibly important and can be a powerful force in evolving humanity. Creating a healthy, effective culture is a tremendous leverage point because people spend so much of their time at work and draw so much of their self-esteem from how they are treated there and what they accomplish. Additionally, organizational culture is integral to the performance and success of your business and truly drives business results.

There is an abundance of leaders who believe in the importance of organizational culture just as we do. Most modern companies recognize how critical culture is to their success and place significant emphasis on talking about it. However, very few know how to actually do anything about it. Because organizational culture is so complex and often misunderstood, many leaders don't quite know how to manage or change it effectively.

> **We created this book as a support for those impactful leaders like you who want to take their organizations to the next level and create great workplaces.**

Many books focus on a single aspect of organizational culture, like employee engagement or accountability. However, few provide a comprehensive framework for understanding and evolving company culture. This book provides an integrated model that does just that and goes beyond the creation of cultural artifacts and extrinsic motivators to produce the desired traits. Because culture is really embedded in the beliefs inside your people, we go deeper. We build on the science of human behavior to manage and evolve organizational culture from the inside out. This means starting inside each employee and supporting the way they see themselves and their organization. Starting with the cornerstones of Self-Awareness, Self-Acceptance, and Self-Accountability, we show organizations how they can link their employees together to create the desired cultural attributes at the individual, personal level. These "missing links" are what previous books have failed to identify and form the roadmap for actionable culture management.

Who is This Book For?

This book is for leaders who believe that culture is important and are willing to invest in developing themselves and their organizations. Culture is important to your individual success and the success of your company. Understanding how to manage it is especially important.

But this book is for others as well. It is for aspiring leaders who want to better understand how to be effective on a broader scale. This understanding will help you increase your performance and improve your career growth opportunities. It is also for human capital professionals engaged in shaping their organization's culture. This book will provide you with a roadmap and model to use as you work across leaders and departments. And finally, this book is for individuals passionate about or wanting to learn more about organizational culture. We know there are some fellow culture nerds out there!

How is The Book Structured?

We have designed this book in three parts. Each part has a specific focus to help provide you with the foundation for the model, build on that foundation to explain the model, and help you with implementation. We have leveraged imagery and symbolism for the model around concepts from genetics. Culture is often seen as the DNA of your organization, and because our purpose is to evolve humanity, representing the model as a DNA strand fits beautifully.

Part one lays the foundation for the science behind the model. This is where we discuss the organization as a system, provide a high-level overview of systems theory, and delve into the psychology and science of human behavior. We also explain organizational culture and how it is created. We will start each chapter with a short story from the creation of the model to provide context for how we came to the conclusions we built it on.

Part two describes the model in detail. Using the metaphor of DNA, we break the model down into individual strands that primarily support a critical trait for effective culture. We define the missing links that, when present, link humans together in a way that produces that emergent trait. Throughout this section, our work after the space shuttle *Columbia* accident illustrates the model's key concepts as they apply to organizational culture.

Part three provides guidance on how to apply the model. This includes the role of leaders in creating the culture and how to effectively lead change in your organization. In this final section, our work as we guided leaders at NASA and other organizations through culture change provides real-life illustrations of what we were able to accomplish using the model.

How Can You Use This Book, And What Action Can You Take?

We hope this book will be more than an intellectual pursuit. We want to evolve humanity, so achieving this goal requires more than thought—it requires action. With a deeper understanding of how culture works in your organization, you will be able to see how your culture is emerging and take steps to intentionally create and manage it.

Throughout the book, we will provide multiple ways to go deeper into these concepts and bring them to your organization through activities, videos, and downloads. Each opportunity is marked by an icon signifying there is bonus content available that coincides with the section you are reading. The URL for the bonus material is also be included in the footer of that page.

These additional resources will help you internalize the concepts and put them into action. It is our desire to create an ongoing partnership with you through this book that allows us to support and encourage you on your journey. Please use the key below for reference.

Keep a close eye out for this icon! It signifies there is additional content that will elevate your reading experience. It may be an assessment, white paper, or something that will help you apply what you are learning to your own life (professionally and even personally!).

You will see this icon at the beginning of each chapter. We realize this book has a LOT of valuable information. Instead of highlighting and dog-earing pages, we've created chapter-specific PDFs for you to download and take notes on. Some pages are in the form of a worksheet and others have writing prompts.

The video icon is frequently used throughout each chapter. It indicates there is additional video content available to deepen your understanding of the concepts.

If you see this icon, it's an invitation for you to join our Insider Edge platform. Once you register, you will have access to exclusive weekly trainings, monthly webinars, an extensive video library, and more—all to help you decrease stress and feel more powerful, confident, and calm in your leadership role and as a human being.

Scan here to access free additional content[1]

Scan here to register for Insider Edge to access expanded book content and more![2]

Already registered? Scan here to access Insider Edge[3]

---

[1] https://gallaheredge.com/themissinglinks
[2] https://gallaheredge.com/themissinglinks#register
[3] https://gallaheredge.com/login

The greatest takeaway should be for leaders to recognize the systemic nature of culture and view themselves and their organizations in a more actionable way through the science of human behavior.

The information in this book can help transform your culture into a competitive edge. When intentionally designed to support the execution of your strategy, your culture can become your most powerful source of sustainable competitive advantage. This is true regardless of industry or company specialty. Because our model is human-centric and based on the science of human behavior, it can help all organizations that employ humans.

PART ONE

Scan here to access free additional content[4]

Chapter 1

Why is Culture Important?

"My fellow Americans, this day has brought terrible news and great sadness to our country. At 9 a.m. this morning, Mission Control in Houston lost contact with our Space Shuttle Columbia. A short time later, debris was seen falling from the skies above Texas. The Columbia is lost; there are no survivors. [...] The cause in which they died will continue. Mankind is led into the darkness beyond our world by the inspiration of discovery and the longing to understand. Our journey into space will go on."
—President George W. Bush

Sixteen Minutes From Home

On February 1, 2003, at approximately 9:00 a.m. EST, the space shuttle *Columbia* disintegrated on re-entry killing all seven astronauts onboard. This matter-of-fact statement, while technically accu-

---

5 https://gallaheredge.com/themissinglinks

rate, does not even begin to capture the magnitude of this tragedy.

The seven human beings who lost their lives on that day were: Colonel Rick Husband, Lt. Colonel Michael Anderson, Commander Laurel Clark; Captain David Brown, Commander William McCool, Dr. Kalpana Chawla, and Ilan Ramon, a Colonel in the Israeli Air Force. They were heroes, scientists, and explorers. They were husbands and wives and fathers and daughters and sons and mothers and friends. And they willingly put their lives in the hands of thousands of engineers who they trusted to deliver them into space and return them safely to earth.

As one of those engineers, I (Phillip) saw this trust as a sacred duty to fulfill. To refer to this as an "accident" is wholly inadequate. Disaster is probably the closest word that captures the depth of emotion I feel when talking about this event and how NASA—and more specifically, I—let these incredible people and their families down.

Many people remember where they were and what they were doing when they heard that *Columbia* and her crew had been lost. Perhaps you remember where you were when you heard the news. If this event can have such a profound effect on people who had nothing to do with the program and had never even met the crew, just imagine the depth of the impact it had on those who spent years of their lives directly working on the shuttle daily and who had worked with and supported members of the crew.

As part of the NASA family, I sat in horror and sadness that morning, but little did I know this tragedy would represent a turning point in my life. In the ensuing investigation, the Columbia Accident Investigation Board (CAIB) found that at 81.7 seconds after launch, foam insulation around an attach point between the shuttle orbiter and the big external fuel tank dislodged and hit the leading edge of the wing. The impact created a six- to ten-inch hole in the reinforced carbon-carbon panel, allowing superheated atmospheric gases to enter the orbiter and melt the internal support structures. This resulted in the orbiter breaking apart and disintegrating over Texas and Louisiana.

But the findings didn't stop there; they went further to identify underlying systemic causes that lay at the heart of the accident. The CAIB stated succinctly, "In our view, the NASA organizational culture had as much to do with this accident as

the foam." This statement was particularly forceful and damning and the most painful finding for me to accept.

> It's one thing to make a mistake because we are doing something extremely difficult that has never been done before. It's another thing entirely when our flawed culture led us to make mistakes.

Because of the CAIB's findings, the shuttle fleet was grounded until NASA could demonstrate to Congress that the organizational and cultural issues that led to the loss of seven lives, the space shuttle *Columbia*, and the STS-107 mission had been corrected. Congress and the American people wanted more from its space agency, and NASA had to give it to them if it were ever to fly again. Faced with such demands, I was asked to lead that transformation for KSC—the critical launch site for all shuttles.

To put this request in the proper perspective, I had just been asked to lead the organizational and cultural changes at NASA's KSC—a 14,000-person workforce comprised of about 2,000 civil servants and 12,000 contractors from multiple companies working on different contracts. This was a high-profile project following a national disaster with a blue-ribbon Congressional Panel providing oversight to ensure we were achieving progress. Congress had to agree that we had made the necessary cultural changes before we were allowed to launch again.

Oh yeah, and I was supposed to lead something "squishy" like culture change here, not a technical project like I was used to. Most of my career had been spent testing payloads and integrating them into the shuttle, designing and operating command and control systems, and helping assemble the International Space Station. Needless to say, I was terrified!

But do you know what scared me the most? It was the fact that NASA was a great organization. In fact, NASA was ranked first in the Best Places to Work in the Federal Government in 2002—the year before the *Columbia* accident. Oddly, it would have made me feel better if I could have pointed to obvious problems to fix. But NASA was by all accounts an excellent organization staffed with highly intelligent employees who were incredibly dedicated to the mission. One of the biggest problems we faced every year was trying to force employees to use their vacation time! How many companies would like to have that as their biggest problem?

This was something that forever changed me. That even one of the best organizations with amazing employees can produce a culture that leads to the death of seven people should serve as a chilling warning for every company.

Ironically, this challenge served as the key to helping me unlock the secret to understanding organizational culture and, consequently, how to change it. It is impossible to control something until you understand it, and as you will see in this book, I believe it is possible to intentionally design, manage, and control your culture. But this all starts from a proper understanding of what culture is and how it works. Few people possess this understanding, which is one reason working on culture is so difficult.

It's also one reason so few companies invest in designing and managing their culture. As humans, we like to feel we are in control, and most CEOs will invest in opportunities where they feel competent and in control rather than something like culture. This is true even if culture is more important if they fear they can't control it, or they don't feel competent in it.

We saw an extreme example of this irrational need for control in 2020 with COVID-19 toilet paper hoarding. People felt out of control because of the pandemic, and although they couldn't control the virus, they could control how much toilet paper they had stored in their basement. So, some people focused on what they could control by hoarding toilet paper. It didn't solve the real problem, just as investing in initiatives that are controllable but not necessarily strategically critical doesn't solve the real problems that many CEOs face.

All Organizations Are Systems, But Are They Complicated or Complex?

To give you the control you desire over your culture, we will provide you with a deep understanding of organizational culture—not only what it is but also what forces work together to produce it within your organization. However, to do this, we must start with a solid understanding of the organization itself.

All organizations are systems. A system is just a combination of interdependent parts working together for a common purpose to convert inputs to outputs, which have a defined boundary allowing them to be viewed as a unified whole. NASA was a system just like the space shuttle was a system. Just like the solid rocket boosters, external tank, and orbiter's main engines all work together in concert to enable the crew to escape gravity, human behavior from a shuttle program manager interacted with the pressures to stay on schedule and under budget as well as the interpersonal insecurities of the technical engineers to produce unhealthy team dynamics and bad decisions.

This realization was the first step in helping me cope with the challenge I was facing. If an organization is a system, then the same principles and tools used to analyze and improve technical systems could address the organizational and cultural issues surrounding the *Columbia* accident.

But it's critically important to recognize that organizations aren't just any type of system— they are complex adaptive systems. These are a special class of systems marked by behavior that is challenging to predict or control and require special methods of analysis. As has been pointed out in several other books, such as Aaron Dignan's *Brave New Work*, there is a difference between *complicated* and *complex*.

Complicated systems require a high degree of specialized knowledge to work on them, but the process can typically be codified and is repeatable. On the other hand, complex systems may require a high degree of specialized knowledge but also require creativity and innovation. Implementing solutions with complex systems requires a unique solution each time which is adapted to the everchanging internal and external environment, so it's impossible to create a codified repeatable process for someone to follow.

As an example, installing a customer relationship management system can be complicated and involve a lot of steps and even specialized knowledge. However, someone skilled in doing this should be able to follow the same steps each time they install the system and be successful. However, delivering a winning customer experience requires creativity and the ability to respond to the different needs and responses of the individual customers. Treating every customer the same is not a winning formula. This same scenario holds true for fixing a car compared to creating a new successful model that consumers embrace.

The *Challenger* accident from 1986 is another example that directly mirrors the issues we're addressing in the *Columbia* accident. It is often oversimplified in case studies and articles as an issue of groupthink when it is analyzed. However, the reality is that the accident occurred within a complex dynamic system where political pressures created by the president's desire to declare the shuttle operational during his State of the Union Address created pressure on the technical community to make the vehicle appear "ready to fly," while also creating arbitrary schedule pressure.

And this was all taking place within an environment where there was extreme budget pressure on the program to decrease the cost per flight by increasing the number of flights per year. This further increased the pressure to launch by adding schedule pressure and fear of future budget cuts if they didn't meet expectations.

Finally, the organizational system was staffed by the most complex adaptive system of all. . .human beings! At the organizational and human level, the program was divided into multiple organizations, contractors, and space centers in different geographical locations. They all had varying degrees of fear about being blamed if something went wrong and were positioning themselves to be protected if something did. And yes, a form of groupthink was present where many people had become so accustomed to certain anomalies that they no longer felt unexpected.

These factors worked together in addition to the technical uncertainty that was present in the decision-making to create the environment in which the bad decision was made to launch on that cold January day. To be clear, it undoubtedly was a bad decision and undoubtedly could have been avoided. But the causes and the solutions to prevent it from happening again are anything but simple or even complicated—they are *complex*.

The primary reason complex adaptive systems are so challenging to work with is that when you push on them, they push back. Unlike other systems, they adapt to whatever you are trying to do to them so you may not get the response you anticipate from your action. An analogy we like to use here is that we can precisely calculate where a rock will land if we toss it, given the precise starting point, angle, and velocity. That is what it is like working with a typical system—you can predict your results, and as long as you execute effectively, you'll get the results you expect.

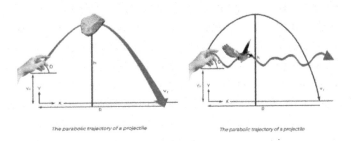

The parabolic trajectory of a projectile
      The parabolic trajectory of a projectile

However, if I replace the rock in this example with a bird, suddenly everything changes. The bird is now an adaptive component of the system. No matter how precisely or accurately you perform the calculations, when you toss that bird, you will be wrong. People in organizations, just like the bird in the example above, have independence. The rock was subject to the laws of physics, but the bird was making its own decisions. Introducing an agent with independence is one of the major differentiators of a complex system. In a noncomplex system, the agents don't possess independence; they perform according to set laws or parameters. However, in complex adaptive systems, we have agents such as humans who possess independence and can make their own decisions.

What makes this challenging is that these decisions may not align with the larger system goals. Multiple competing goals can emerge within the system agents at different levels: individual, team, department, and organizational.

Often these competing goals exist within us as individuals because, after all, we are complex organisms. You can recognize that a change makes sense for the organization and still have an emotional feeling of loss associated with that change. We often see this with reorganizations where individuals recognize that the company needs to change how it is structured due to growth or a shift in strategy, but the new structure results in them having a different supervisor, which is scary because they like and are comfortable with their current one. So, their individual goal of maximizing their personal comfort conflicts with the organizational goal of the reorganization.

When working with a complex system, rather than trying to force the solution through throwing the bird where we want it to go (which will likely just increase policy resistance), a more effective approach is to understand the systemic drivers or motivators of the individual agents and use these to help achieve the larger goal.

Understanding the individual motivation of the bird, the best strategy is probably to place a pile of birdseed at the location you wish the bird to land, release the bird, and let it fly there on its own. Depending on how broadly we draw the boundaries of our system, we may even want to consider protecting the birdseed from being raided by squirrels and perhaps even protecting the bird from predators when it's feeding on the birdseed. We can fold as many layers of complexity into this example as we want.

Why Does Complexity Matter?

 This independence and adaptation lead to a phenomenon called policy resistance, where complex systems exhibit behavior that resists the intent of a particular course of action or strategy by leaders. The picture above shows a great example of how people have pushed back and made the traffic gate completely ineffective.

We see this all the time in social systems where a policy aimed at changing a behavior actually has the opposite effect. One painful example most of us are familiar with is the incessant road projects that increase the number of lanes on the road, only to see people quickly realize the benefit of changing their commute to take that route shortly after it is open. This swells the traffic on that portion of the roadway to consume the available capacity negating any benefits gained by making the improvements.

Another term commonly used for policy resistance is unintended consequences. These consequences can be difficult to predict in advance and typically produce undesirable results that were never intended by those who designed and implemented the solution.

At the root of this complexity and turbocharged by the adaptation within the system lie feedback loops; a thermostat is a great example of a feedback loop most people understand. The thermostat measures the temperature of the air (input) to produce hot or cold air (output). When the temperature hits the designated setpoint, the output pauses and waits for the next change in the input.

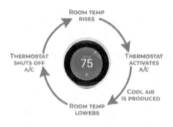

Feedback loops like this are also major contributors to policy resistance in organizations, and when leaders fail to recognize the presence of these feedback loops, they increase the probability that their policies and solutions will cause unintended consequences. A simple feedback loop we see in organizations deals with communications. Sometimes a leader will lament that employees aren't open with him and don't share their concerns. This is a linear view of the situation that subtly places the blame on the employees. Because this is a common situation, you probably immediately wonder how well that leader *actually* receives feedback.

There is a feedback loop at play where—at the simplest level—the employee is sharing, and the leader is listening. A linear view sees the problem as "they aren't open with me." However, recognizing this system as a feedback loop, we see that the leader now has accountability in the system and can contribute in a meaningful way to the solution. From both science and experience, we can tell you that nothing increases another person's willingness to be open and share than sitting across from a world-class listener.

Taking this system's view allows us to go from a blame-based belief of the problem to a more complex position that recognizes the contribution of both sides and allows for a more complete and effective solution. The full feedback loop may look like this: "As I listen more to my employees, they feel more heard, and it increases how open they are with me."

Feedback loops are a large part of what create problems for us in analyzing and understanding the system because they introduce nonlinearity which we aren't adept at handling as humans. Nonlinear means that the behavior of the system doesn't follow a straight line. We tend to estimate assuming a constant rate of growth or change, which is linear.

When feedback is present, growth or decay can be exponential, and time delays can be introduced. Each creates nonlinear relationships, which we are notoriously poor at estimating. You can test this on yourself with this simple puzzle: If I placed a penny on the first square of a chessboard and doubled the sum for each successive square, how much money would I have when I reached the final square of the board? To help you out, there are sixty-four squares on a chessboard. Don't read any further until you've thought of a number.

OK, so if you take $0.01 and double it sixty-four times, how much money will you have? Do you think you'll have $100? Maybe $1,000? Did you go as high as $1 million or even $1 billion? When we have done this with groups, we have never had an individual go as high as $1 trillion. The answer to the problem is:

$92,233,720,368,547,800 (over $92 quadrillion!)

To save the skeptics out there from doing the math, here's a table that shows how the penny grows to the ridiculous sum of over $92 quadrillion in just sixty-four moves.

1	$0.01	22	$20,971.52	43	$43,980,465,111.04
2	$0.02	23	$41,943.04	44	$87,960,930,222.08
3	$0.04	24	$83,886.08	45	$175,921,860,444.16
4	$0.08	25	$167,772.16	46	$351,843,720,888.32
5	$0.16	26	$335,544.32	47	$703,687,441,776.64
6	$0.32	27	$671,088.64	48	$1,407,374,883,553.28
7	$0.64	28	$1,342,177.28	49	$2,814,749,767,106.56
8	$1.28	29	$2,684,354.56	50	$5,629,499,534,213.12
9	$2.56	30	$5,368,709.12	51	$11,258,999,068,426.20
10	$5.12	31	$10,737,418.24	52	$22,517,998,136,852.50
11	$10.24	32	$21,474,836.48	53	$45,035,996,273,705.00
12	$20.48	33	$42,949,672.96	54	$90,071,992,547,409.90
13	$40.96	34	$85,899,345.92	55	$180,143,985,094,820.00
14	$81.92	35	$171,798,691.84	56	$360,287,970,189,640.00
15	$163.84	36	$343,597,383.68	57	$720,575,940,379,279.00
16	$327.68	37	$687,194,767.36	58	$1,441,151,880,758,560.00
17	$655.36	38	$1,374,389,534.72	59	$2,882,303,761,517,120.00
18	$1,310.72	39	$2,748,779,069.44	60	$5,764,607,523,034,230.00
19	$2,621.44	40	$5,497,558,138.88	61	$11,529,215,046,068,500.00
20	$5,242.88	41	$10,995,116,277.76	62	$23,058,430,092,136,900.00
21	$10,485.76	42	$21,990,232,555.52	63	$46,116,860,184,273,900.00
				64	**$92,233,720,368,547,800.00**

So, as you can see, it can be very difficult to estimate exponential growth, and our estimates can be wildly inaccurate. This can lead to errors with forecasting, strategy, analyzing the causes of issues, and designing effective solutions.

Cause and Effect Are Difficult to Determine, But Why?

Another major challenge with complex adaptive systems is that cause and effect are difficult to determine because they may not be close in time and space. We expect the cause to closely precede an event in time and happen relatively closely in space. If we see something happen, we rarely assume that it's happening because of something that occurred six months ago on another continent.

But with complex adaptive systems, the multiple feedback loops that exist within the system and the time delays that exist within those loops can create just such a scenario. The butterfly effect, where a butterfly flaps its wings in Tokyo and determines whether there's rain or sunshine in New York the next day, is a classic example. In organizations, we frequently see examples of leaders making decisions where the true impacts aren't seen for months or years. If these decisions turn out to negatively impact the organization, the leader rarely connects the negative impacts to the decision they made and thus doesn't learn from it.

A great example of a decision NASA struggled with in the past is outsourcing entry-level positions to its contractor workforce. In the short term, this decision has no negative impact on organizational performance. However, as experienced employees retired and NASA filled senior-level positions, they were forced to select from individuals who had never worked in the entry-level positions, where the hands-on experience with flight hardware was gained. This created an important gap in the understanding of some key positions.

This is a highly complex problem with many factors, but the key point here is that the time delay between when the decision was made and when the problem surfaced was several years in duration. The net effect of this—in addition to making it difficult to determine the true cause of an issue—is that organizational learning can be slow, difficult, and sometimes nearly impossible unless the underlying system dynamics are surfaced and included in the analysis. The feedback loops and nonlinear dynamics must be accounted for in analyzing the organization.

How Organizational Performance Emerges

From the combination of each of these elements of a complex adaptive system emerges organization performance. In complexity theory, *emergence* essentially indicates that the whole is bigger than the sum of its parts. More specifically, emergence is a behavior or property of a system that cannot be discerned from the individual constituent parts which produce it.

Our favorite example of emergence is the taste of sugar. It is impossible to discern the result-

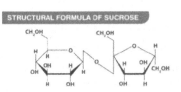

ing taste of sugar by licking the individual carbon, hydrogen, and oxygen elements. The taste emerges from the structure of the system formed by the sugar crystal when the elements are combined in the right way. You could easily create something that tastes very different from those exact same elements.

Emergence depends as much on the relationship between the elements as it does on the elements themselves. Breaking the elements apart destroys the emergence. Traditional reductionist methodologies for solving emergent problems don't work. Unfortunately, this is exactly the type of problem-solving that was drilled into our heads as we were growing up—break a problem down into its smallest parts, solve those, and sum the results to get the answers. What seems like traditional wisdom is actually a recipe for failure.

Many complex systems exhibit *path dependence* and emergence. To understand path dependence, consider an example of a snowflake. You've most likely heard that every snowflake is unique. The reason that's true is that the shape of a snowflake is an emergent property with path dependence. The final shape depends on the specific path taken as it falls and how that path takes it on a journey through the sky, bringing it into contact with other snow crystals and experiencing changing atmospheric pressures and temperatures. The growth and shape of the crystalline structure are so sensitive to changes in temperature and pressure that no two snowflakes take the same journey. This is why there is such extreme variation between snowflakes.

Path dependence means that the specific path taken and history involved in producing the emergent behavior is significant and affects the final outcome. The possible options or solutions at a given time depend on the decisions previously made, so a purely repeatable process may not exist.

One of the most iconic NASA examples of path-dependent emergent culture comes from the *Apollo 13* mission. Intended to be NASA's third landing on the moon, an explosion that vented much of the crew's oxygen into space made bringing them home almost impossible. NASA snatched victory from the jaws of defeat and refused to give up in the face of overwhelming odds.

Whether Gene Kranz actually said the now-famous phrase, "Failure is not an option," that sentiment has been branded onto the soul of the NASA workforce who willingly accept any challenge. As we will see, this can be a two-edged sword enabling the agency to succeed at challenges that have never been attempted but also leading them to agree to undertake projects with clearly an insufficient budget.

This is the essence of path dependence—*Apollo 13* was a singular mission in the storied history of NASA's lofty accomplishments, yet NASA's culture cannot be adequately described without its mention.

Culture is an Emergent Property

Now that we have laid a solid foundation for understanding an organization as a complex adaptive system and all the nuances involved, we are ready to make our real point. It's important to recognize that organizational culture is an emergent property that arises from the organization's adaptive complex system. Specifically, it is produced by the interactions of the commonly held beliefs and attitudes of the employees as they work together to accomplish the organization's goals.

This emergence is produced by feedback loops that exist as employees interact with and adapt to each other and the organization, exerting their own independence to produce complex patterns of behavior that are difficult to tightly control or predict. These feedback loops possess the classic trademarks of nonlinearity and exist at multiple levels and between multiple groups and entities. Most interestingly, a feedback loop even exists between the culture and the employees who create it, which is why cultural attributes can persist for long periods of time, seemingly impervious to change and also change quickly with little notice.

As Ruth Benedict wrote in *Patterns of Culture,* "No individual can arrive even at the threshold of his potentialities without a culture in which he participates. Conversely, no civilization has in it any element which in the last analysis is not the contribution of an individual."

Organizational culture also possesses path dependence, and its emergence is very aware of its history. Cultures between organizations are as unique as snowflakes, and it is impossible to merely pick up and transplant the culture from one company to another.

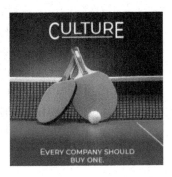

For a while, this seemed like a popular endeavor until too many companies realized the futility of attempting to do so. They would find a company that reportedly had an excellent culture, study them, and try to copy their practices in an attempt to copy their culture. As a result, we would see companies running out and buying ping pong tables for their employees to mimic a Silicon Valley culture and see similar innovations.

Somehow, the ping pong table didn't do the trick.

There is far more to creating organizational culture than duplicating the surface artifacts or even the practices and espoused values of a company. There must be a meaningful fit between the culture and the strategy of the company for the performance benefits to be realized. But that's for another chapter.

For now, the point we want to make is that organizational culture is unique, and its uniqueness is created by what the history of the organization has taught the employees to hold dear and how it has shaped their common beliefs, attitudes, and behaviors. This is embedded in the stories and the core values of the organization—the true core values—which may not be what are on the wall in the lobby.

Earlier, we pointed to the *Apollo 13* success as a source of stories that created path-dependent cultural beliefs around "failure is not an option." We also pointed out how this is a two-edged sword. Part of the emergent culture at the time of the *Columbia* accident was around how leaders were developed and rewarded. Possessing this "failure is not an option" attitude was rewarded and a subtle part of the leadership philosophy.

We believe this belief system played into the *Columbia* accident in a very critical way and worked against the mission manager, Linda Ham, during the STS-107 mission. Her inability to accept the possibility of failure made her resistant to request on orbit imaging of the wing to find out if there had been any damage from the foam. Since she believed that nothing could be done prior to reentry, she would rather remain ignorant of the problem than live with the knowledge of certain failure.

We will discuss this in more detail in a later chapter, but culture both affects and starts with our beliefs which include our beliefs about who we are and what choices are available to us.

Good Organizations Can Do Bad Things

Understanding organizational culture and ultimately develop the ability to change, design, or manage it requires taking a holistic approach. As we cautioned earlier, typical reductionist methodologies won't work, so you will want to adopt a systems perspective of your organization and learn to look for how the structure contributes to the behavior while looking at how all parties involved contribute rather than asking who's to blame.

---

6 https://gallaheredge.com/login/

One way to think of this is stipple art, which is made from thousands of tiny dots used to create a picture. If you stand too close to the picture, all you will see is a collection of tiny dots, but a beautiful picture will emerge when you stand back.

To further illustrate how this works, let's return to where we started with the *Columbia* accident. Remember I said I was terrified because NASA was such a great organization with smart, dedicated employees, and I could see no obvious problems to solve? Well, I also said that this turned out to be the key to helping me understand organizational culture.

Because of this apparent contradiction, I began looking at the problem from a systems perspective and realized that culture was actually an emergent property. That meant that looking at properties like "smart employees" and "dedicated to the mission" in isolation was misleading. I was using reductionist methodologies on an emergent problem. I had to look at how these factors were combining to produce specific cultural attributes that could lead to an accident such as *Columbia*.

Again, it wasn't that the culture was toxic. As I've stated before, many things about the organization and the culture at NASA were positive. But because NASA is a high-reliability organization with razor-thin margins for error, being good wasn't good enough. And because of the complex nature of organizations and culture specifically, an organization can have many positive attributes and a generally positive culture while also having specific areas where their culture works against them.

A critical measure of a culture's effectiveness is how well it supports an organization's specific purpose and strategy. For NASA, this meant that the culture at NASA had to support a mission-critical, high-reliability organization through effective risk management and strong safety practices and beliefs.

One example I found was that the employees' strong link between their identity and the NASA mission, combined with their high self-accountability, was interacting with an environment of constrained resources and a perceived threat of program cancellation. This created a strongly held belief that they had to "save the program" and that actions they took could potentially mean the difference between the shuttle continuing to fly or not. In simple terms, they loved the shuttle so much it was like their baby. They were living in constant fear that they would lose it and felt it was their responsibility to save it.

To help you see how this type of decision bias works, imagine that I took you up to the top of the Empire State Building, where a long beam was cantilevered out into open space. Out at the end of this beam is taped $1,000 in cash, and if you walk out to the end of that beam unassisted, you can have it. Would you do it? Most people wouldn't. The risk of falling from that height versus $1,000 isn't a good trade for them.

Now, imagine the same scenario, but this time at the end of the beam is your child or loved one. Would you walk out there to get them? In this case, most people would go without hesitation. What changed?

Whether we're conscious of it or not, we are conducting a risk/reward trade-off calculation in our minds. Whenever we take one side of the equation and essentially set it at infinity (say by placing the value equivalent to the price of our child's life), we lose the ability to effectively evaluate the risk against the reward and will accept more and more risk.

This is what was happened to the shuttle workers when they got into the mindset that they had to save the program. In essence, their baby was at the end of that beam, and they were trying to make decisions regarding risk in that situation. How effective do you think they were being?

The effect of these beliefs on the culture was subtle. It impacted decision-making and the ability to effectively make risk trade-offs resulting in the unconscious acceptance of more risk. The really scary thing about this whole situation is that they weren't even aware that their decision-making was compromised. They were still the smart, well-trained, highly logical engineers they always were, and they were using the same processes they had always used, so why should they think anything was wrong?

But fortunately, the fix was relatively easy. Awareness was required to fix this issue because no one involved wanted to be making bad decisions. We just had to educate everyone on the cognitive bias and train them to watch for the words "save the program." Any time those words were said during a meeting, a time-out was called, and a discussion was held about why it was said, what that meant, and how decisions could be compromised.

The Journey Begins

As you can see, while culture is an emergent property of the organization, it exists between the ears of the employees.

Engineering and complex systems provide the architecture and tools for analyzing and managing organizational culture, but the ability to make the necessary connections to create and manage culture comes from the field of psychology. In and of themselves, humans are complex and create a whole field known as psychology and, more specifically, organizational psychology. I knew it would be important to leverage the science of human behavior, including what needs and desires were the biggest drivers of human behavior in organizations. For that reason, I hired organizational psychologists to work with me in managing the culture at KSC.

Twenty-nine months after the accident, NASA was given the green light to launch again, but this only marked the beginning of my journey. I have continued to study culture and have worked with companies to develop and transform theirs. Together, Laura and I studied how the science of human behavior works to create an organizational culture and how these behaviors are rooted in our own self-concept and need to defend and protect that self-concept.

This has enabled us to identify the missing links for creating and maintaining an effective culture created from the inside out.

"A nation expresses its heartfelt grief for the loss of these brave astronauts who have entered the long line of heroes who gave their lives for America. This terrible loss is a reminder that we can never take for granted the sacrifice of heroes."

—Sen. John McCain, R-Arizona

---

7 https://gallaheredge.com/login/

Chapter 2

The Science of Human Behavior

"We don't see things as they are;
we see them as we are."
—Anaïs Nin

Welcome to NASA

On her first day of work as a civil servant at NASA, Laura was handed the Columbia Accident Investigation Board (CAIB) Report. Part two, which described how organizational and cultural factors contributed to the accident, immediately grabbed her attention. It was especially significant because later that same day, we met with the Organization Design Team for the newly forming directorate at KSC: Engineering.

While it wasn't uncommon for the directorates (also called "organizations") across the Space Center to

---

8 https://gallaheredge.com/themissinglinks

be reorganized to optimize for mission success, this was a reorganization that was affecting nearly two-thirds of KSC. Due largely to the findings and recommendations of the CAIB report, the technical functions that supported each of the programs, including Space Shuttle Processing and the International Space Station, were being pulled out of those programs and into a consolidated engineering organization. Both the scope and the impact of this reorganization were far-reaching and critically important.

Laura was learning that the organization's design played a role in the tragedy and ensuring that engineering was its own directorate was a critical step in changing human behavior to support effective decision-making.

The engineering directorate would become a matrix organization, with their technical engineers reporting functionally to the engineering leadership while supporting the programs and projects they were most closely aligned with. Laura's learnings about matrix organizations told her that they were one of the most challenging designs because it can feel like each person has two bosses; the ability for those leaders to work effectively together depended heavily on strong interpersonal skills.

And as a psychologist, the thing that fascinated Laura the most was that to manage interpersonal relationships effectively, each leader needed to first build a better relationship with themselves by growing their self-awareness.

On top of that, Laura began working on a change management training designed to create space for each person going through this organizational change to understand the reasons for the change, the impact of the change on them personally, and to internalize what this all meant for them as an individual. This reorganization was creating feelings of loss for people, particularly engineers who had been working in the shuttle organization for their whole careers. It created a sense of pride to be associated with such an impressive vehicle like the shuttle. Losing that, even though much of the work stayed the same, was triggering resistance that they needed to work through.

By the end of her first week, Laura realized there were many levels to think about when it came to creating organizational culture.

Organizational Culture From the Inside Out

Culture and organizations are complex so, leading and developing organizations can be a daunting task. There are so many pieces and parts working together to produce the results. Sometimes the interactions between components are difficult to understand or even recognize. With so many moving parts and complex interactions, how can you possibly lead a successful organization while growing it and developing it into an awesome workplace? Even if you aren't leading an organization, just figuring out how to be happy and successful within one can be confusing.

Before we created the Missing Links Model, we developed a simple framework based on the work we did at KSC, which addresses a myriad of challenges like leadership, accountability, change, alignment, culture, and organization design. We wanted a simple way to communicate to our clients outside of NASA the foundation of our approach. This model is the key to transforming your organization. Its power lies in one simple truth—at its core, everything starts with the self.

Our Inside Out Model starts with the Self at its core, moves to the team level, and then organizational culture level—it is bidirectional. These layers affect each other; the behavior of one individual can affect the organization, just as organizational factors can affect individual behavior. We'll start with an explanation of this model because it formed the foundation of many concepts in the Missing Link Model.

First Up: Organizational Culture

We can best illustrate how the model works by walking through it backward. At the outer level, we have organizational culture, which is an emergent property and encompasses nearly everything about how the organization works. You can think about this level of the model through the acronym SET: strategy, execution, and talent.

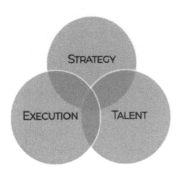

The first is strategy. The relationship between strategy and culture goes both ways and is vitally important. Leaders will want to be clear about what their strategy is to accomplish their goals. Feeling clear about strategy positively impacts organizational culture because it creates a unified direction that enables greater success. And that success has a positive impact on how people feel and behave in the organization.

The second element of our organizational culture level of the model is execution. Here we focus on designing the organization in a way that promotes

---

a culture that supports the *execution* of the strategy. But when you break that down, it all comes back to human behavior. How the organization is designed, which includes its structure, how decisions are made, processes, policies, and systems—affects how people feel and behave. For example, if a key strategy is agility and the ability to quickly respond to customer needs, leaders will want to design the organization to ensure that people are empowered to make decisions at their level, or they will fail to execute the company's strategy.

The last piece of the organizational culture level of the Inside Out Model is talent. This refers to aligning the talent management processes to support the culture and the strategy. This includes getting clear about the core values of the organization, the behavioral expectations of the people, and aligning everything from the talent acquisition processes (e.g., recruiting, hiring, and onboarding) to the talent management processes (e.g., rewarding, developing, promoting, and firing) to the desired culture and strategy.

But it's not enough to just lay out a process. People form beliefs based on their experiences in the organization, and based on those beliefs, they behave in a particular way, which ultimately produces the culture and results of the organization. This means that how processes are executed is defined as much by what people believe as by how the process is laid out. When processes are executed by multiple people or interface with other processes, these differences in beliefs and behaviors can lead to team dysfunction and poor performance. So, let's take a look at how teams can work so it is intentional and supports great culture.

Next Up: Team

If your organization is larger than one person, unless it's comprised of robots (which could be the future), the execution of these organizational processes will also invariably require people to work together. Consequently, to have a great organization, you must have great teams. It is very difficult to achieve anything of consequence today without good teamwork. Teamwork is comprised of a lot of factors, and numerous books have been written on this topic. To make the subject manageable, we have distilled this down into three primary components of a great team which create the acronym ACT: alignment, collaboration, and trust.

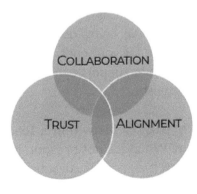

First is **alignment**. For a team to function effectively, its members must be on the same page and working toward a common goal and vision. It is surprisingly easy for misalignments to arise within a team. For that reason, it is useful to look at alignment as a process as well as an out-come. The process of alignment means going out of your way to make sure that you are surfacing differ-ent views from people on the team. This means in-cluding people with different experiences and back-grounds and keeping the conversations respectful when there are disagreements, so each perspective is heard. This kind of healthy conflict is usually nec-essary to achieve an outcome of true alignment, which best-selling author, Patrick Lencioni, invites leaders to consider as binary: you're either aligned or you're not.

The second component of the team level of our model is **collaboration**. The ability to work well together, accept and integrate each other's suggestions, and synergize the efforts of multiple individuals is the visible hallmark of a great team. Collaboration is what enables a team to be greater than the sum of its parts. Collaboration requires skills, and too often in organizations, these skills are overlooked. Leaders come to believe that collaboration is just something that you do, rather than seeing it as a combination of specific behaviors, including being open about your intentions, accountable for your contributions to the situation, and willing to support others with what they want to accomplish.

The final component is **trust**. Trust within a team is like oxygen in a room. When it's not present, it's the only thing people can focus on. Trust acts as a lubricant for interpersonal interactions, making it easier and faster to communicate and support one another, even on difficult topics. Trust is multifaceted, and as Stephen Covey highlights in his book, *The Speed of Trust*, we can break trust down into trust in competence (believing that somebody can accomplish results) and trust in character (believing that somebody is truthful in their intentions). In both cases, the presence of trust reduces fear between people on a team, which enables them to perform at higher levels. While fear is a motivator for humans, it will never yield better outcomes than when people can put their full energy and attention toward problem-solving without getting bogged down in fear of judgment from others or the fear of being let down by others.

And understanding how fear impacts human performance can be examined at the individual and final level of our Inside Out Model: the self.

The Shining Star: Self

When we focus on the core of our Inside Out Model—the Self—fear can become any culture's worst enemy. The elements of our Self Model describe the outcomes associated with humans who have overcome or learned how to effectively cope with the fears that come up for us in interpersonal interactions.

The Self level does not have a nifty acronym like the elements before it, but it has a nice alliteration of self-acceptance, self-awareness, and self-accountability. In creating this level of our model, we were heavily influenced by the work of Dr. Will Schutz and *The Human Element*. [10] We will do a deeper dive into each of these in chapter 5 but briefly overview them here.

Self-acceptance is the foundational piece of the core of our Inside Out Model. Self-acceptance means accepting yourself exactly as you are, including all your flaws and imperfections. If you make a mistake and find yourself being (humanly) imperfect, you don't get mired down in guilt, self-blame, or blaming others.

When you are OK with your flaws and imperfections, you allow yourself to see those flaws and imperfections more clearly, making you more self-aware. Your self-awareness extends to learning how your fear is driving ineffective behavior, which negatively affects trust and collaboration, so you can become more self-accountable.

---

[10] Will Schutz, The Human Element: Productivity, Self-Esteem, and the Bottom Line (Jossey-Bass 1994).

Self-accountability means understanding how you are contributing to every situation you find yourself in, rather than deflecting or avoiding responsibility for your own actions. Identifying your own contributions improves your ability to make conscious choices about how you'd like to behave differently to be more effective.

It can be easy to think that individual performance only means what technical or physical outputs a person can produce. However, individual performance extends to how people respond to and interact with other teammates. This is where many organizations get into the trap of focusing too heavily on the technical capabilities of an employee and overlooking the damage they are doing through their behavior toward other employees.

The Inside Out Model shows the dependence of the team on its individuals and the dependence of the organizational culture on its teams. And because culture exists between the ears of the individuals, it serves leaders well to better understand what goes on between those ears—what is called psychology. In the context of organizations, we focus on organizational psychology.

Our understanding of human behavior in organizations has evolved over the years.

Historically, managers subscribed to what Douglas McGregor calls Theory X of management. Theory X of management assumes that people don't enjoy working and therefore need to be pressured and controlled into achieving organizational goals. This resulted in roles that were designed with a very narrow scope—managers who literally and metaphorically peered over the shoulders of the workers and essentially treated them like robots or small children. Theory Y, in contrast, assumes a much more positive opinion about humans, both in terms of their motivation and what they are capable of accomplishing under the right conditions.

Organizational psychologist Chris Argyris extended this theory of human motivation by applying it to management behavior. Argyris argued that holding assumptions consistent with Theory X created a conflict with a mature human personality and urged leaders to design organizations that support employees as they grow along the Maturity spectrum. He asserts that leaders can actually get the most out of the people in the organization when their behavioral patterns align with the assumptions that people enjoy work and will accept responsibility under the right conditions. They will work hard to achieve a goal they accept, are inherently creative, and are motivated by the desire to realize their own potential.

Tapping into some of the most fundamental motivations as humans is a key way to fix the incongruence that Argyris described in his work. It is absolutely possible for leaders to bring the cultures of their organizations into alignment with what humans want.

So, what do humans want—or need—to perform at their best?

Tapping Into the Needs of Your Employees

Sometimes we say that organizations are just groups of people. Another perspective is that organizations exist to serve human needs. This is certainly true from a customer or client perspective. An organization serves its customers, who are humans seeking something to fulfill a need. But what about serving the needs of the humans within the organization?

Let's take a look at the word "need" for a moment. You're probably aware of Maslow's hierarchy of needs, as many of us learned about it in a psychology 101 class. The original model includes five levels, starting with the base level of needs which help us stay alive. But three of the five levels in his model are of a social nature. These social needs comprise our focus when we refer to human psychological needs.

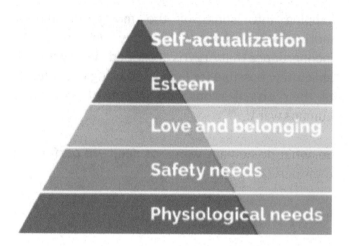

The Basic Psychological Needs Theory (BPNT) posits that there are fundamental requirements for humans to be well-adjusted and have overall well-being. While the absence of these psychological needs may not cause imminent death like an absence of food or water, an absence of fundamental psychological needs creates a higher risk of ill-being. For example, having a lower quality of relationships, higher stress, and less happiness can negatively impact physiological needs through poor eating habits, sleep deprivation, and higher blood pressure (Bartholomew et al. 2011, Ryan et al. 2016).

While Maslow specifically highlights physical safety in his model, he only *implies* psychological safety as a human need. Psychological safety is defined by Amy Edmonson as a *belief* that one will not be punished or humiliated for speaking up with ideas, questions, concerns, or mistakes. The *Columbia* tragedy is a powerful example of what can happen if an organization lacks psychological safety. Creating psychological safety in the culture could have given people the confidence to speak loudly and confidently through dissenting opinions and multiple layers of management.

While not all organizations face life and death consequences when they lack psychological safety, all organizations will benefit from cultivating an environment where people are willing to speak up, disagree, and provide feedback. In his best-selling book, *Think Again*, organizational psychologist Dr. Adam Grant describes his involvement in a study of high-performing teams at Google: "...the most important differentiator wasn't who was on the team or even how meaningful their work was. What mattered most was psychological safety." For our purposes, we pay attention to the drivers that contribute to an environment of psychological safety from which effective culture emerges.

A whole branch of psychology—evolutionary psychology—examines how we may explain human behavior based on how we have evolved as a species. Evolutionary psychology is built on an implicit assumption that social behavior between humans serves a function. At the most basic level, it is reproductive; however evolutionary psychologists posit that it extends beyond that.

For example, you've probably heard the phrase "It takes a village" when referring to raising children. Even conceptually, imagine thousands of years ago, having a newborn baby and simultaneously hunting for food. This is overly simplistic, but it's far too much for any one person to do on their own and not only survive but thrive. When you compare people in groups with high interdependence and high cooperation, they are more fit to survive than those who are solitary.

Additionally, this perspective supports the notion that these drivers are truly inherent and run deeper than any individual differences when it comes to age, gender, ethnicity, or personality. This suggests that humans are very motivated or driven to fulfill these psychological and social needs. For that reason, we call them "drivers."

Creating an Effective Culture: The Drivers

There are four fundamental human drivers in organizations: growth, belonging, connection, and identity. When leaders design their cultures in such a way that these human needs are met, they can tap into these intrinsic drivers to create an effective culture.

While there are nine criteria to determine that a psychological need is fundamental, we focus here on the three that feel most critical for our contexts:

1. Inherent—that the need ties back to our evolution as a species

2. Directional—that humans are motivated to fill that need and
3. Essential—that humans experience ill effects if the need is not met

We include inherent because we exist to evolve humanity and find that it serves us well to understand where we came from to continue evolving forward. We focus on directional because leaders continuously seek to understand how to create cultures where humans are intrinsically motivated. Finally, we focus on the criterion of essential to highlight that neutral is not neutral. When these needs aren't met, humans begin actively detracting from the culture you want to create.

The First Driver: Growth

We define the driver of growth as a fundamental human motivation to continuously expand our capacity, capability, and understanding to cope more effectively and thrive in the world.

From an evolutionary perspective, our ability to grow and learn enabled us to survive in our environments. Growth enabled us to develop new tools and ways to cope in the world to increase our ability to provide for our children.

In Maslow's hierarchy of needs, growth is best captured at the self-actualization level, which means it fulfills us from a spiritual sense. From the perspective of the Basic Psychological Need Theory, growth is best represented in competence which refers to effectiveness and achieving mastery to avoid feeling helpless.

Humans Are Motivated For Growth

The idea of mastery as a motivator is echoed in the work of Dan Pink in his book, *Drive*, where he identifies humans are motivated less by a carrot or a stick and more by purpose, autonomy, and mastery. He explains a study conducted by Edward Deci, who found that when people were asked to solve puzzles, those who were not provided an extrinsic reward of money actually spent more "free" time working on the puzzle in the long run, providing evidence that the learning and growth from working through the puzzle was its own reward. Improving a skill or more fully understanding an idea is a source of joy and fulfillment for humans. In fact, dopamine, a feel-good hormone, is associated with the moment of learning something new. So, your brain literally rewards you for your growth.

Humans Suffer Without Growth

Everything in the universe is expanding or contracting, so if you're not growing, you're dying. Dr. Daniel Amen, a psychiatrist and best-selling author, explains that when humans stop learning, they literally start dying.[11] He cites research showing that

---

[11] Daniel Amen, MD, "When You Stop Learning, Your

continuing to work past retirement age decreases the risk of getting dementia, largely because work keeps people mentally stimulated and growing. Of course, people can engage in learning and growth outside of work behaviors, but maintaining growth is essential to avoid the ill effects of cognitive decline.

Successful organizations focus on the individual development of humans. Without this, team building and organizational development will hit a plateau. Growth within teams and organizations is capped by the capacity of the leaders and individuals who comprise them. Unless you're growing the individuals, you are capping the growth of your organization—just one more reason that the "self" is at the core of our Inside Out Model.

[12]

The Second Driver: Belonging

We describe the driver of belonging as a fundamental human motivation for our authentic selves to be accepted by others in our environment.

Brain Starts Dying," LinkedIn, March 6, 2017, https://www.linkedin.com/pulse/when-you-stop-learning-start-dying-dr-daniel-amen/.

[12] https://gallaheredge.com/themissinglinks

From an evolutionary perspective, belonging to a group (or a tribe) used to keep humans alive. Belonging meant that you were afforded benefits of group membership, including protection from possible harm, which increases the likelihood of survival. It also meant an increased chance of long-term relationships resulting in having children who also can survive and thrive among the elements.

In Maslow's hierarchy of needs, once humans are past the physiological and physical needs to stay alive, belonging is the most foundational of the social needs. We are actively motivated to feel included in social groups where we form relationships to avoid problems like loneliness, depression, and anxiety.

Humans Are Motivated for Belonging

Baumeister and Leary (1995) reviewed decades of research on belonging. They report evidence of humans' motivation to belong is so strong that people work actively to hold onto relationships, "even if there is no material or pragmatic reason to maintain the bond and even if maintaining it would be difficult." They describe one study of human behavior where people sent holiday cards to strangers simply because they *received* a card from them. An abundance of evidence highlights the multitude of ways that humans are motivated for belonging, like our societal rituals such as weddings to honor a relationship. Even in situations when humans reject a bond (such as in unrequited love), we tend to feel distress and pain during the experience, showing how core belonging is to our existence as humans.

Humans Suffer Without Belonging

Brené Brown describes what can happen when humans feel deprived of belonging, which is a sense of shame. She defines shame as "the intensely painful feeling or experience of believing that we are flawed and therefore unworthy of love and belonging."[13] And feelings of shame lead to all kinds of ill effects like anxiety, depression, and self-destructive behaviors like addictions and self-isolation. Research from Kiecolt-Glaser and colleagues offers evidence that a lack of belonging leads to reduced immune system functioning,[14] and other research has linked loneliness to a higher incidence of illnesses, cancer, and even death.

Belonging appears to be a major differentiator in how we experience our lives and is clearly a fundamental human need. Organizations that create an environment where people feel they belong will benefit from greater energy and output from those

---

[13] Brené Brown, "Shame V. Guilt," Blog Post, January 14, 2013, https://brenebrown.com/blog/2013/01/14/shame-v-guilt/#close-popup.

[14] Janice K. Kiecolt-Galzser, PhD et al., "Urinary Cortisol Levels, Cellular Immonocompetency, and Loneliness in Psychiatric Inpatients," Psychosomatic Medicine Vol. 46, No. 1 (January/February 1984).

employees, as they are free to bring their whole selves to their work.

The Third Driver: Connection

We describe the driver of connection as a fundamental human motivation to have shared experiences, relatable feelings, and develop confidence with others.

Humans are hard-wired for connection. We are tribal creatures, and evolutionarily speaking, we literally used to depend on one another for survival. In tribal times, if a hunter was injured while on the hunt, he depended on his tribe to provide him with food and healing care until he was ready to get back on his own two feet and resume providing. When a hunter was unable to hunt and provide for the tribe (the hunter not giving something), the tribe was still there to care for him and nurture him back to health (the hunter taking something). It's the hard-wired nature of our brains for that connection that kept us together as humans, increasing our chance of surviving, adapting, and evolving.

Even today, when our dependence on one another can feel different from tribal times, we depend on each other.

_____

[15] https://gallaheredge.com/login/

Connection is best equated to Maslow's third level, which combines love and belonging, which is met by friendship and intimacy. In BPNT, relatedness is the experience of warmth, bonding, and care and is needed to avoid feeling alienated or lonely (Ryan and Deci 2017).

Humans Are Motivated By Connection

Humans devote an enormous amount of time and energy to connect with one another. A popular dating app, Tinder, had its highest amount of activity (3 billion swipes) when the COVID-19 pandemic hit the United States in 2020.[16] Other apps also saw significant increases over the next couple of months when social distancing regulations were enforced and people stopped spending time together like they previously had. While it is easy to argue that dating apps or other technology like social media actually create disconnection in our society, it's hard to deny that humans are intrinsically motivated to act in order to connect with each other.

Creating a connection between humans leads to improved health and brain function. For example, when mothers are nursing their babies, the bonding hormone oxytocin is released, which decreases

---

[16] Fortune Editors, "Activity on Dating Apps Has Surged During the Pandemic," Fortune, February 12, 2021, https://fortune.com/2021/02/12/covid-pandemic-online-dating-apps-usage-tinder-okcupid-bumble-meet-group.

blood pressure, increases generosity, and improves performance even during a stressful task. As adults, engaging in a twenty-second hug has been shown to result in an increase in the hormone oxytocin, which can reduce your blood pressure and improve your mood.

Humans Suffer Without Connection

Numerous studies have connected loneliness or the absence of human connection with premature death and other negative physiological symptoms. Research has shown that a baby who is not held and not loved, even if they are being fed and having basic needs met, will fail to produce sufficient amounts of the human growth hormone, their immune system development will suffer, and in some cases, they will even die.[17]

When humans create connection in an organization, they are motivated to work beyond minimum requirements. Organizations that foster connection between leaders and employees create cultures that fulfill this basic human need, enabling those humans to lean in toward one another, increasing collaboration, compassion, and Community.

---

[17] Maia Szalavitz, "How Orphanages Kill Babies—and Why No Child Under 5 Should Be in One" Huffington Post, November 17, 2011, https://www.huffpost.com/entry/how-orphanages-kill-babie_b_549608.

The Fourth Driver: Identity

We describe the driver of identity as a fundamental human motivation to feel ownership of ourselves as individuals and how we fit into the world.

From an evolutionary perspective, identity was critical to help people know who they could rely on with minimal risk of betrayal. If, for example, you knew you were in the same tribe as another human, you could feel confident that they would do what is in your best interest. Alternatively, if they were from another tribe, you might need to question if they were looking to acquire your resources or harm you to benefit their own tribe.

In Maslow's hierarchy of needs, identity is most closely related to esteem, which is about esteem for oneself (similar to individual identity), as well as the desire for status or prestige from others (similar to social identity).

Humans Are Motivated for Identity

The question of who we are—our identity—is so intriguing for humans. The Cambridge Analytica scandal involved exploiting humans' motivation to better understand their own identity by asking Facebook users to take a personality test called "This is Your Digital Life." Over 87 million users traded their personal information for an answer to this question around their identity. In 2019, personality tests were a $500 million-industry.[18] People are hungry to understand themselves and grow their awareness of their identity, as it is a source of comfort and utility. Knowing who we are helps us know what to do and how to behave.

Social identity can be defined as a person's sense of who they are based on their group memberships. According to Tajfel & Turner (1979), social identity theory includes three elements: social categorization, social identification, and social comparison.

In early life, children look to those around them to develop their identity. They learn how to categorize others—social categorization—usually oversimplifying in the process. Social identification means applying one or more categories to oneself as an individual, which leads to the third element: social comparison. This social comparison creates a basis for how we feel about ourselves or our self-image. Humans are motivated to have a positive self-image, which means they will evaluate their own social identity with high regard.

---

[18] Emma Goldberg, "Personality Tests Are the Astrology of the Office," New York Times, September 18, 2019, https://www.nytimes.com/2019/09/17/style/personality-tests-office.html.

Humans Suffer Without Identity

When humans lack a clear identity, they are generally described as having an identity crisis. It could include a lack of clear identity or an identity conflict. Identity crises have been linked to negative symptoms such as depression, fatigue, and issues with motivation and concentration.[19] Identity serves as an internal compass, guiding you to have a sense of what you are supposed to do. Living in alignment with one's identity or true self is a source of happiness. When people are living out of alignment, behaving to please or impress others, it is exhausting.

Developing a strong sense of identity is something we crave as humans because it brings us a sense of comfort. Whether your identity is attached to your alma mater, your favorite sports team, or your organization, identity is often a source of pride. Personal and social identities guide how we live our lives and make choices, giving us a sense of direction. Without direction, nothing matters.

 20   21

---

[19] Jamie Elmer, "What's an Identity Crisis and Could You Be Having One?" Healthline, January 22, 2019, https://www.healthline.com/health/mental-health/identity-crisis.

[20] https://gallaheredge.com/login/

[21] https://gallaheredge.com/themissinglinks

Tying It All Together

Tapping into some of our most fundamental drivers is a key way to fix the incongruence that psychologists like Argyris described in his work. It is absolutely possible for leaders to bring the cultures of their organizations into alignment with what humans need and want. The *Columbia* tragedy is a powerful example of what can happen if basic psychological human needs are not met.

When individuals do not feel psychologically safe, they fail to have the courage to speak up, disagree, and be vulnerable in a group of peers and leaders. Using concepts from the Inside Out Model and our understanding of drivers, we were able to see where NASA needed to shift its culture.

An effective culture can help an organization support the needs of the teams and individuals within it. With an organization like NASA, an effective culture can accomplish larger goals, starting with protecting and improving the lives of others. Consider for a moment: what kind of culture do you think would emerge in your organization when each of these four drivers is fully met?

Chapter 3

What is an Effective Culture?

"Alice: I just wanted to ask you
which way I ought to go.
Cheshire Cat: Well, that depends on
where you want to get to.
Alice: Oh, it really doesn't matter, as long as I g...
Cheshire Cat: Then it really doesn't matter
which way you go!"
Alice in Wonderland [22]

Why is Culture Important?

It was November 12, 2003, and a headline in *The Washington Post* read, "NASA Blasts to the Top of Workplaces Ranking." This article was commenting on the results of the Office of Personnel Management's survey conducted from May to August 2002—a mere six months before the February 1 *Columbia* accident.

---

[22] https://gallaheredge.com/themissinglinks

An excerpt from the article read:

"An unlikely agency landed atop a non-profit group's new rankings of the top federal workplaces: NASA. The 45-year-old agency, racked since the fatal space shuttle *Columbia* disaster, nevertheless emerged in the No. 1 spot on the Partnership for Public Service's inaugural Best Places to Work in the Federal Government rankings.

"What the data tells us is that NASA's workforce is the most engaged, the most committed of any in the federal government," said Max Stier, president of the partnership, which tries to stimulate interest in government service."

This surfaced an apparent contradiction between the findings of this survey and the findings of the CAIB, which blamed NASA's culture for the accident as much as the foam that hit the wing. To resolve this contradiction, it is necessary to be very intentional about defining the objective for culture. So, while NASA had what many would consider a good culture, the real question is whether it had an *effective* culture. For NASA, this had to mean more than an engaged and committed workforce. It meant our astronauts had to return safely to earth.

This is a deceptively simple truth: to optimize something, you must first know what you are optimizing.

How to Determine an Effective Culture

Organizational culture is an extremely complex attribute of an organization. It's difficult to analyze, difficult to measure, difficult to change or manage, and even difficult to define. However, to create the results you want in your organization, we must start by defining what is meant by an effective culture. Failing to fully define and understand the nature of organizational culture leads to a lot of failed attempts to effectively leverage it to drive company performance and success.

Three criteria can be used to determine whether an organization's culture is effective. An effective organizational culture:

1. Drives business results
2. Increases employee engagement
3. Improves lives

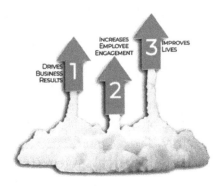

Drives Business Results

An effective organizational culture must drive business results. Organizations exist to create value and generate profits for their owners/shareholders. Federal agencies such as NASA exist to deliver public value. Both types of organizations can have critically important safety or other performance criteria intricately linked to their mission. So, one of the goals of an effective culture is to assist the organization in achieving these outcomes. The best way to evaluate how well the culture supports the organization's ability to achieve business results is by assessing it through the lens of the company strategy.

Company strategy captures how a company intends to compete and deliver value while maximizing profit. Consequently, assuming that the company has accurately developed a strategy that enables it to compete and win (which we define as accomplishing its goals), an effective culture is one that is aligned with this strategy. When there is alignment between the strategy and the culture, the attitudes, beliefs, and resulting behaviors of employees are naturally those that are required to execute the strategy. This removes the need for burdensome enforcement mechanisms to drive the needed behaviors, like adding multiple layers of approvals into a process or requiring reams of documentation and record-keeping. Such mechanisms not only deplete the energy and resources of the company, they also often fail. This is exactly why Peter Drucker famously said, "Culture eats strategy for breakfast." It doesn't mean that strategy is unimportant.

On the contrary, an effective strategy is critically important to organizational success; rather, it means that when the two are in conflict, culture always wins.

Therefore, one goal in creating an effective culture is to intentionally design it around your strategy. This statement sounds much more linear than it is. In reality, there is a feedback loop where your culture naturally influences the strategy you select, and the strategy influences the design of your culture. Consequently, it can be an iterative process, especially if neither is well established. We recommend starting by defining your strategy and ensuring that it is perfectly clear, understood and supported by the leadership team. Once this is done, it becomes the North Star for aligning your culture and your organization design.

John Kotter and James Heskett conducted a longitudinal study of 207 US companies across twenty-two industries that spanned an eleven-year period. This study comprised one of the most comprehensive analyses of the impact of corporate culture on performance. The results from this study are astounding:

	INEFFECTIVE CULTURES	EFFECTIVE CULTURES	DIFFERENCES
NET INCOME INCREASE	1%	756%	755%
REVENUE INCREASE	166%	682%	516%
STOCK PRICE INCREASE	74%	901%	827%
WORK FORCE EXPANSION	36%	282%	246%

From this, we can see that not only is culture an important part of creating a positive work environment that drives retention and employee engagement, it also has a direct impact on the bottom line. Digging into the numbers above, we see that companies with ineffective cultures grew their revenue by 166 percent while only increasing net income by a mere 1 percent. In essence, these companies were extremely inefficient at converting revenue into profit. They have to continually grow revenue by almost 166 percent just to maintain their current profit.

Compare that to the effective cultures, and we see revenue increase by 682 percent (more than four times that of ineffective cultures) with a corresponding increase of 756 percent net income. These companies both outperformed companies with ineffective cultures by a factor of four and became more efficient in the process—growing profit by a greater percentage than they grew revenue. As we all know, it's not how much you make but how much you keep that determines success!

Increases Employee Engagement

The second criterion is that an effective culture must drive employee engagement. Arguably, this criterion could be merged with the former due to its tremendous impact on business results. One Gallup study[23] found that companies with the highest levels of employee engagement were 22 percent more profitable and 21 percent more productive, while another study[24] found that companies with engaged employees outperformed their peers by 147 percent in earnings

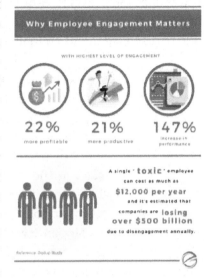

per share. Furthermore, the opposite of engaged isn't necessarily a neutral state; it is active disengagement, which is toxic. A single "toxic" employee

[23] Susan Sorenson, "How Employee Engagement Drives Growth," Gallup, June 30, 2013, https://www.gallup.com/workplace/236927/employee-engagement-drives-growth.aspx.

[24] Gallup, "A Global Pandemic. And its Impact on Global Engagement, Stress and the Workforce," Accessed August 6, 2021, https://www.gallup.com/workplace/349484/state-of-the-global-workplace.aspx?g_source=EMPLOYEE_ENGAGEMENT&g_medium=topic&g_campaign=tiles.

can cost as much as $12,000[25] per year, and it's estimated that companies are losing over $500 billion[26] due to disengagement annually.

While these figures are astounding, we believe that engagement is significant and unique enough to warrant discussion as a separate criterion. Including engagement as a criterion allows us to focus on one of the key elements of performance that produce the business results in the first criterion. Here we are looking at the extent to which employees feel passionate about their jobs and how committed they are to the company, which determines how much they will go above and beyond in their work. Engagement is a fascinating combination of heart and mind composed of an intrinsic emotional connection to the business and its purpose, along with a rational evaluation of the benefits, conditions, and quality of employment.

As with culture itself, the specific formula for engagement at a given organization is as unique and diverse as the employees who work there and is shaped by the values and purpose they share.

---

[25] Michael Housman and Dylan Minor, "Toxic Workers," Harvard Business School, 2015, https://www.hbs.edu/ris/Publication%20Files/16-057_d45c0b4f-fa19-49de-8f1b-4b12fe054fea.pdf.

[26] Susan Sorenson and Keri Garman, "How to Tackle U.S. Employees' Stagnating Engagement," Gallup, June 11, 2013, https://news.gallup.com/businessjournal/162953/tackle-employees-stagnating-engagement.aspx.

Regardless, the overwhelming factor in driving engagement is organizational culture. A quote about creating engagement we like is, "Culture is king. Compensation is key. Good leadership is gold."[27] This quote helps to illustrate the head and heart connection involved in engagement while emphasizing culture's leading role. Given the important and far-reaching implications of engagement and the central role that culture plays in its creation, an effective culture must increase engagement.

Improves Lives

The third and final criterion of an effective culture is that it must improve lives. This may sound somewhat idealistic, but we do believe that providing a healthy and engaging work environment for people to come to every day greatly improves their lives. Companies have a role and a responsibility beyond just earnings, both within the lives of their employees and society. The idea of corporate social responsibility has gotten a lot of traction in recent years, and most companies are practicing some form of this. We don't feel it is a stretch to say that companies can change the world to make it a better place and improve people's lives. An effective organizational culture supports and produces this type of social responsibility as an extension of the company.

---

[27] Emplify, "Why People Value Culture More Than Compensation Now," Accessed August 6, 2021, https://emplify.com/blog/value-culture-over-compensation.

Even without such lofty goals, an effective culture will still improve lives because of its impact on the individuals within the organization. We spend a tremendous amount of time at work—roughly one-third of our lives—and the quality of the work environment directly impacts the quality of our lives. For many, that impact reaches beyond the walls of the office as they take it home with them. So, when we create a healthy work environment through an effective culture, oftentimes, we are improving the lives of both the employees and their families.

The improvement in people's lives comes through a combination of psychological, emotional, and physical benefits. These elements are often so intertwined that it's impossible to separate them. A CareerBuilder survey[28] on stress in the workplace found that 61 percent of employees are burned out, and 31 percent of the respondents reported extremely high levels of stress at work. This survey also shows how that stress resulted in poor physical health (tired, aches and pains, weight gain, high blood pressure) and compromised mental health (anxiety, depression, anger). By creating a positive work

---

[28] Career Builder, "Do American Workers Need a Vacation? New CareerBuilder Data Shows Majority Are Burned Out at Work, While Some Are Highly Stressed or Both," May 23, 2017, https://press.careerbuilder. com/2017-05-23-Do-American-Workers-Need-a-Vacation-New-CareerBuilder-Data-Shows-Majority-Are-Burned-Out-at-Work-While-Some-Are-Highly-Stressed-or-Both.

environment and reducing the negative impacts of stress and burnout, an effective culture can have a tremendous positive impact on people's lives.

29

Four Traits Essential to Effective Culture

Now that we have defined the criteria for an effective culture, the next question becomes, what does an effective culture look like? This is actually a more complex question to answer than it may seem. Recall that culture is an emergent property of organizations created by the interaction of common attitudes, beliefs, and behaviors held by its employees. This definition highlights the two-fold challenge of working with organizational culture: First, it can take on many shapes and permutations as every organization is unique. Second, it is based on the attitudes and beliefs inside the heads of individuals.

Because culture is unique for every organization and inextricably linked to the humans that comprise it, learning and applying best practices from other companies can be challenging. In fact, it is typically an abject failure when one organization tries to copy the culture of another organization. Often, this results in copying cultural artifacts (remember

---

29 https://gallaheredge.com/login/

our joke about a ping pong table in the office as the ultimate example of this) or trying to copy and espouse values and other sentiments that don't have meaning or exist within the individual belief systems of employees.

To help navigate this quandary, we have identified what is unique versus common across highly effective cultures. Based on our criteria of organizational effectiveness, we have identified four traits essential to an effective culture:

1. Maturity
2. Diversity
3. Community
4. Unity

A Sturdy Foundation: Maturity

The first trait of an effective culture is Maturity. While it is important for all traits to be present to truly achieve effectiveness, Maturity is foundational and has a significant impact on the other three traits. We define Maturity as a culture where individuals manage themselves and their behavior to enable consistent, efficient production of products while effectively communicating and interacting with others. The process of achieving Maturity is a journey we all are on. We recognize that Maturity is an area where all humans—the authors included—can continue to grow. Furthermore, we recognize that regardless of how far along we are on this journey, our behavior can be immature at times. This is especially true when we are tired and hungry or when someone triggers our feelings of insecurity around our self-concept.

Driving Business Results

If you've run a business of over thirty people (or even worked in one), our definition of Maturity probably sounds extremely appealing, and you can probably see immediately how this trait would drive business results. To fully appreciate the dramatic impact that Maturity has on an organization, we point back to chapter one and think of the organization from a systems perspective.

In an organization that lacks Maturity, employees have difficulty regulating their emotions in challenging situations. This will cause some to shut down; others will lash out and become terse in their communications. Employees will also avoid having difficult conversations, so resentments will build and over time, cliques will form.

As we describe these behaviors, think in terms of feedback loops and how those will create escalation, downward spirals, and lock the organization into negative patterns of behavior. It will become difficult to get things done, and the working environment will not be fun! This will decrease the ability to solve problems, innovate, and respond quickly to challenges. All of this grows in that exponential fashion we described as it is multiplied across the employees in your organization.

You may be asking yourself, "But how does this really affect my business results?" Honestly, the business results we describe above could almost be considered as the answer to this question. The behaviors associated with this trait have such a pervasive and overwhelming impact on a company's performance, it would be fair to credit them with much of the success or failure associated with the business results. Another way to look at this is purely from a "time is money" standpoint. When an organization lacks Maturity as described above, it sucks time and resources away. Time is lost because employees avoid each other, or fail to communicate, or spend time in unproductive meetings. Whenever the employees in an organization are spending time on unproductive things, and errors are increasing because of poor communication, it affects the bottom line.

Finally, one hallmark of Maturity is the presence of self-awareness. Employees behave in a more mature manner when they possess self-awareness because they see their own contribution to situations and recognize the impact of their behavior on others. Unsurprisingly, research shows that this capability is good for business and drives results. Korn/Ferry

International studied[30] the stock performance of 486 publicly traded companies and found that those with strong financial performance had employees with higher levels of self-awareness than the poorly performing companies. Employees at the poorly performing companies had 20 percent more blind spots and were 79 percent more likely to have low overall self-awareness than those at high-performing companies.

Increasing Engagement

As Maturity increases within your employees, communications, team dynamics, and organizational performance will skyrocket. Those feedback loops we mentioned will become positive, producing healthy interactions among your employees and increasing employee engagement. This increase in engagement comes from two sources. First, it comes from greater enjoyment of the work environment and commitment to both the organization and fellow employees. Second, it comes from a greater sense of self-actualization driven by the growth in self-acceptance, self-awareness, and self-accountability. This also leads to increased engagement stemming from a greater perception of control over their

---

[30] Korn Ferry, "Korn Ferry Institute Study Shows Link Between Self-Awareness and Company Financial Performance," June 15, 2015, https://www.kornferry.com/about-us/press/korn-ferry-institute-study-shows-link-between-self-awareness-and-company-financial-performance.

life and workplace. When we have a strong relationship with ourselves, we are fully alive and present, which keeps us engaged while working and brings the best we have to offer to our jobs.

One of the most important creators of employee engagement is the manager-employee relationship. The fact that 81 percent of HR professionals surveyed in HR.com's State of Employee Engagement 2019 report[31] identified employees' trust in their organization's leaders as the top contributor to employee engagement highlights this point. The level of Maturity in an organization has a great impact on how well this relationship works by ensuring both parties have the self-awareness and self-accountability to see and own their contribution to situations that arise in the workplace. Additionally, it is a critical component for the ability to hold effective crucial conversations, which are the key to quickly resolving both work

---

[31] HR. "The State of Employee Engagement in 2019: Leverage leadership and culture to maximize engagement," May 2019, https://www.hr.com/en/resources/free_research_white_papers/hrcom-employee-engagement-may-2019-research_jwb9ckus.html.

and interpersonal issues so everyone can get back to being productive.

Because of its ability to influence both the quality and effectiveness of every relationship within an organization, Maturity positively contributes to numerous other drivers of employee engagement, including:

- Feeling their work is meaningful
- Feelings of empowerment
- A sense of belonging
- Recognition
- Purpose
- Fulfilling work relationships
- Autonomy

Improving Lives

The ability to meaningfully influence relationships goes well beyond the job, however, and permeates every aspect of the individual's life. We often hear from clients that our work has made as great an impact in their personal lives as it did at work. Despite what some may think, we are whole, integrated individuals. Compartmentalization is rarely successful, and when it is, it's typically destructive to the individual. When we work with our clients to grow their Maturity, we are improving the lives of those people. The knowledge, skills, and abilities they learn help them become more effective at dealing with all aspects of their lives—

at work, home, and everywhere else. It also helps them become healthier and happier individuals because they learn to deal with feelings they had been ignoring or expressing in unhealthy ways. They also learn more effective behaviors, which make them more effective individuals. And perhaps most important, they gain a greater ability to love and accept themselves, which is the key to making everything else in life better.

All Are Welcome: Diversity

The second trait of an effective culture is Diversity. We define this trait as a culture that actively seeks, invites, and involves people with various skills, experiences, backgrounds, and perspectives while accepting them for who they are. To meet this definition, it is necessary to create an organization representative of the broadest possible demographic profile where individuals across that spectrum are included on teams, in decisions, and at all levels of leadership. This has always been a critically important trait in an organization because of its importance in creating an effective culture. However, the events of 2020 made it clear to anyone paying attention that Diversity was critical for civil, social, and humanitarian reasons beyond mere organizational performance. While we will stick to our core expertise and focus primarily on the contribution of Diversity in creating an effective culture, we did want to acknowledge the importance of these other aspects. We encourage you to seek experts in those areas to learn more.

Driving Business Results

It's somewhat ironic that so much effort must be put into creating Diversity within organizations because the business case for it is so strong. Countless studies have shown that bringing together a broad variety of individuals with different skills, experiences, backgrounds, and perspectives in an inclusive and accepting manner produces bottom-line results. These results stem from a higher quality of decision-making when more perspectives are involved, and a wider set of experiences and perspectives contribute to the solution. And research confirms this benefit extends to social Diversity as well as educational/ disciplinary Diversity. McKinsey & Company's 2018 Delivering through Diversity Report confirmed once again that not only was Diversity a driver of business results but that the lack of Diversity actually served as a penalty. According to their study:[32]

- Companies in the top-quartile for gender Diversity on their executive teams were 21 percent more likely to have above-average profitability than companies in the fourth quartile.

---

[32] Vivian Hunt, Sara Prince, Sundiatu Dixon-Fyle, and Lareina Yee, "Delivering Through Diversity," McKinsey, January 2018, https://www.mckinsey.com/~/media/ McKinsey/Business%20Functions/Organization/ Our%20Insights/Delivering%20through%20diversity/ Delivering-through-diversity_full-report.ashx.

- Companies in the top-quartile for ethnic/cultural Diversity were 33 percent more likely to outperform on profitability.
- Companies in the fourth quartile on both gender and ethnic Diversity are 29 percent more likely than the other three quartiles to underperform on profitability.

Diversity also produces greater innovation and an increased ability to adapt. This ability to adapt comes from both an enhanced ability to detect the need for change and an increased ability to respond to the change. And in today's environment, the ability to quickly adapt is key to survival.

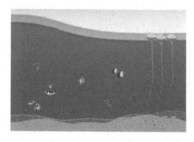

Imagine, for example, the importance of being able to predict a tsunami. The Bureau of Meteorology uses deep ocean tsunami detection buoys to confirm the existence of tsunami waves that result from undersea earthquakes. These buoys can report changes in the sea level minute by minute. But this technology would not work if there were ten buoys clustered together (representing homogeneity). This lack of Diversity would fail to acknowledge pattern shifts and meaningful differentiations across a large span of water. If the buoys are clustered together, they will only be able to detect meaningful change—and trigger the alarm to do something about it—when it happens right where they are. But undersea earthquakes can occur in a variety of places, so the buoys must be spread out to increase the chances that it will detect that change, alerting you to take action.

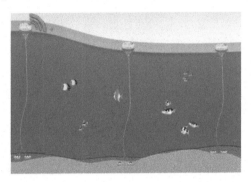

Organizations work in the same manner. Diversity within your organization and your leadership team increase the likelihood that humans will detect changes and the need to adapt to stay ahead of them. If your whole leadership team thinks alike, comes from the same background, and is literally or metaphorically in the same place, the chances are much greater that you will miss important signals that enable you to stay ahead of your competition and continue to add value to a changing world.

To experience the benefits of Diversity, we want to not only invite in a wide variety of perspectives, backgrounds, and experiences but also include and involve them in meaningful ways. This involvement drives business results because it helps to ensure maximum utilization of your workforce. This matters because your payroll costs are likely one of your largest expenses, and it's silly to let your talent sit there underutilized while paying their salaries. This is obviously a double whammy when most companies feel resource-constrained and constantly starved for talent.

Increasing Engagement

In addition to the direct effect that Diversity has on costs, it also increases engagement. When individuals are appropriately included, they feel valued and motivated to provide their contributions. A 2015 study by Deloitte found a statistically significant relationship between Diversity practices and employee engagement for all employees. And specifically, the researchers concluded that promoting inclusion in an organization was an important means of increasing employee engagement.

Ultimately, the strong link between engagement and inclusion, as well as with Diversity in general, comes down to employee experience. But not just the employee's own experience. Employees take their own experiences and beliefs about the experiences of other employees and construct a belief about how the company values its people. If leaders in the organization treat another employee poorly, then they might do the same to them. This belief eventually decreases the trustworthiness of the company in the mind of the employee. Engagement is decreased through the head/heart equation for engagement, as we discussed earlier, as the employee decides exactly how much extra to give to the company. They are also deciding how much they can safely give the company.

When psychological safety is created, Diversity works to increase engagement. This type of environment where people feel supported, included, and at one with their psychosocial workplace environment decreases individual anxiety and allows them to bring their whole self to work. This idea of "whole self" is central to engagement because it is difficult to be fully engaged when you are expending energy to hide or suppress some aspect of yourself. Furthermore, it is hard to feel enthusiastic about a workplace that requires this type of charade. Creating a culture of Diversity is a powerful way for companies to increase engagement.

Improving Lives

Creating organizations that proactively invite people to be who they are and involve them in meaningful ways at all levels of the organization does improve lives. Although we began this section by cautioning that we would not be approaching Diversity from a largely social perspective, organizations have an inherent social responsibility and play a powerful role in shaping today's society. It is incumbent on every organization to continually strive toward improving Diversity while dismantling systemic racism within its sphere of influence. This not only improves the lives of immediate employees but can have impacts well beyond the boundaries of the organizational chart.

A Sense of Camaraderie: Community

Our third trait of an effective culture is Community. We define this as a culture where individuals know and like each other, feel a sense of camaraderie, and express genuine concern for one another with a corresponding desire to help. This trait embodies much of what people often think of when they describe a "good" culture. It possesses many of the hallmark traits of effective teamwork and positive working relationships and describes what it feels like when working on a team just clicks. Individuals openly share information about both the work and themselves, trust each other, are empathetic, and want to help one another.

Driving Business Results

When individuals feel a strong sense of Community within their organization, they feel compelled to drive business results. Research from Gallup has shown that only about 20 percent of people "strongly agree" that they have a best friend in their workplace.[33] However, if that were to go up to 60 percent, organizations would recognize numerous benefits, including 12 percent higher profit and 36 percent fewer safety incidents. Community provides a means of support. While we are not as

---

[33] Annamarie Mann, "Why We Need Best Friends at Work," Gallup, January 15, 2018, https://www.gallup.com/workplace/236213/why-need-best-friends-work.aspx.

tribal now as we once were as a species, our need for other people has not gone away. Whether it is receiving encouragement from a teammate, getting advice from somebody who has gone through your challenge before, or somebody simply pitching in to get things done, more work is getting done by teams now. And humans can accomplish so much more as a team. These days, it is virtually impossible to accomplish anything as a lone individual, so the effectiveness of your organization is determined by the effectiveness of your teams.

A metaphor can be pulled from the sports world, specifically looking at how Community contributes to the performance of a team. According to Tefu Mashamaite, a South African association football player (that's soccer to us Americans), "The success of a team sport is more dependent on the cohesion of the sum individuals in the team than just individual brilliance, and yes, it's very important that proper relationships and interactions are forged between various footballing stakeholders. As the adage goes, the team is only as good as its weakest link; one can argue that the strength of the chain depends mainly on the relationship, i.e., trust, reliability, coachability." Sounds a lot like he's talking about emergence, doesn't it?

Clearly, Tefu sees a direct link between the Community that exists on a team and its ability to perform, but he doesn't stop with the relationship between just the players. "Players need a good and healthy relationship with the coach because it reinforces a sense of belief and alleviates all unnecessary stresses. A sense of belonging builds self-confidence, and a confident team can overcome any obstacle. Therefore, as a player, knowing that a coach has your back whether win, lose or draw gives one more energy to fight."

Increasing Engagement

This energy to fight translates into increased engagement. When we feel we are in that fight together, we will strive longer and harder than if we feel we are in it alone. Consider this popular example of synergy. A single draft horse can pull up to 8,000 pounds on its own, but when two draft horses work together, they can move up to 24,000 pounds—well over double what one of them alone can do. And this weight can be further increased through training the pair of horses to work together. Community is the key to unlocking that synergy and enabling one plus one to equal three or even four. And during times of extreme turmoil or uncertainty, Community can serve as the force that pulls the organization together.

As we've referenced, the space shuttle *Columbia* tragedy in 2003 was a big turning point for NASA. The presence or absence of Community could have been the difference between this organization pulling itself together or pulling itself apart. From Phillip's perspective, employees at NASA felt a strong sense of Community as they worked to recover the debris that was scattered across Texas and Louisiana following the tragedy. Every single

NASA employee and contractor felt they owed it to the fallen crew to find every possible piece of debris so they could reconstruct the shuttle as fully as possible to best understand exactly what happened. There was no such thing as an organizational barrier or red tape during that entire process. Multiple states, multiple space centers, and even multiple federal agencies worked together to get things done quickly. Everybody just came together—no squabbling or arguing over jurisdiction or politics. While cultural factors contributed to the accident, NASA's sense of Community was very strong.

Improving Lives

This sense of Community within the NASA family also helped many of us process the tragedy and cope with the many challenges associated with the investigation and return to flight. Community improves lives by providing people with much-needed support. As humans, we need other humans. In the United States, the Bureau of Labor Statistics reports that productivity per worker has increased 400 percent since 1950 and that 65–85 percent of Americans work more than forty hours a week.[34] With such a significant portion of our lives spent in the workplace, the ability to create Community and provide support is an important contribution

---

[34] G.E. Miller, "The U.S. is the Most Overworked Developed Nation in the World," 20 Something Finance, January 13, 2020, https://20somethingfinance.com/american-hours-worked-productivity-vacation.

to people's lives and can significantly enhance their health. Studies, such as the one found in the American Journal of Lifestyle Medicine have shown that feelings of support and connection with those around us can lead to positive health benefits.[35]

The Glue That Binds: Unity

The final trait of an effective culture is Unity. We define this trait as a culture where individuals work as one with a high degree of alignment around purpose, direction, goals, and behaviors. This trait enables an organization to transform from a collection of pieces and parts into a coherent system that functions in a coordinated manner. The less an organization possesses, the more it devolves from a state of complexity toward chaos.

Driving Business Results

Unity's ability to drive business results lies in focus. One quote that illustrates this particularly well by Harry Emerson Fosdick is, "No steam or gas ever drives anything until it is confined. Niagara cannot be turned into light and power until it is tunneled." The same is true of the resources in your organization,

---

[35] Jessica Martino, Jennifer Pegg, and Elizabeth Pegg Frates, MD, "The Connection Prescription: Using the Power of Social Interactions and the Deep Desire for Connectedness to Empower Health and Wellness," American Journal of Lifestyle Medicine 11 (6) (Nov/Dec 2017): 466-475.

which, as we said, is essentially just a system that turns inputs into outputs. When organizations lack Unity, the energy is being converted into strife, arguments, working at cross purposes, waste, turf wars, politics, and sabotage. Conversely, the power of Unity is revealed in the absence of these destructive behaviors. When all that energy is focused back into the direction the organization has decided they want to go, the results can be astounding. Rather than scattered light, you now have a laser.

Unfortunately, creating this laser focus and alignment can be much harder to do than it sounds. As we've already discussed, an organization is a complex adaptive system. So, getting it to move in unison in a singular direction requires a systems view of both the task and the organization. Just consider trying to get six people to move a boulder by pushing on it. Now, this particular boulder is so big, it will only move if all six people are pushing in the same direction. As the leader, you can organize your team to accomplish this task easily, right?

Well, not so fast. This boulder is also roughly spherically shaped. So, when two people are standing next to each other, they are actually pushing at a slight angle to each other. The angles which people push with respect to each other increase as they move further from each other. The net result of this is that enough force is diverted away from the direction you actually need your team to push in that the boulder won't budge, as shown in the graphic on the next page.

To succeed at this task, it will be necessary to create a system to align the force of your team to ensure that they are all pulling in the same direction. Perhaps you could attach a rope to a single point on the boulder and then have everyone pull on the rope. The point is, without creating an organizational system to properly align and guide the efforts of the team, misalignments will create inefficiencies that will bleed energy out of the system, silently robbing you of resources and sabotaging your results. These misalignments occur naturally as a form of organizational entropy, not because anyone is trying to misalign the system, but because it takes less energy to operate that way than it does to keep things tightly aligned. It's important that leaders constantly stay vigilant about ensuring they create and maintain the alignment required to effectively and efficiently execute their strategy.

Often leaders will comment to us that, "It seems like we have more people than ever, are working harder than ever, but are getting less done!" A lack of Unity drains the energy, joy, and momentum from the organization and has a direct and measurable impact on the bottom line. The financial impacts are far-reaching but consider this simple example.

If you have a monthly payroll of $1 million and misalignments within your organization result in 10 percent unproductive time (an extremely conservative estimate—a 2016 study by Global Corporate Challenge found it is to be 25 percent),[36] you are losing $100 thousand per month or $1.2 million per year! That is just in payroll costs and doesn't account for lost sales, increased operations costs, waste, and employee turnover.

Increasing Engagement

Compare that with an organization where everyone is truly on the same page regarding the vision, goals, and how they plan to get there and who's doing what. This type of Unity increases people's engagement because they buy into where the organization is going and how it is getting there. And let's face it, it just feels so much better to be a part of an organization where everybody is on the same team *and* the same page. Imagine being on a team where you hit that traction point in the game of tug of war—and BOOM—you win. That feeling. Imagine that feeling happening again and again. As a team and as an organization, you enjoy the journey. This is also how Unity increases engagement—by helping

---

[36] Sandy Smith, "Presenteeism Costs Business 10 Times More than Absenteeism," EHS Today, March 16, 2016, https://www.ehstoday.com/safety-leadership/article/21918281/presenteeism-costs-business-10-times-more-than-absenteeism.

individuals see greater progress and experience the surge of momentum.

Unity reduces unhealthy conflict, which oftentimes is actually the result of systemic influences. Think back to the boulder example. What if the individuals on the far outside edges noticed that they were almost pushing in different directions and then, under the influence of the hot sun, the fundamental attribution error—the tendency to attribute another's negative behaviors to some flaw in their character—kicked in, and each decided that the other one was doing it because they were stupid or trying to be difficult? The resulting accusatory statements led to a heated argument which then, well...does this sound like any turf wars in your organization?

Leaders aren't immune to these influences either. What if you had gotten mad at the individuals on your team because you had told them all to push in one direction and they weren't? But it was because of the shape of the rock and not some act of rebellion or laziness? What would that have done to team morale? Would it have rallied the team and inspired them to push harder? It's likely that the individuals pushing on the boulder thought they were doing what they were asked to do and were probably pushing as hard as they could and already felt frustrated because they were giving it all and seeing no progress. Being reprimanded would have just been pouring salt into the wound. How the leader responds and the organization's ability to create Unity will either produce engagement or disengagement in these individuals.

Improving Lives

An organizational culture with the trait of Unity improves people's lives by reducing negative and unhealthy conflict within the organization and creating a more enjoyable journey. As described above, when people feel the surge of momentum working in their favor, it is an uplifting experience and can add energy and excitement to the work environment. And everyone loves being on a winning team. The feelings of alignment and shared purpose among team members can be strong motivators that make work feel like a shared journey.

Furthermore, creating a strong sense of Unity greatly decreases frustration and burnout. As we described earlier, burnout is a significant concern, and reducing it greatly improves the lives of individuals. To further illustrate how significant this impact can be, one study[37] analyzed the evidence of physical and psychological consequences of job burnout across thirty-six studies. It found, "Burnout was a significant predictor of the following physical consequences: hypercholesterolemia, type 2

---

[37] Denise Albieri Jodas Salvagioni et al., "Physical, Psychological and Occupational Consequences of Job Burnout: A Systematic Review of Prospective Studies," PLoS One, 12 (10) (October 2017), https://www.ncbi.nlm.nih.gov/pmc/articles/PMC5627926.

diabetes, coronary heart disease, hospitalization due to cardiovascular disorder, musculoskeletal pain, changes in pain experiences, prolonged fatigue, headaches, gastrointestinal issues, respiratory problems, severe injuries, and mortality below the age of forty-five years. The psychological effects were insomnia, depressive symptoms, use of psychotropic and antidepressant medications, hospitalization for mental disorders, and psychological ill-health symptoms."

In today's organizations, it may be that the single greatest contribution leaders can make to improving the lives of their people is to create Unity. This can't happen without corresponding Maturity, as we've said previously. However, creating a workplace that is free from negative conflict, where employees are pulling in the same direction with a strong sense of purpose, clear goals, and focus eliminates the destructive feelings of frustration and burnout and produces positive feelings of momentum and winning. And as the study above shows, this clearly improves lives.

The Missing Links

As we saw with NASA, it's possible for an organization to have the most engaged and committed workforce and still fail at executing its mission. It's not enough to have a great culture; you must have an effective culture. Although all cultures are unique, effective cultures produce four common traits. These common traits of Maturity, Diversity, Community, and Unity are emergent properties produced by the interactions of shared beliefs of employees. One of the biggest challenges of working with organizational culture is learning how to shape, manage, and change it when culture ultimately lives between the ears of employees. However, by combining the science of human behavior with the principles of complex systems, we have developed a model that shows how to successfully shape and create an effective culture. The key to this model lies in what we call the missing links of organizational culture.

 38

---

38 https://gallaheredge.com/themissinglinks

Chapter 4

The Missing Links

"The meeting of two personalities is like the contact of two chemical substances: if there is any reaction, both are transformed."
—*Carl Jung*

[39]

Discovering What Was Always There

It was a beautiful Sunday morning in 2019, almost fifteen years to the day since I (Phillip) had been asked to lead the organizational and cultural changes for return to flight after the *Columbia* accident. Those intervening years had taken me on an amazing journey of exploration into organizational culture and the science of human behavior I never would have imagined when I first started. But through it all, one quest had remained singularly constant. From day one, I began striving to better understand organizational culture, and perhaps even more important, to simply, clearly, and effectively explain it to others.

---

[39] https://gallaheredge.com/themissinglinks

Transforming organizations is not the work of one person. It requires the involvement and support of a wide variety of people in different capacities within the organization, from the CEO and executive team to the team leading the change to the leadership across the organization, key stakeholders, and ultimately, every employee. The ability of these people to effectively analyze the organization, communicate the cultural challenges and need for change, and implement the prescribed solutions is critical to achieving success. Furthermore, due to the complex nature of culture issues, it must be clear how and why the prescribed solutions will address the identified challenges to gain full buy-in.

I could not find any model or framework that addressed the challenges we were facing at NASA after the *Columbia* accident, so I ultimately made my own models. One challenge I always struggle with is the inherent tension between simplicity and accuracy when dealing with complex systems. As an engineer, it often feels hard for me to distinguish between a lack of accuracy and lying. This is something that I've had the help of many good mentors to work on and one of the ways Laura still challenges me to grow regularly.

My initial attempts were painfully crude and incredibly complex. An early version, called the Systems Wheel, was just a big circle of different cultural drivers that affect employee behavior. I would sit for hours with the organizational psychologists and talk about the different drivers of behavior and culture and how the science of human behavior created organizational culture. Together, we would continually update and refine our models, simplifying and using them with organizations. This allowed us to gather real-world feedback about what worked, what was clear, and what made sense so we could improve them. One iteration used root cause models that analyzed the specific contributors to challenges we were facing and solutions that could mitigate those contributors. Eventually, we created causal loop diagrams based on my study in business dynamics at the Massachusetts Institute of Technology (MIT), even traveling to MIT to get their input on our model.

A Systems View of the Ladder of Inference

While this causal loop model proved very instructive for us as consultants and researchers, it still did not meet the goal of being simple, clear, and easy to understand for the average person off the street. Fortunately, NASA was committed to changing its culture and ensuring that another *Columbia* accident never happened again, whether I could clearly explain organizational culture or not. The tools we created and the dedicated people we had across KSC succeeded in improving the culture and continue to make KSC's culture highly effective.

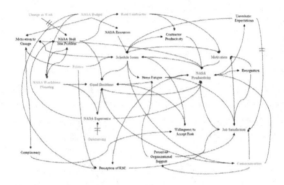

Meanwhile, Laura and I continued to develop and refine models we used with clients outside of NASA to help them develop and maintain effective cultures. One we've already introduced you to is the Inside Out Model. This model definitely meets the criteria for clarity and simplicity. We love how well it communicates one of the most important truths about organizational culture—that everything starts with the Self, and even if you are dealing with an organizational issue, you will want to begin by considering how the Self level is influencing that issue.

Unfortunately, the Inside Out Model was too simplistic once it came to working with clients on their organizations. The Inside Out Model was missing one final requirement: the ability to connect a solution to the issues within an organization and understand how and why they were going to work. We needed something more, but not too much more. How do you take the knowledge and lessons of fifteen years of work with numerous PhDs across a wide variety of organizations—not to mention the shoulders of innumerable giants we were standing on through research and study—and distill that down into a clear, simple, yet comprehensive model?

So, there I was, fifteen years later, sitting in church on a warm, sunny Florida Sunday. As I listened to the pastor, the words of the sermon seemed to wash over me like soothing waves. On this particular morning, it felt like they contained a special secret message meant only for me. That somehow, they held the key to unlocking a box in my mind that held a deep secret—one I had been trying to access for fifteen years. At that moment, it became clear how we could organize the model around the traits of Maturity, Diversity, Community, and Unity, and how these four traits created a clear, concise, and easy-to-communicate model that was comprehensive in covering all the work we had done. I could see how these traits could be grounded at the individual level through innate human drivers.

Perhaps most spectacular of all, I could see how the work that Laura and I had been doing with organizations to help them create effective cultures came together to create the four traits of Maturity, Diversity, Community, and Unity. I could see how it all worked together.

Is this how it feels for all major discoveries? I was wandering around the hallways of my brain and stumbled upon it lying on the floor as though it had been there all along. Just waiting to be discovered, but I'd just never turned down that particular hallway before. Is this how Edison felt when he finally figured out how to make a working lightbulb (not that I'm comparing the magnitude of the two discoveries)? It felt the same for Laura when I explained it to her. It just felt right. She instantly got it and was able to add to it and make it better. We felt tremendous energy and creativity around defining the model and how quickly it had developed and been understood by both of us. We actually struggled more trying to determine the right metaphor to communicate the model than we did with trying to create the model itself. Ultimately, we chose the metaphor of a DNA strand because we felt it both signified the role culture played as an organization's basic genetic material and because we felt it aligned with our company's "why" of existing to evolve humanity.

The true test of the model, however, was not what we thought about it; the true test was how clients would respond to it. We tested it with existing clients to see how they would react and whether they would quickly and easily grasp the concepts. To our delight, they loved it. We then moved quickly to use the model with prospective clients, and the results were just as positive. We feel very confident in presenting this model as an effective way to diagnose, explain, and address organizational culture.

How Does Your Culture Taste?

To intentionally create an emergent culture, leaders can create opportunities to develop the missing links between the people in their organization by tapping into the drivers of human behavior. The fact that culture is created by the relationships between the humans in your organization is often overlooked and poorly understood. This is why we call them "missing links." In reality, they aren't missing at all—they exist to varying degrees between the people in every organization. These links are similar to the bonds between the hydrogen, carbon, and oxygen elements that create the sugar molecule we described in chapter one. When they are present and hold those elements together in the right relationships, it produces the emergent taste of sugar. However, if you change the structure or relationship of those elements, you could just as easily end up with gasoline, which would have a quite different emergent taste.

The missing links within your organization are no different. Although they may be present, the degree to which they exist, the strength of the bond, and how the link is constructed can vary greatly from organization to organization. The differences in the links create the differences between the cultures of various organizations. Some of the differences are what make the culture of an organization unique and special. However, other differences transform the nature of the culture from one that tastes like sugar to one that tastes like gasoline.

To effectively establish these links between the humans, you want to have something to which the links connect. This is more powerful and much easier to accomplish when linking to an innate human driver—something that is naturally present and compels us at an instinctual level. This is why we focus on connecting the links to the drivers of growth, belonging, connection, and identity that we discussed in chapter 2. This creates a strong attachment point for the link and a source of energy and motivation for its maintenance.

The Missing Link Model allows leaders to create an emergent culture of Maturity, Diversity, Community, and Unity by tapping into the drivers of growth, belonging, connection, and identity to develop the missing links between the humans in their organization.

The Missing Link Model

To guide leaders through the process of creating an effective culture, we have created the Missing Link Culture Model. This model shows how the traits of Maturity, Diversity, Community, and Unity emerge at the cultural level, while their drivers of growth, belonging, connection, and identity are fueled at the individual level by connecting your people through the Missing Links. This creates four individual strands that produce the desired cultural traits. The Missing Link Model, with its four strands and the missing links, is shown below:

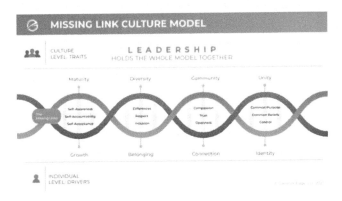

Each strand connects an individual driver to a cultural trait through a combination of three missing links. These links work together synergistically to produce the emergent cultural trait. Without all three links, it will be impossible for the trait to fully emerge. Additionally, while we did our best to create a model where the strands are independent, the emergent nature of culture is such that there is linkage and overlap between the strands. Increasing self-awareness throughout an organization, for example, will certainly have an impact on openness, influencing the emergence of both Community and Maturity. So, it is important to understand the model both from a strand perspective as well as a holistic perspective. We must never lose sight of the fact that we are working with a complex adaptive system whose behavior is both emergent and path-dependent. Reductionist methodologies shouldn't be used to analyze or apply the model by looking only at a strand in isolation.

Below are high-level descriptions of each strand and the links that comprise them.

Maturity

Leaders can create a culture where individuals manage themselves and their behavior to enable consistent, efficient production of products while effectively communicating and interacting with others. This is accomplished by tapping into the driver of growth to develop **self-acceptance, self-awareness,** and **self-accountability** between the people in their organization. We define these links as:

Self-Acceptance: being fully OK with everything about who you are, including flaws and imperfections as well as the ability to honor your strengths and talents

Self-Awareness: the ability to see yourself as you really are, fully acknowledge your own experience, and recognize your impact on others

Self-Accountability: taking full responsibility for the choices you have made to co-create every situation as well as the ownership of how you will contribute to creating what you want

Diversity

Leaders can create a culture that actively seeks, invites, and involves people with various skills, experiences, backgrounds, and perspectives while accepting them for who they are. This is accomplished by tapping into the driver of belonging to develop **differences**, **respect,** and **inclusion** between the people in their organization. We define these links as:

119

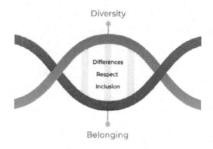

Differences: possessing a variety of ideas, backgrounds, perspectives, ethnicities, skills, beliefs, genders, and age groups as well as many other dimensions that contribute to making each of us unique

Respect: treating others with the esteem due to all humans

Inclusion: involving and engaging individuals in meaningful ways that allow them to contribute fully

Community

Leaders can create a culture where individuals know and like each other, feel a sense of camaraderie and express genuine concern for

one another with a corresponding desire to help. This is accomplished by tapping into the driver of connection to develop **compassion**, **trust,** and **openness** between the people in their organization.

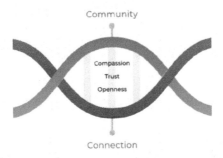

Trust: believing firmly that someone has your best interest at heart and has the ability and commitment to do what they said they would do

Compassion: an understanding of how others feel with a corresponding desire to take action to support

Openness: a willingness to be vulnerable by disclosing your awareness of your own experience or what feels true for you

Unity

Leaders can create a culture where individuals work as one with a high degree of alignment around purpose, direction, goals, and behaviors. This is accomplished by tapping into the driver of identity to develop **common purpose**, **common beliefs**, and **control** between the people in their organization. We define these links as:

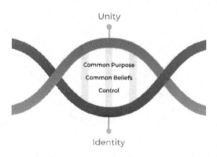

Common Purpose: a compelling reason for the existence of your organization that inspires people to make the world a better place

Common Beliefs: a shared world view that defines how people will behave toward one another

Control: the boundaries and mechanisms that determine how the organization functions and achieves its goals

We will describe each strand in great detail throughout part two and explain how the driver is ideally suited to support each trait. We will also go into a thorough discussion of each link and how leaders can intentionally develop them between their people. This will provide a thorough understanding of the model and how it can be applied within an organization.

The Tie That Binds: Leadership

The true key to applying the model, however, is leadership. In fact, we say that leadership is what holds the whole model together. This is because it is the leaders' responsibility to create the culture, and their words and actions can have a disproportionate effect on shaping and changing it, so much so that we often refer to leadership as the engine for culture change. We will take a much deeper look at the role leadership plays in managing and changing culture in part three. For now, we will summarize with a quote from the CAIB Report, "Leaders create culture. It is their responsibility to change it."

You can go to The Missing Links resources page to take our Missing Link Quick Assessment now to receive a personalized report for your organization.

40

Possessing a Greater Capacity to Adapt

In part three, we will also explore how an organization's ability to adapt is actually an attribute of the culture and not merely an accident. This means that when a culture has the traits of Maturity, Diversity, Community, and Unity, it will possess a greater capacity to adapt. This capacity is critical to the survival of the organization. In today's world, an organization's internal capacity to adapt must be greater than the rate at which the external environment is changing. Otherwise, the company will get left behind. This internal capacity is found

---

40 https://gallaheredge.com/themissinglinks

primarily in its people and culture. One of the main functions of leadership is to lead change, and an organizational culture designed for adaptation will make this job a lot easier. Companies with effective organizational cultures will enjoy a significant competitive advantage due to their ability to quickly adapt to changes in the environment and outpace their competition.

Humans Are Gloriously Complex

The Missing Link Culture Model is a powerful tool for assessing, managing, and changing organizational culture. It is particularly effective for communicating how culture is created within an organization and what leaders can do to make positive improvements. It is heavily grounded in the science of human behavior and based on well-documented research in organizational psychology. These theories are applied through a lens of complexity theory which recognizes the organization as a complex adaptive system and culture as an emergent property. So, while it remains both simplistic and relatable in its construction, it contains sufficient depth and complexity to accurately describe and address the true nature of organizational culture. Because of this, our biggest challenge in writing this book was restraining ourselves from offering only the content presented on these pages. The subject matter itself is surely as deep and fascinating as the human being itself in all its glorious complexity.

PART TWO

Scan here to access free additional content[41]

---

[41] https://gallaheredge.com/themissinglinks

Chapter 5

The First Strand: Maturity

"The battles that count aren't the ones for gold medals. The struggles within yourself—the invisible, inevitable battles inside all of us—that's where it's at."
—Jesse Owens

See No Evil...

The decision to look at the foam strike as an in-flight issue or post-flight issue is a critical one in the case of *Columbia*. Before *Columbia*'s final mission, STS-107, the Program Review Control Board (PRCB) classified the occurrence of foam striking the orbiter as a post-flight issue, which means the immediacy to resolve it as a threat to the lives of the astronauts goes away.

---

42 https://gallaheredge.com/themissinglinks

This was a flawed decision based in part on inaccurate information presented to the decision-making body. Shuttle program manager Linda Ham didn't verbally question the decision at the meeting, but she later referred to the rationale for the decision as "lousy." And yet, when various teams were investigating the foam strike that occurred during the launch of STS-107, despite believing the decision had a lousy rationale, Ham's sentiments and questions were not focused on understanding the in-flight risk for the current mission. In a Mission Management Team Meeting, chief mission evaluation room manager Don McCormack shared with Ham and the team that they were analyzing the extent of the damage and discussing what their options were if they *did* discover damage to the orbiter. Ham's reply included the following quote: "I don't think there is much we can do, so it's not really a factor during the flight because there is not much we can do about it."

She redirected the team away from assessing the risk and exploring solutions. Several engineers initiated requests for imagery that would allow them to better assess the risk, but Ham didn't support those requests and shut them down. Given that Ham found the rationale for the decision to be lousy, one might expect that she would have been more prone to understand the in-flight risk. But she also expressed a belief that there was no solution to the problem if they did, in fact, find there was a problem from the foam strike. Ham's belief that there was no viable solution to the problem could have subconsciously influenced her opinion about whether it was truly an in-flight problem worth exploring.

If you don't believe you have the power to do anything impactful to solve a problem, you may subconsciously convince yourself that it is not a problem, which is a defense mechanism. It can take an incredible amount of inner confidence to have the vulnerability to say, "This could be a real problem, and I don't yet know how to solve it." But without strong inner confidence or a high degree of self-acceptance, you can experience a gap in self-awareness, such as convincing yourself that no problem exists. And with decreased awareness, self-accountability drops. If you're not allowing yourself to be fully aware of a problem, then you won't make the choice to explore solutions to that problem.

Throughout her career, we don't doubt that Linda Ham always wanted to make the absolute best possible decisions for NASA and that she cared deeply about the lives of the astronauts. At the time, Ham was married to an astronaut, and arguably, nobody could have had more care and dedication to the safe execution of the mission. This is a powerful example of how leaders with the best intentions can still make poor decisions that shut down problem-solving.

Why We Start With Maturity

Maturity is the first strand in our Missing Link Culture Model, and it won't surprise you to know that our choice to place it there is by design. Our

Inside Out Model has Self at the core and includes the elements of self-acceptance, self-awareness, and self-accountability. This is mirrored in the Maturity strand and reflects, once again, the simple truth that everything starts with the self.

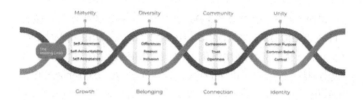

Once or twice over the years, we agreed to clients' requests to go straight into facilitating conversations around competitive strategy or organization design and skipped over the workshops that facilitate individual growth in self-awareness. The problem with this approach is that whatever communication issues held the team back from reaching effective decisions when we weren't there were still present when we were. We would pause the conversation, bring in a useful tool to help leaders understand how they were subconsciously showing up defensively, and return to the dialogue, only to repeat this pattern minutes later.

Most of the time, when leadership teams are struggling to make decisions, *how* they are communicating with one another is a very big part of the problem, and it is one that many people choose not to address directly. The last time you felt a conversation was going off the rails or feeling ineffective, did you pause to call out what you were noticing and shift the conversation to discuss the interaction itself? Or did you keep pushing through the conversation, hoping it would resolve itself? Most people do the latter because it can feel strange or at least unfamiliar to call out the interaction itself. And this becomes a repeated problem.

In an HBR article[43] that describes why strategy execution fails in organizations, ten of the twenty reasons are connected to humans' ability to effectively communicate with one another (e.g., unclear communication, lack of commitment, resistance to change). Sometimes the most important problem to solve is the communication problem (or problems). Then the rest of the discussions yield much more information with better shared understanding and better decisions with much stronger team alignment.

Even in the work we do around strategy and organization design, we tell our clients that a description of the strategy is only one of the products we deliver. The other two are an aligned team and executive development. Together, we align the team by surfacing resistance and vetting decisions so that each person on the team can commit, with heart, to

---

[43] Jeroen Kraaijenbrink, "20 Reasons Why Strategy Execution Fails," Forbes, September 10, 2019, https://www.forbes.com/sites/jeroenkraaijenbrink/2019/09/10/20-reasons-why-strategy-execution-fails/?sh=644c2edd1ebe.

the decisions that are being made. This requires a level of Maturity, and that is why we always begin with this strand.

The Power of Maturity

We define a culture of Maturity as one where individuals manage themselves and their behavior to enable consistent, efficient production of products while effectively communicating and interacting with others. While organizations are complex adaptive systems, it's useful to remember that organizations are just groups of people. How those people regard one another, feel about each other, and behave toward one another ultimately comes back to how they feel about themselves. Maturity emerges when leaders tap into the driver of growth to develop self-acceptance, self-awareness, and self-accountability between the people in their organization.

Focusing on creating a culture of Maturity is invaluable for an organization. When you think of your role as a leader, how many times in any given week do you find yourself dealing with the "people" issues that come up? Whether it's an accounting employee going around her boss to express frustration with how he is micromanaging or a sales manager whose department has a reputation for steamrolling people because they're the revenue engine and think they can get away with it, every leader knows these challenges. A lack of Maturity in an organization creates additional problems beyond the existing problems that the organization already exists to solve. A lack of Maturity includes people triangulating about each other—talking behind others' backs—and talking over each other because nobody is truly listening, or people are avoiding one another because they don't get along. The time and energy that is wasted on ineffective management of people issues translates to thousands or even millions of dollars lost each year.

Not only does a higher level of Maturity in an organization yield positive business results, but because the interactions between people are much healthier, engagement also increases. When people feel good about who they are (high self-acceptance), know themselves fully (high self-awareness), and take responsibility for the circumstances of their lives (self-accountability), everything about their lives improves, and they contribute positively to society, their families, and their organizations.

Linking Growth to Maturity

Growth is our fundamental human motivation to continuously expand our capacity, capability, and understanding to more effectively cope and thrive in the world. Our desire for growth is built into our human DNA because, evolutionarily speaking, learning how

---

44 https://gallaheredge.com/login/

to navigate the world was essential to our survival. Our human ability to survive the elements, prepare ourselves for challenges, and continuously decrease the likelihood of succumbing to our environment is how we have continuously evolved.

From this intrinsic desire for growth emerges Maturity. Whether you consider a toddler growing their language skills to enable more mature interactions with parents (asking for what they would like rather than simply crying as babies do) or you think about an adult focusing deeply on learning skills to be more effective in relationships, real growth always leads to higher levels of Maturity.

All growth is emotional. The activity of learning any new knowledge set or skill takes humans through an emotional process. Think of the last new thing you learned. What emotions did you experience? Curiosity? Determination? Confusion? Frustration? Satisfaction? Joy? Pride? When we grow as humans, our emotions are key.

Neurologist Antonio Damasio worked with a patient he calls "Elliott" who suffered in his life after a brain tumor was removed from his frontal lobes. The surgery impacted the part of his brain that processes emotions. So, while he was intelligent in a cognitive sense, his life seemed to be falling apart because he struggled to make even basic decisions.[45]

---

[45] Antonio Damasio, Descartes' Error (New York: Penguin Press: 2005).

Our decision-making, as humans, is a very emotional process. Even those of you who feel you are very logical, creating cost/benefit analyses or pros/cons lists rely on your emotions to gauge what to include in the analyses and what to give weight to.

Maturity is also intricately linked with emotions as it requires a level of emotional intelligence. Humans are very emotional creatures. In their book *Burnout*, authors Emily and Amelia Nagoski explain that Positron Emission Tomography (PET) imaging has clarified humans are very emotional beings who sometimes think, rather than being very logical beings who sometimes feel. Everything about how we're showing up connects back to our ability to manage our own emotions. Whether it's staying calm and centered while in a conversation that feels adversarial and confrontational or keeping frustrations in check while untangling headphone wires, humans engage with the world more maturely when they have been able to grow.

As you help the individuals in your company grow—of course, always starting with yourself—you will see higher levels of Maturity emerge across the organization.

How Do You Create Maturity?

Maturity is created by tapping into the driver of growth to develop self-acceptance, self-awareness, and self-accountability between the people in your organization.

Self-acceptance means you choose to accept yourself, with all your flaws and imperfections, as well as all your strengths and talents. When you choose to accept yourself, it makes it easier for you to see those flaws, imperfections, strengths, and talents, increasing your self-awareness. And as you become more self-aware, you recognize that you have so many more choices in terms of how you want to behave and show up in the world. You're more self-aware of your own choices, and you're more willing to be fully responsible for those choices. You're also empowered to make the choices you want to make to create more of the life you want for yourself and those around you (self-accountability).

Missing Link: Self-Acceptance

Self-acceptance happens when you decide you are fully OK with how you are, right now, in this moment. Let's begin with a brief explanation of self-esteem. Think of one circle that represents how you see yourself today (your self-concept), and another circle that represents you in your ideal state. See the illustration on the next page, which represents these constructs as two circles in a Venn diagram. At the simplest level, the extent to which these two things overlap represents how high your self-esteem is.

---

[46] https://gallaheredge.com/login/

Self-acceptance, how-
ever, is more nuanced.
Self-acceptance is *how
you feel* about the gap between who you are today
and who you want to be.

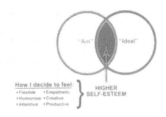

On the one hand, if you look at the gap and believe
it is evidence that you are not enough and are de-
ficient in some way, you'll experience lower self-acceptance. If, on the other hand, you look at the gap
and feel good about both where you are and the
direction that gap represents, you will experience
higher self-acceptance.

When you have higher self-acceptance and accept
yourself as you are, you show up with more flexibility.
You are more creative and open. You are more
humorous. You are more attentive to others. You are
productive because your energy is focused
outwardly on problem-solving.

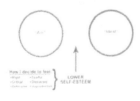

When you experience
lower self-acceptance,
you show up with more ri-
gidity. In those moments,
you are consumed, con-
sciously and subcon-
sciously, with fear of how you are perceived and fear
of how you feel about yourself, and that prevents
you from being attentive to others. You are focused
on self-preservation rather than on problem-solving. You will lack humor and be less productive.

We describe self-acceptance as the key to making everything in your life easier, but it is often misunderstood.

Self-Acceptance Contributes to Growth

One of the most dangerous myths about self-acceptance is that it leads to an absence of growth or self-improvement. This stems from the belief that self-acceptance is on the opposite end of the spectrum of self-improvement. In reality, self-acceptance and self-improvement can and do co-exist. And you are your best self when you choose to be high on both.

Research shows that higher levels of self-acceptance actually accelerate your growth. Soo Kim and David Gal found that higher levels of self-acceptance led to more actions aligned with self-improvement. In their study, participants were briefed on self-acceptance and asked to write about a time when they felt high self-acceptance and describe the importance of unconditional acceptance of self. Others were simply asked to write about their last trip to get groceries. Next, all participants were asked to write about a time when someone had power over them. When participants are asked to reflect on a time when they felt powerless, it can trigger a desire to compensate in ways that aren't actually helpful, like paying more money for a luxury item to help them feel better about themselves. That happened for participants who were *not* primed toward self-acceptance (they expressed a willingness to pay more for luxury items). However, participants who *were* primed toward self-acceptance were not triggered to engage in compensatory activities. Instead, they were more likely to express a willingness to buy a product to help them improve (a book that could help them develop a skill—*Power and Influence for Dummies*). Their findings suggest that self-acceptance does not lead to an absence of self-improvement but rather increases the likelihood that people will seek self-improvement resources.

Recognizing the paradox of self-acceptance and self-improvement is a game-changer. Instead of believing that self-acceptance will lead to complacency and that you *need* the fear of not being

enough to drive you to grow, recognize that self-acceptance will help you grow faster and easier.

You probably have things about yourself that you would like to improve upon. The reality is, you will never get to a place in your life where you feel that you are "done" developing, learning, or growing. You will always find things you want to change or improve. Therefore, just because you can identify things you would like to improve upon is no reason to not accept yourself exactly as you are.

Imagine two kids at the batting cages. One of them, Joey, has low self-acceptance. When he swings to hit the ball and misses, it triggers all his fears about not being good enough. His inner critic starts to rage about his mistake. On the outside, Joey grips the bat tightly, twists his face up into anger, and he screams in frustration. His coach tries to calm him down and offers advice, which takes a good thirty seconds before Joey is calm enough to hear the advice to help him learn and grow. But he's still not fully calm. He's trying to listen, but he's holding tension in his body in ways he's not even aware of, and his mind is still spinning, beating himself up, and feeling stress. So, as his practice session continues, he struggles to incorporate the advice and coaching, and his growth is stalled.

The other child, Jamal, has high self-acceptance. When he swings to hit the ball and misses, he feels disappointed for a moment but doesn't subconsciously internalize. After all, he's here to learn!

He looks at his coach, who says, "No worries, buddy; just choke up a little on the bat and turn your head so you can watch the ball all the way until it makes contact with your bat."

"OK!" he replies confidently.

And just like that, there's growth. Joey might also grow. He could eventually calm down and shake off the frustration so he can hear the advice. Or he may decide that hitting is too hard and he hates it (because he doesn't feel good about himself when he does it) and quit. If that's the case, he won't grow in this area.

This is an example of "toddler mentality," a valuable piece of self-acceptance. A toddler just learning to walk doesn't negatively judge herself because she can't walk perfectly. When she attempts to walk and then falls, she doesn't call herself "stupid" and feel embarrassed about the failure. The toddler just gets up and tries to walk again. As adults, however, we often treat ourselves as though we should be experts at everything—even things we have never attempted before. One result of this is that we work to avoid failure in an attempt to avoid the negative feelings about ourselves that it produces. Unfortunately, however, this typically means that we learn very slowly or not at all.

The same is true when it comes to our tendencies to learn and grow in a new functional area at work or our ability to receive feedback on how we can improve our interpersonal skills. When you have higher self-acceptance, this actually fuels your ability to grow, rather than impeding it.

Imagine yourself in a meeting, presenting your work on a project, and somebody makes a comment that you experience as harsh criticism. You notice an emotional reaction in the moment, and as much as you want to take it constructively, you find yourself distracted for the rest of the meeting. Subconsciously, you don't like the insecurity this comment has triggered, so you're distorting what's happening and struggling to stay focused. You're worried about what others think of you because of the feedback you received, and you're stuck in your head, either feeling angry and defensive about what was said, or maybe you feel sad and defeated. Either way, in this state, you're less likely to learn and grow until you can get to a place where you feel better about yourself in the moment.

When you have high self-acceptance, you're able to internalize the feedback while still feeling good about yourself, accelerating your ability to learn and grow.

Linking Humans With Self-Acceptance Creates Maturity

When individuals in an organization have high self-acceptance, the nature of their interactions is mature. Working in an organization yields all kinds of stressors, such as balancing workload, making strategic decisions, and working with different types of people. But how people cope with those stressors makes all the difference in how the culture emerges. If people do not feel good about themselves at work, they will subconsciously interpret what's happening around them as threats. A looming deadline threatens to reveal incompetence. A coworker's tendency to gossip threatens one's sense of likability. Being left out of meetings can threaten one's sense of importance.

But when individuals have a high degree of self-acceptance, they are less likely to internalize what is happening around them as evidence of their own inadequacies. Instead, they will be more effective at assessing the situation. And because they feel good with themselves—even with their flaws and imperfections—they'll be able to better understand how their flaws and imperfections are contributing and make effective adjustments. People with high self-acceptance have a stronger ability to regulate their emotions during difficult times.

Research by Dimitri Agroskin found that individuals who feel better about themselves actually have more gray matter in the areas of the brain that help people regulate their emotions. This is further evidence that self-acceptance contributes to the emergent trait of Maturity because Maturity is characterized by managing their behavior and their interactions with others effectively. Emotional regulation is correlated with the quality of relationships (Gross and John, 2003), and it is key to a culture of Maturity.

Let's return to the hypothetical example of you sitting in a meeting, having just received feedback that felt like harsh criticism. What's the most mature way you could respond? You likely imagine yourself staying calm, focusing on the person giving you feedback, thanking them for their input, asking a follow-up question to understand his thought and ascertain the most meaningful and valuable part of his input. Your calm, collected, authentic style probably also calms down any emotions he was experiencing, and as a result, you both feel more connected.

Not only do higher levels of self-acceptance accelerate growth and create mature interactions, they also facilitate higher levels of self-awareness. When you are OK with yourself as you are, with all your flaws and imperfections, it's easier for you to see yourself as you truly are: self-aware.

Missing Link: Self-Awareness

We define self-awareness as the ability to see yourself as you really are, fully acknowledge your own experience, and recognize your impact on others. All humans suffer from self-deception (the opposite of self-awareness). There are things about yourself that you do not let yourself know, such as convincing yourself that health is important to you while eating fast food five times each week and exercising once per quarter. Or you may deceive yourself into thinking that your coworker is "such a jerk" for criticizing your project ("everybody thinks so, right??"), rather than recognizing that fear is actually triggered in you (I fear Jane thinks I'm not good at my job because deep down I'm afraid I'm not good at my job). Self-awareness allows you to reduce self-deception and see yourself and the world more accurately. How can people increase their self-awareness?

We are Licensed Human Element® Practitioners, and when we work with our clients, the work of The Human Element® is a big piece of the work we do to help them increase their self-awareness.

The Human Element® is built around the Fundamental Interpersonal Relations Orientation (FIRO) theory developed by Dr. Will Schutz. FIRO is a theory of human behavior that connects how humans behave to the desire to feel significant, competent, and likable. The theory looks at humans as onions, having layers to explain how we show up. FIRO asserts that our behavior is categorized into inclusion, control, and openness (ICO). And those behaviors predominantly align with the feelings of significance, competence, and likability (SCL).

BEHAVIOR	INCLUSION	CONTROL	OPENNESS
FEELINGS	SIGNIFICANCE	COMPETENCE	LIKABILITY
FEAR	IGNORED ABANDONED	HUMILIATED EMBARRASSED	REJECTED DISLIKED

For example, you may be more likely to feel *significant* to a coworker when they *include* you in things, like getting to know you as a person, inviting you to meetings, or including you in emails. You may be more likely to feel *competent* in the presence of your boss when she delegates *control* to you, allows you to influence her decisions, and empowers you to run your department. And you may be more likely to feel *likable* when your coworkers are *open* with you, share their personal thoughts and feelings with you, and regard you with warmth. When you don't feel as significant, competent, or likable as you'd like to feel, this subconscious feeling can trigger defensiveness, which yields immature emotional reactions that destroy collaboration and teamwork.

Let's say, for example, that your coworker, Bob, has ignored your emails for the last two weeks. Subconsciously, if this triggers a fear of insignificance in you, you will experience a defensive reaction. You may feel a desire to blame ("Bob is such a jerk!"), or you might feel like a victim ("Why is Bob doing this to me?"). As humans, we can be creative and stealthy when it comes to how our defenses manifest. One of the most common tools we use with our clients is a Signs of Defensiveness Survey. Check out The Missing Links book resources page[47] to download and complete the survey for yourself to increase your own self-awareness.

---

[47] https://gallaheredge.com/themissinglinks

When defenses are triggered, it may seem like you are defending yourself against Bob for his unjust treatment of you and your emails, but you're actually defending yourself against your own harsh judgments of yourself. Each of us has a psychological immune system that subconsciously protects us from things we don't want to see or hear. First, your brain creates a story in your head about how Bob feels about you (e.g., "Bob's ignoring me because he doesn't think I'm important enough" [insignificance]). But the onion goes one level deeper than the story in your head about how Bob feels about you. Most of the time, that story about Bob's behavior will only trigger defensiveness in you when it hits on a deeper fear and insecurity you have about yourself (your self-concept).

This psychological immune system causes you to distort what you see. The work of The Human Element® calls this distortion defensiveness. When you distort what you see, you inhibit your ability to learn and grow, take in new information, adjust your perspective, and make good decisions—so you can get stuck. It can be hard to hear different views and take in what they're saying when we're distorting reality.

When we talk about self-awareness, we are not simply talking about seeing yourself the way others see you—although that is a valuable piece of awareness and is a part of the work we do with our clients. We are talking about allowing yourself to know yourself fully and completely, practicing awareness of your whole experience (thoughts, feelings, beliefs, assumptions, physiological sensations, memories, intentions, and more). This includes allowing yourself to surface the subconscious stories that trigger you, the emotional archeology to uncover what past experiences helped create those stories, and what tools can help you rewrite the narrative that leads to higher self-acceptance.

Self-Awareness Fuels Growth

The individual driver of growth is our fundamental human motivation to continuously expand our capacity, capability, and understanding to cope more effectively and thrive in the world. It almost goes without saying that increasing self-awareness contributes to growth. Because humans have a psychological immune system to prevent us from feeling the pain of our own harsh judgments, without self-awareness, each of us would struggle to grow. We would blame the world for our bad feelings and circumstances we're unhappy with in our lives and be blind to how we are contributing to every situation we're a part of.

> "The range of what we think and do is limited by what we fail to notice. And because we fail to notice that we fail to notice, there is little we can do to change; until we notice how failing to notice shapes our thoughts and deeds."
>
> —R. D. Laing

Becoming more self-aware is the key to unlocking how you can grow. If you are not aware of your tendency to listen poorly when you feel stressed, it won't even occur to you to develop the skills of emotional regulation to reduce stress and the skill of active listening. Research by Anna Sutton found that greater self-awareness is correlated with greater self-development, improved decision-making, and better job performance (Sutton, Williams & Allinson, 2015).

When Laura first attended The Human Element® in 2009, she had a profound self-awareness awakening. She learned a lot of things about herself, but what stood out to her most through the feedback she received and the experiences she went through was that others were not as open with her as she wanted them to be. Laura learned that her subconscious defensiveness manifested in ineffective behaviors that shut others down. Specifically, she did not always listen very well, especially if she felt stressed out or felt a strong disagreement with what she was hearing. While it was very challenging for her to learn this about herself and become more self-aware, it was instrumental in helping her grow. She was able to grow as a leader, better understand her own reactions to situations, and align her behavior with her intentions. The experience also helps her empathize with clients when they struggle with the same feelings and behaviors. This self-awareness was and continues to be pivotal to her growth.

Linking Humans With Self-Awareness Creates Maturity

When you think about the moments in your organization when people lack self-awareness, what comes to mind? Perhaps it's the well-meaning high achiever who has no idea how much she steamrolls other people when she's leading a project. Or maybe it's the verbose leader who thinks that he's fantastic at running meetings but actually just talks the whole time and feels satisfied with how that felt. Or maybe it's the seasoned employee who is convinced that he has been passed up for promotion because his bosses are threatened by him when everybody else can see he has major interpersonal gaps that he needs to fill before becoming an effective leader. In every instance where people lack self-awareness, you probably think, "If only they could mature their thinking" or "It's just an emotional Maturity issue."

On the flip side, when you imagine people who are very mature and able to manage themselves effectively, you likely think of people who know themselves well, understand how they feel in various situations, and are aware of their impact on others. They give and receive feedback effectively, they talk through disagreements calmly while keeping their highest intentions clear in their minds, and they collaborate on even the toughest problems. This is what Maturity looks like, and it is created when humans are linked together through their self-awareness.

Psychologist Anna Sutton teamed up with Helen Williams and Christopher Allinson to study the impact of an intervention designed to increase self-awareness. They measured the effectiveness of the training over a period following the intervention and found that participants demonstrated improved communication, confidence, and better relationships—all key attributes of Maturity.

In working with us, one client discovered that one of his triggers was feeling insignificant. This happened if he felt like others were not valuing his time. This could be when they wanted to complain about a decision they already spent time making together, when they wanted him to jump in and help with work when he was on vacation, or if they were going to him to solve a problem instead of working through the established reporting structure. Often, when he felt triggered like that, he would withhold what he was thinking and feeling. Sometimes, he would even pull back from an email conversation for multiple days because he felt so bothered by it.

When he uncovered the source of his trigger—fear of not being respected or regarded as significant—he noticed that it decreased his emotional intensity, and he felt more able to show up effectively in the interactions. His increased self-awareness allowed him to voice what he was feeling and create a more mature interaction.

This self-awareness will help you develop more mature interactions in part because they facilitate your ability to set effective boundaries. If you find yourself triggered and responding defensively to a situation, you may think that you are setting boundaries in that process. But setting boundaries is done most effectively when you are calm, clear, self-aware, and able to communicate to somebody how you'd like to be treated. You teach people how to treat you. Boundaries are deeply connected to self-acceptance, self-awareness, and self-accountability. Part of what enabled the mature interaction was not just our client's self-awareness but also his ability to make a more effective choice, increasing his self-accountability.

Missing Link: Self-Accountability

We define self-accountability as taking full responsibility for the choices you have made to cocreate every situation and the ownership of how

---

48 https://gallaheredge.com/login/

you will contribute to creating what you want. Self-accountability is the final link we discuss in the Maturity strand because it is dependent on the other two. To be accountable for your choices, you have to be aware of the choices you have made. To be aware of the choices you have made, you have to be self-accepting enough to let yourself see your choices. Once you are aware of the choices you are making, then you'll be more empowered to make choices aligned with the direction you want to go.

The concept of choice is another cornerstone of the work of The Human Element®. Acknowledging choice and, specifically, believing you have a choice allows you to lead a purposeful life and increases self-accountability. The belief that you can't do something immediately makes your inability true since you stop any attempts to overcome your self-imposed limitation.

In his book, *The Human Element*, Dr. Will Schutz explains that the concept of choice includes both conscious and subconscious choice. Sometimes your choices are conscious, in that you're giving your active attention and energy to them in the moment, and you're aware of the processing in your mind as you reach a decision. Perhaps you're thinking through who to invite to a project planning meeting, and you're thinking through the functions involved and the skill sets required as you choose who to include. Other choices are not made consciously. For example, maybe in developing the invite list for the meeting, you forgot to include your boss. You may write that off as "just a mistake" that only happened because it was so obvious, you weren't thinking about it. It's also possible that you were making a subconscious choice to exclude her because you feel eager to take more control over this project without feeling like she might start to micromanage you.

The concept of self-accountability is critical because it invites you to look at all your choices, conscious and subconscious, and align your choices with the outcomes you are seeking.

Self-Accountability Contributes to Growth

Usually, the biggest thing holding us back is ourselves. If you don't believe you have a choice in a matter, you will give up trying to affect it and relieve yourself of any accountability for the outcome. Having personal accountability and owning your contribution to a situation are critical components to understanding how you create the outcomes you get and can therefore change them.

Psychologist Carolyn Dweck writes about the differences between having a "fixed" mindset and

---

[49] https://gallaheredge.com/themissinglinks

a "growth" mindset.[50] When you have a growth mindset, you believe that effort and learning matter and find feedback helpful. In contrast, when you have a fixed mindset, you believe that you are born with a certain level of ability and effort doesn't really matter—which makes feedback dangerous.

Dweck teamed up with researcher Yuxiang Zhao in 1994 to investigate how students' mindset affected their learning. They found that people with a growth mindset were far more likely to engage in new approaches to help them learn and grow compared to those with a fixed mindset. Those with a fixed mindset were more likely to exhibit helpless coping strategies, such as trying to get out of the situation. This mindset is so strong that it can even be induced. People who are (falsely) led to believe that their abilities are fixed will demonstrate less learning than those who are led to believe that their abilities can be developed (Plaks & Chasteen, 2013).

Believing you can grow and develop is a key aspect of self-accountability, and it applies not only to tangible skills like riding a bike or computer programming but also in the case of shifting elements of your "personality." In his best-selling book, *Personality Isn't Permanent*,[51] Dr. Benjamin Hardy writes about

---

[50] C.S. Dweck, Mindset: The New Psychology of Success (New York: Random House, 2006).

[51] Benjamin P. Hardy, Personality isn't Permanent: Break Free from Self-Limiting Beliefs and Rewrite Your Story (2020).

his personal dislike of personality assessments. If you pair the results of a personality test with a fixed mindset, you'll stop yourself from growing as a leader, a member of the team, and as a person.

The extent to which you believe you can make choices that will impact the outcome you want is a huge predictor of your tendency to engage in learning for your own growth.

In the case of *Columbia*, had the Mission Management Team shared a common belief that they *could* choose to develop a solution for the damage to the orbiter, they might have been more willing to look at the situation and explore all different possibilities. Even if the possibilities they explored to solve the problem would have failed, the simple mindset of believing that something can be done could trigger tremendous learning and growth for the organization and for space travel as a whole.

When an oxygen tank exploded during the infamous *Apollo 13* mission, NASA leaned heavily into the slogan of "Failure is not an option." The team on the ground was determined to do everything they could to bring the astronauts back safely, and they focused their energies on learning and creating solutions to dozens of problems they had never dealt with before. If they didn't believe that they could make choices to save the astronauts, they would not have learned all that they did.

Recognizing the ways that you are contributing to every situation that you're a part of, through your action or inaction, will absolutely fuel your level of growth.

Linking Humans With Self-Accountability Creates Maturity

When you picture a culture of Maturity and then think of the word "accountable," what do you picture? You probably imagine a culture where each person takes the initiative, admits when they don't know the answer to something, apologizes for their mistakes, and actively contributes to the organization's goals.

What you're picturing is an organization filled with self-accountable people.

Arti Trevedi conducted a literature review on individual accountability in 2013 and reported that compared to people who demonstrated accountability, people who engaged in unaccountable behaviors such as blaming or avoiding were less effective, more stressed, unhappy and frustrated, and less collaborative. Individuals who engaged in accountable behaviors have higher efficiency and effectiveness and greater confidence than those who engage in unaccountable behaviors.

One client struggled with how to handle a situation in his organization. A very expensive mistake had occurred, and his team was battling blame and frustration. We guided him through a Human Element® exercise focused on self-accountability where each person takes a turn saying what they did or did not do to prevent a solution to the problem. This structured exercise creates an environment where each person acknowledges how they played a role, and nobody is engaging in blaming or other helpless behavior. He reported after this exercise, they not only learned so much more than prior conversations about the problem but the whole atmosphere and environment were also different. Because people were so much more likely to see how they were a part of the problem, it became easier for them to work together to see how they can be part of the solution. They felt more like they were on the same side, working against the problem, and what emerged was a greater level of Maturity.

Tying It All Together

At the intersection of self-acceptance, self-awareness, and self-accountability resides Maturity. As individuals work to feel accepting of themselves, exactly as they are, it becomes easier for them to see themselves as they truly are. Self-awareness expert Dr. Tasha Eurich writes, "Where self-esteem means thinking you're amazing regardless of the objective reality, self-acceptance (also called self-compassion by some researchers) means understanding our objective reality and choosing to like ourselves anyway."[52] This self-awareness combined with self-acceptance facilitates self-accountability, where the person feels empowered to make choices that help them to be the person they want to be. The combination of these elements of Self is reinforcing in nature. As you make more choices to align yourself authentically, it becomes easier to feel self-accepting in the face of any additional shortcomings, which creates greater self-awareness and, then again, greater self-accountability.

By combining self-accountability, self-awareness, and self-acceptance, we tap into our inherent driver of growth to gain the courage and clarity of vision to face our world as it is and take the necessary steps to shape it into what we want it to be.

---

[52] Tasha Eurich, Insight: Why We're Not as Self-Aware as We Think, and How Seeing Ourselves Clearly Helps Us Succeed at Work and in Life (2017).

Chapter 6

The Second Strand: Diversity

"Inclusivity means not just 'we're allowed to be there' but we are valued. I've always said: smart teams will do amazing things, but truly diverse teams will do impossible things."
—Claudia Brind-Woody

[53]

Hear No Evil...

The day after *Columbia*'s final launch, two engineers at the Marshall Space Flight Center working in the Intercenter Photo Working Group noticed the foam strike on the left wing of the orbiter. Within an hour, personnel at KSC had also seen the impact on higher-resolution images. These pictures showed that a large piece of foam from the external tank

---

[53] https://gallaheredge.com/themissinglinks

had hit the orbiter's left wing about eighty-one seconds after liftoff, but nobody could see exactly what the damage was or even precisely where the impact occurred.

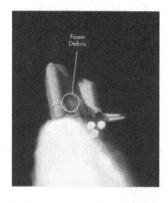

Foam
Debris

The Intercenter Photo Working Group members were very concerned, and because they didn't have any of their own pictures or video that could accurately show the extent of the damage, they requested ground-based imagery of *Columbia* on orbit. Unfortunately, this working group didn't have direct access to the mission manager. So, they requested this support through Wayne Hale, the shuttle program manager for Launch Integration at KSC. This was the first of three requests for imagery made during the STS-107 mission.

Once word got out that debris had impacted the orbiter during launch, a Debris Assessment Team was created to evaluate the risk. Oddly, the Mission Management Team—and specifically the mission manager—was not actively involved in directing its efforts or openly communicating with it.

Ultimately, the Debris Assessment Team came to the same conclusion and made the second request for imagery. Again, due to a lack of participation by the Mission Management Team, a decision was made to pursue the request through the Engineering Directorate at the Johnson Space Center. In his request, the cochair of the team, Rodney Rocha, asked, "Can we petition (beg) for outside agency assistance?" Rocha believed there were ways they could explore reducing the risk if they better understood the damage. We don't know if his ideas would have ultimately prevented the disaster, but it shows there were things that could have at least been explored.

Despite the relatively little attention or support they received from the Mission Management Team, the Debris Assessment Team almost succeeded in getting their imagery request approved through the Department of Defense (DOD). However, according to the CAIB report, when Linda Ham found out about it, she began questioning Mission Management Team Members and other Shuttle Program senior leaders instead of going directly to the Debris Assessment Team members. When they were faced with a challenge to produce a requirement for imagery, none could do so, and a response was given to the DOD that there was no "official" request for imagery.

Had Linda Ham included the people in the conversation who were the closest to the problem, she may have made a different decision as she would have better understood the potential severity as well as possible mitigation strategies. During critical moments of problem-solving, it's common to have different opinions given different sources of information, different areas of expertise, and different ways of thinking. Staying respectful and inclusive of those differences is crucial to creating a culture of Diversity.

How Maturity Links to Diversity

A culture of Maturity is necessary to enable a culture of Diversity because the more we mature, the less threatened we are by people or ideas different from who we are or what we believe.

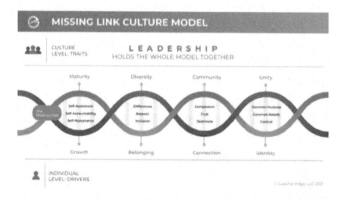

The level of Maturity within an individual is directly related to their ability to respect differences between people. If you struggle to fully accept yourself, whether you're aware of it or not, the presence of an idea or person who represents a difference from you could be perceived by your psychological immune system as a threat to what you believe, what you value, and who you are.

However, once you accept yourself, allow yourself to be more aware, and develop self-accountability, you will have the Maturity to treat all kinds of differences with respect. With Maturity comes the ability to recognize that other people's behavior is not about you, which makes it easier to be inclusive and respectful to others, even when they're different. The idea that we can all belong, even when we are different, continues to create the psychological safety needed for Diversity to emerge.

The Power of Diversity

As a reminder, we define a culture of Diversity as one that actively seeks out, invites, and involves people with various skills, experiences, backgrounds, and perspectives while accepting them for who they are. You can see from this definition that we refer to a variety of ways in which we differ from one another when we talk about Diversity.

A culture of Diversity drives business results, increases engagement, and improves lives. We previously cited research that has shown that organizations perform better when they have more Diversity in their organization and, specifically, in their leadership teams. Diverse perspectives lead to more creative solutions and a greater ability to detect the need to adapt, which is what keeps companies not just surviving but thriving.

A culture of Diversity also signals to all employees that they are welcomed and accepted just as they are. Just as trust in one's company is damaged by a lack of Diversity, one's trust and willingness to engage increase when one sees that all types of people are welcomed and given equal opportunity to succeed. In the words of Martin Luther King, Jr, "Injustice anywhere is a threat to justice everywhere" highlights this point.

How Belonging Links to Diversity

Belonging is a key driver of human behavior. We define belonging as a fundamental human motivation for our authentic selves to be accepted by others in our environment.

We previously quoted Brené Brown's definition of shame ("the intensely painful feeling or experience of believing that we are flawed and therefore unworthy of love and belonging"). Dr. Brown also describes the difference between fitting in and belonging. On the one hand, fitting in means changing things about how you present yourself to seem more like those around you. When people are focused on fitting in, they suppress their individual differences, resulting in an artificial sense of homogeneity. Belonging, on the other hand, is about

---

[54] https://gallaheredge.com/login/

being who you truly are and feeling accepted as your authentic self. When people show up as their authentic selves, the differences between them become more evident, leading to a culture of Diversity.

Our fundamental human driver for belonging enables the Diversity between us to emerge. Leaders can tap into their team's drive for belonging to create an emergent culture of Diversity.

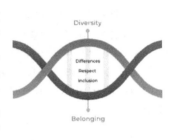

How Do You Create Diversity?

Leaders can develop Diversity in their culture by tapping into employees' drive for belonging through including and respecting people with differences.

Missing Link: Differences

It feels too simplistic to say that you must have differences to have Diversity in your culture, so we'll elaborate. Specifically, we define the missing link of differences as possessing a variety of ideas, backgrounds, perspectives, ethnicities, skills, beliefs, genders, and age groups, as well as many other dimensions which contribute to making each of us unique.

Differences Fuel Belonging

In the context of an organization, honoring the uniqueness in each person contributes to our human drive to belong. This is precisely how leadership at Gilead Sciences views differences. In their initiative to create an environment where people can be themselves without fear, they are specifically inviting people to *be* different and express conflicting views. When you enter into a space where people differ from one another and are encouraged to be different, it makes it easier for you to feel that you belong.

An article in *Scientific American* confirmed this effect by highlighting a study that showed that when teams have created space for different viewpoints, it contributes positively to our human driver of belonging because it invites each person to be their authentic self.[55]

Linking Humans Through Differences Creates Diversity

This same study also highlighted how differences between us lead to the emergent trait of Diversity by triggering group members to anticipate different viewpoints. This expectation leads people to prepare

---

[55] Katherine W. Phillips, "How Diversity Makes Us Smarter," Scientific American, October 2014, https://www.scientificamerican.com/article/how-diversity-makes-us-smarter.

better and anticipate that the conversation and decision-making will require more effort. And not surprisingly, the more effort we put into something, the more likely we are to achieve better results.

Differences enable humans to reduce confirmation bias. Confirmation bias refers to the tendency to seek out information that aligns with existing beliefs and subconsciously filter out conflicting information. This creates a reinforcing loop where your beliefs can become even more entrenched, and it is even harder to see a different perspective or challenge what you think you already know. You'll probably continue to look at the same problem in the same way and struggle to see a viable solution. It's like Einstein famously said: "We cannot solve our problems with the same thinking we used when we created them."

When you include people with different ideas, skills, and backgrounds, then as a team, you're less likely to suffer from the poor decision-making that results from confirmation bias. Organizational psychologist Chris Argyris developed the Ladder of Inference to illustrate the poor decision-making that results from confirmation bias and a lack of Diversity.[56] Argyris explains that humans have an available pool of data from which they select data, paraphrase it, name it, evaluate it, and then decide what to do. Each step is

---

[56] C. Argyris, "The Executive Mind and Double-Loop Learning," Organizational Dynamics, 11(2) (1982): 5-22.

affected by our own assumptions and the inferences we make from data. We create mental models—explanations about how we think things work in the real world—and base our decisions on them.

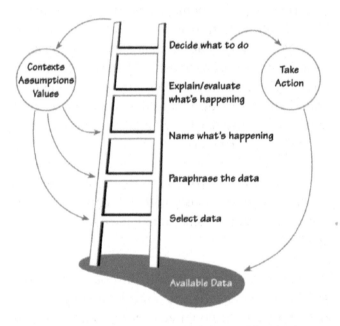

Even our attempts to make decisions objectively can be subject to confirmation bias and other biases. For example, one study gave different teams the same data set of the interaction between soccer players and referees to determine if red cards were given to dark-skinned players more than light-skinned players. Even when analyzing data statistically and scientifically, so many decisions are made, like what variables to include and what statistical assumptions to make, that some teams concluded there was a statistically significant difference and others did not.[57]

But because Diversity is so critical to our capacity to innovate and problem-solve, it is imperative in your culture that you intentionally bring different perspectives to avoid the debilitating trap of confirmation bias.

Differences between people also change our ability to understand situations. In primatology, early researchers were male, and they focused on the male primate behavior in mating situations. It was not until female primatologists studied primate behavior that they uncovered that female primates took a much more active role and even had sex with multiple males. Men were more likely to dismiss that female behavior as a fluke, whereas women were more likely to pay attention to it to learn about it.[58] Sociocultural differences matter as well. Japanese researchers paid more attention to hierarchy in primates than US primatologists because those values hold more importance in Japanese culture.

---

[57] R. Silberzahn et al., "Many Analysts: One Data Set: Making Transparent How Variations in Analytic Choices Affect Results," Association for Psychological Science 1, no. 3, (2018), https://journals.sagepub.com/doi/10.1177/2515245917747646.

[58] Megan Bang, Carol D. Lee, Douglas Medin, "Point of View Affects How Science Is Done," Scientific American, October 1, 2014, https://www.scientificamerican.com/article/point-of-view-affects-how-science-is-done.

These mental models of how interactions happen strongly influenced what these researchers were likely to observe. Bringing people together with different mental models is useful for avoiding the pitfalls of our human tendency to confirm existing beliefs, where we miss things. When leaders can link people together through their differences, Diversity emerges.

Different experiences or even industry backgrounds can lead to the power of Diversity, too, as evidenced by the partnership between Coca-Cola and the US Department of Health and Human Services during the COVID-19 pandemic.[59] Coca-Cola Consolidated developed cryotubes to supply preforms for COVID-19 testing kits throughout the country. That partnership, which was facilitated by Oak Ridge National Laboratory, helped these industries come together to support a national and global crisis, and yet most of us would not think of a soda company as a solution provider to a global pandemic.

Missing Link: Respect

We define respect as treating others with esteem due to all humans. This definition is particularly

---

[59] Coca-Cola, "Coca-Cola Bottlers Dedicate Production Capability to Support COVID-19 Test Kits," GlobeNewswire, June 1, 2020, https://www.globenewswire.com/news-release/2020/06/01/2041439/0/en/Coca-Cola-Bottlers-Dedicate-Production-Capability-to-Support-COVID-19-Test-Kits.html.

important to us because respect, like many words, means different things to different people. Some believe that respect is earned through accomplishments or credentials. Others believe that respect is a commodity given and received through behaviors such as arriving on time or cultural rituals such as bowing in some Asian cultures. But we are talking about respect at the most foundational human level—the acknowledgment that each human has worth simply because they exist.

Respect Fuels Belonging

This is a perspective that, unfortunately, not all humans support. Some people believe that not every human deserves respect, and this view negatively impacts culture. In a session with one of our clients, we were using a psychometric instrument to uncover how the leaders feel about "people." One of the leaders emailed us to find out what we meant by "people." He argued that if he was answering for all of humankind, he would answer one way, but if he was answering for his coworkers, he would answer another way. As you might imagine, his scores on the instrument suggested that he did not have high regard for others' level of significance.

If we accepted his perspective, we could talk about respect that is due to each person because they have been invited into your organization, suggesting that there are "others" out there who are not worthy of respect because they lack knowledge, expertise, or skills, or because of how they behave and mistakes they have made. But there are two key reasons this is problematic. The first is that how you feel about people as a whole will always have carryover effects on how you regard people in an organization, especially as it grows, and you will lose the ability to form a deep relationship with each person.

This is problematic because knowledge and skill gaps happen in organizations regularly as industries evolve, strategies change, and new roles emerge. So, looking at what one "brings to the table" as a means to decide if they are worthy of respect would mean that respectful treatment is fickle and inconsistent. Similarly, all humans are imperfect and make mistakes, so if you use one's mistakes as a reason to no longer treat them with respect, that reduces psychological safety and detracts from a sense of belonging.

Consequently, respect contributes to our human need for belonging.[60] A study by Simon and Sturmer (2005) showed that when individuals received respectful treatment, it increased their perceived acceptance into the group.

---

[60] Erica Volini et al., "Belonging: From Comfort to Connection to Contribution," Deloitte, May 15, 2020, https://www2.deloitte.com/us/en/insights/focus/human-capital-trends/2020/creating-a-culture-of-belonging.html.

Diversity Emerges When We Link People Through Respect

When we link people through respect, Diversity emerges as a cultural trait. A study by Anita Williams Woolley and colleagues showed that social sensitivity, which includes social respect, is a key ingredient that leads teams to perform better on a diverse set of cognitive tasks. This social sensitivity was a stronger predictor of performance than intelligence.

In all the research about the benefits that Diversity brings to organizations, the key differentiating variable is respect. A homogenous team will never yield the maximum performance possible. Heterogeneity on teams is necessary to maximize performance. But a heterogeneous team can yield the worst performance or the best performance—the distinction between the two is respect for those differences. When there is respect for differences, we're able to engage in healthy conflict to enable the best decision-making. For more information on healthy conflict and to download a copy of our Organizational Conflict Styles matrix, check out The Missing Links book resources page.[61]

---

[61] https://gallaheredge.com/themissinglinks

The ability to respect differences of opinions, different backgrounds, different skills, and different ideas is crucial to maximize organizational performance. If you don't have a culture of respect, that's a problem.

One client asked for our help because they had a lingering culture of disrespect. The organization was fairly homogenous historically, both demographically and on world views. Because, historically, nearly everybody in the company had similar viewpoints on religion and politics, even the leaders in the organization would convey disrespectful messages about people who held a different viewpoint. When this disrespect is pervasive and comes from the top, it creates an environment where people feel they need to hide who they are or what they believe, meaning *they, personally,* won't be respected.

> **The absence of respect squashes Diversity, and the presence of respect allows it to flourish.**

 62

Missing Link: Inclusion

We define Inclusion as involving and engaging individuals in meaningful ways that allow them to contribute fully. Because this kind of culture honors people for who they are and individual differences are seen as a source of strength for the organization, Diversity emerges.

Inclusion Fuels Belonging

This inclusion feeds each human's drive to belong. Researchers Baumeister and Leary indicate that including people is one of the main mechanisms of reinforcement or reward to show them they belong. So, what does it mean to be inclusive?

One of the key elements of inclusion is listening. When footage of the *Columbia* accident revealed that foam had struck the orbiter, senior shuttle program leader Wayne Hale realized that his failure to listen contributed to the accident. He remembers the day that engineers showed him the video of the foam striking the orbiter and felt fairly dismissive. And this is not because he didn't care about the risk. Prior shuttle missions had also experienced foam strikes, and each time, the shuttle returned safely and simply required time to repair the damage between launches. This pattern worked against him in this instance as he leaned more on past experiences and less on listening to what was presented to him. In hindsight, he could see that had he listened more effectively and pushed past his initial assumptions—

that he was right and they were wrong—perhaps he could have increased his understanding of the situation and better understood their concerns. In his own blog where he recounts his experiences working with the shuttle program, he says, "Defer to expertise rather than leaders. Check your ego at the door. Too many people are so busy passing out their point of view that they fail to hear the warnings that are coming at them. Listening is not enough; comprehending and acting are also required." Instead of believing that somebody else is "wrong" when they present a different perspective, lean into curiosity, and see what you can learn when you listen.

There are so many positive outcomes to listening. Robert Kramer found that what he calls "leaderly listening" accounts for 40 percent of what makes successful leadership. When humans are speaking and feel that the person they're speaking to is listening, they become more articulate and share more than they thought they would. The people listening learn significantly more. And the level of trust in the relationship between the two people increases.[63] As relationships improve, the sense of belonging is enhanced.

---

[63] Tamm, J. W. and Luyet, R., Radical collaboration: Five essential skills to overcome defensiveness and build successful relationships. (Pymble, N.S.W., Australia: HarperCollins, 2004).

In the aftermath of the *Columbia* accident, Hale realized how critical it was that he practice active listening to create a more inclusive culture at NASA.

Diversity Emerges When We Link People Through Inclusion

An inclusive culture has a powerful effect on an organization's results. Deloitte's Global Human Capital Trends survey found that an inclusive culture leads organizations to be six times as innovative and agile while also exceeding financial targets far beyond what noninclusive cultures hit.

Inclusivity between humans leads to an emergence of Diversity. Differences in perspective that lead to Diversity not only contribute to innovative solutions but also to our ability to detect a need for change.

You are likely familiar with the Indian parable about a group of blind men who encounter an elephant and, upon feeling different parts of its body, argue about what it is. To make this parable more applicable to the modern business environment, let's imagine this is a lion and it's sitting in the lobby of your office building. A group of your employees from various departments wanders into the lobby blindfolded (who knows why they would be blindfolded but just go with us on this one), and the story unfolds similar to the original parable.

Diversity is what enables your company to feel the various parts of the lion so you can figure out that it's a lion. Inclusion is what enables you to put those pieces together into a meaningful picture so you know what action you should take. In the absence of Diversity, all of your employees have very similar shared backgrounds, experiences, and mental models. Consequently, they will receive very similar inputs from the environment (feel the same part of the lion) and come to the same conclusions. In the absence of inclusion, even the information you do have won't be openly shared, and you will be unable to figure out that there's a lion sitting in your lobby.

In many organizations, what actually happens is that you, as the CEO, begin slowly receiving intelligence reports from various departments. These reports trickle in at different times and through different channels depending on the reporting structures and IT systems used by the different departments. Your first report is about some spikes that appear to pose a threat from a clamping force with a recommendation to develop some form of armor for protection. A secondary report comes in discussing musculature and perceived strength and speed with recommendations around developing quick and maneuverable vehicles.

Just as you start to rally the troops to respond to this threat, a third report comes in describing the lovely soft fur and encouraging you to make sure you stop by the lobby to experience this wonderful sensation. This report recommends a strategic alliance. Finally, the fourth and fifth reports arrive together. One seems to support the first report about spikes but states that they seem to work in a swiping motion. It supports the recommendation for armor. The other claims not to have felt anything but did hear a rumbling noise that might have been threatening. It recommends commissioning a six-month study to look at the problem and recommend options.

You've already lost significant time just getting the reports, and you still don't have a clear picture. You're not sure if you should attack, defend, partner or study! What about acting quickly? Does it help to act quickly if you act in the wrong direction? This is what leaders face every day and why Diversity and inclusion are critical to effective leadership and decision-making. As we said, the ability to adapt requires both the ability to detect the need to change as well as the ability to adapt quickly! The different reports won't matter for you unless you are inclusive. When you include each different perspective, Diversity can emerge.

And we cannot imagine talking about Diversity and inclusion without paying special attention to the topics of antiracism and egalitarianism in our society because organizations are a part of society; they are not apart from it.

181

Antiracism and Egalitarianism

Shockingly, even when organizations have hired a chief diversity officer, 27 percent of individuals in those roles still have to make the case for diversity, inclusion, and equality in the workplace. While topics of racism, sexism, and other forms of prejudice and discrimination on the basis of demographic variables are not our primary area of expertise, it is an incredibly important body of work.

We have already made the case for the power of having Diversity in your organization in terms of how it drives business results and increases employee engagement. And given the extremely disturbing history of the United States with our treatment of Black people and horrifying incidents of racism against Japanese Americans during WWII, against Middle Eastern people after 9/11, and against Latinx people as immigration has increased over time, we want to specifically call out the importance of Diversity for improving the quality of employees' lives.

In an essay written for *Harvard Business Review*, authors Laura Morgan Roberts and Anthony Mayo offer a compelling case for purpose-driven capitalism. After centuries of injustice and horrifying treatment of Black people, what if leaders focus less on (short-term) profit and focus more on what is right?

It was over 400 years ago that White people began the human trafficking of Black people in the land now known as the United States of America. And it was only seventy years ago that Elmore Bolling was murdered for being "too successful to be a Negro," according to a statement given to a newspaper reporting on the incident at the time. And in 2020, shortly after the COVID-19 pandemic rocked the United States to its core, we watched in horror as a White police officer, Derek Chauvin, murdered a Black man, George Floyd, in the streets of Minneapolis in broad daylight in front of dozens of witnesses while being filmed. This crystal-clear footage of a completely unjustified murder of a Black man by White police sent shockwaves through the nation and inspired more White people than ever before to join in the fight for the Black Lives Matter movement.

And yet, leaders in organizations still question, "Should I say something?"

If your goal is to not appear prejudiced, then you're starting from a flawed position. This can lead you to performative allyship or "strategic color-blindness" that prevents you from having to talk about race. Whether it is conscious or not, many managers actually fear they lack the skills to have the difficult conversations they anticipate when discussing race and racism.

But Desmond Tutu has beautifully said, "If you are neutral in situations of injustice, you have chosen the side of the oppressor." Research has shown that when there are major events in the press around racism in the country, how the leaders in the organization respond makes a difference. A lack of support will lead minority employees to feel there is a more interpersonal and institutional bias against them.

Imagine, for a moment, that you are telling your leader that somebody close to you has just died. And imagine that he responds "neutrally." Perhaps he makes no comment or has a neutral facial expression as you share this news. Neutral is not neutral. And it is no longer OK to not speak up.

Too many leaders are allowing fear to stop them from having the conversation. They fear saying "something wrong" or they fear feeling "attacked." But, in the words of Roberts and Ella Washington, "Remember that comments on systemic inequalities are not personal attacks."

Strong parallels between the resistance come up for leaders to talk openly about antiracism and the broader defensiveness that hinders productive conversations. Now, more than ever, we want to invite all leaders, especially White leaders, to practice self-acceptance, grow their self-awareness, and increase their self-accountability when it comes to fighting against racism and other forms of prejudice and discrimination.

> **Have the conversations. Take a stand. Do what is right.**

Tying It All Together

While it may not feel necessary to call this out explicitly, it feels important to state that the emergent trait of Diversity requires all three of these missing links to work together.

The key to getting a rocket off the ground is to ensure that you have three things: fuel, oxidizer, and spark. Any two and nothing happens. But if you combine all three, KABOOM! For Diversity to get off the ground, you must have all three links. Any two and nothing happens. The fuel in this metaphor is the differences between people. This is the main ingredient and what Diversity "burns" as it's taking off. Without differences, you have nothing to fuel your Diversity and you're going nowhere. Respect is the oxidizer (oxygen) of the group. It is what the fuel consumes as it burns. If you remove the oxidizer or respect, the flame will choke itself out regardless of how much fuel or differences are present. Respect creates the space (oxygen) for the differences to burn by establishing psychological safety. And finally, inclusion is the spark. You can have all the differences and respect in the world, but without inclusion, the explosion will never happen. That explosion occurs when the spark of inclusion brings the differences together in an environment of respect.

To simply have people with differences between them in the organization without respecting those differences and actively including them is actually worse than not having differences at all. Similarly, if you have an organization where everybody is respected for who they are, but everybody is very similar to one another, even inclusion won't bring out Diversity because everybody is holding the same part of the elephant/lion.

If you have differences between people and each person is respectful of one another, but there is no active inclusion, people could naturally self-select out or end up being excluded from conversations or decisions. The decision to include must be active and intentional.

But when you have all three together, the interplay is powerful and beautiful, where each person can show up as their full, authentic self, respect both what is similar to and different from themselves and contribute fully to the mission of the organization and to one another's growth through intentional inclusion.

Chapter 7

The Third Strand: Community

"The greatness of a community is most accurately measured by the compassionate actions of its members."
—Coretta Scott King

64

Speak No Evil...

Senior program manager, Wayne Hale, was sitting in a room, watching a screen while an engineer named Bob Page from the debris team showed him a video of *Columbia*'s final launch. Something dislodged from the external tank and went "poof" on the orbiter. This was a problem he was familiar with. Foam has fallen off during the launch and sometimes hit the orbiter before,

---

64 https://gallaheredge.com/themissinglinks

187

more than once. In the past, it had meant there would be some damage to repair when the vehicle was being processed for its next flight. This anomaly was so familiar to him that he initially dismissed it as an in-flight concern and risk to the mission, especially with other concerns to attend to, such as schedule and budget.

But engineers at NASA were concerned, based on the data from their modeling and simulation work, that *Columbia* might not survive the re-entry process due to where the foam struck the orbiter (which was not completely clear). Page's decision to approach Wayne was one of three indirect requests made for imagery that would allow the engineers to better assess the risk.

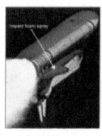 

Rodney Rocha (cochair of the Debris Assessment Team) had sent a message to Paul Shack, a senior shuttle engineer at Johnson Space Center, expressing his concern that the damage could fall anywhere "between acceptable *to not-acceptable to horrible, and no way to reduce uncertainty.*" This indirect request for imagery was made in hopes of reducing that uncertainty, but it was shut down.

And finally, Bob White, a NASA contractor from United Space Alliance, asked Lambert Austin, manager of systems integration, to assist. Linda Ham approached Lambert directly about the request for imagery but did not speak directly to Bob White or members of the Debris Assessment Team or the Intercenter Photo Working Group. Nor did the members of that team or that working group approach Linda Ham directly.

This game of triangulation, where people communicated using indirect channels to express their concerns and make their requests, no doubt, lost effectiveness and clarity in the messaging.

When Linda Ham shut down the request for imagery, the concerned employees interpreted that to mean there would be no further exploration of the issue. At that point, they allowed their fears of being seen as "the boy who cried wolf" or a "troublemaker" to quiet their voices.

It would have taken incredible courage, vulnerability, and personal risk to still push for the imagery request, reach out to Linda Ham directly to explain the concerns about safety, and explicitly fight against her decision to shut it down. And so, at a certain point, they didn't. They were not equipped with data to prove that there would be a disaster; in fact, they were seeking the information that would allow them to increase their certainty one way or another.

In Wayne Hale's blog, he recounts one of the most important lessons from the accident. "Letting a mistake go unchallenged has other consequences: funerals, program shutdown, and life-long regret. Make your choice wisely—speak up rather than remain silent. If the organization can't stand that, it's the organization that needs to change."[65]

Had there been a stronger sense of Community across NASA's culture, this accident may not have occurred. When people have high trust and communicate openly and directly, even *about* their fears about being open and direct, that decreases the likelihood that this kind of accident would ever happen again. Triangulating or indirect communication nearly always reduces the clarity of the message, muddling decision-making. More openness, instead of withholding, could have saved lives in this incident.

Community Requires Diversity

In the last chapter, we described our human need for belonging, which comes when we feel respected for our individual differences, rather than when we feel we are hiding who we are and conforming to "fit in." If you are part of an environment where you find yourself questioning if you will be welcomed as your true self, you'll likely struggle to show up in an

[65] Wayne Hale, "After Ten Years: Enduring Lessons," Blog Post, January 31, 2013, https://waynehale.wordpress.com/2013/01/31/after-ten-years-enduring-lessons.

authentic way, inhibiting your ability to connect with other humans. But once you believe that you belong, because the organization has created an inclusive culture of Diversity, that lays the foundation for connection, another human need.

The Power of Community

A culture of Community is one where individuals know and like each other, feel a sense of camaraderie, and express genuine concern for one another with a corresponding desire to help.

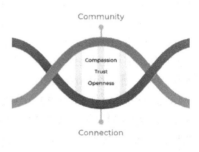

Community provides a means of support. Whether it is receiving encouragement from a teammate, getting advice from somebody who has gone through your challenge before, or somebody simply pitching in to get things done, more and more work is getting done by teams now. And humans can accomplish so much more as a team. These days it is virtually impossible to drive meaningful business results as a lone individual.

Consider Thomas Edison as an example. Edison is frequently given credit for his invention of the light bulb. In reality, it was an entire team of researchers working for years to develop a functional light bulb.

And perhaps the more important idea Thomas Edison brought to the human race was an invention factory. Not just one person working alone in a laboratory like a mad scientist, but a team of people collaborating, iterating, bouncing ideas off of each other—essentially an early-day research and development lab.[66]

Specialization has always been around in our human race, but it looks different now. Instead of specializations like hunters and gatherers, now we have front-end designers and back-end developers. We have digital marketing strategists and people who specialize in Google AdWords, consultants who specialize in designing sales funnels, and consultants who specialize in aligning culture. It's time to let go of the myth of the genius coder or genius scientist toiling alone as the basis for amazing breakthroughs in technology and problem-solving. Our ability to work together is essential to our collective success.

A culture of Community also increases employee engagement. Think about your own work history. When there was a sense of camaraderie, you likely felt a desire to collaborate with others, help people accomplish their goals, and support your coworkers as humans. Research supports this

[66] Michelle Stone, "How Edison's Invention Factory Pioneered Team Collaboration," Autodesk, accessed August 6, 2021, https://www.autodesk.com/products/eagle/blog/how-edisons-invention-factory-pioneered-team-collaboration.

connection between a sense of Community and employee engagement. Jessica Methot and her colleagues found a correlation between the number of friendships within an organization and that individual's performance, suggesting that working with people you like increases your engagement (and success!) in your work.[67]

Ultimately, a culture of Community where people feel a sense of connection, have a reliable source of support, and a feeling of camaraderie improves their lives.

[68]

Linking Connection to Community

Connection is an inherent human need. Even today, when our dependence on one another can feel different, numerous studies have shown a correlation between loneliness—the absence of

---

[67] David Burkus, "Work Friends Make Us More Productive (Except When They Stress Us Out), Harvard Business Review, May 26, 2017, https://hbr.org/2017/05/work-friends-make-us-more-productive-except-when-they-stress-us-out.

[68] https://gallaheredge.com/login/

human connection—with premature death and other negative physiological symptoms. [69] [70]

Humans are hardwired for connection. We are tribal creatures. Recall our example of the hunter in tribal times; if he were injured while on the hunt, his tribe would care for him until he was able to resume providing.

So even when a hunter was unable to hunt and provide for the tribe (the hunter not giving something), the tribe was there to care for him and nurture him back to health (the hunter taking something). It's the hard-wired nature of our brains for that connection that kept us together as humans, increasing our chance of surviving, adapting, and evolving.

---

[69] Nicole K. Valtorta et al., "Loneliness and Social Isolation as Risk Factors for Coronary Heart Disease and Stroke: Systematic Review and Meta-Analysis of Longitudinal Observational Studies," Heart 102 no. 13 (June 2016), https://heart.bmj.com/content/102/13/1009.short.
[70] Laura Alejandra Rico-Uribe et al., "Association of Loneliness with All-Cause Mortality: A Meta-Analysis," PLoS One, 13 no. 1 (January 2018), https://www.ncbi.nlm.nih.gov/pmc/articles/PMC5754055.

Years ago, anthropologist Margaret Mead was asked by a student what she considered to be the first sign of civilization in a culture. The student expected Mead to talk about fishhooks or clay pots or grinding stones.

But no. Mead said that the first sign of civilization in an ancient culture was a femur (thighbone) that had been broken and then healed. Mead explained that in the animal kingdom, if you break your leg, you die. You cannot run from danger, get to the river for a drink, or hunt for food. You are meat for prowling beasts. No animal survives a broken leg long enough for the bone to heal.

A broken femur that has healed is evidence that someone has taken time to stay with the one who fell, has bound up the wound, has carried the person to safety, and has tended the person through recovery. Helping someone else through difficulty is where civilization starts, Mead said.

"We are at our best when we serve others. Be civilized."

—Ira Byock, The Best Care Possible: A Physician's Quest to Transform Care Through the End of Life (Very, 2012)

In today's times, our dependence on one another looks different. Our interdependence has become more transactional in nature. For example, you probably depend on your grocery store to provide you with the food you desire, and you probably use money you have earned to pay for that food. That is transactional interdependence.

But our hard-wired need for connection has not gone away.

In an organizational context, it can be easy to think of examples of interdependence or times when we need each other to get our work done. The sales department needs Sales Qualified Leads (SQLs) from the marketing department to hit their revenue numbers. The customer experience department needs clarity from the sales department about what promises have been made to the customer, so they can fulfill those promises. The product team needs information from the sales department to know what the target market is saying they want from the product so they can evolve the product to grow their sales.

Organizations are filled with interdependencies. So, what is the difference between doing things at a transactional level and creating a real sense of Community?

It's the difference between gears that are turning like cogs in a machine and actual human beings.

Because we apply the science of human behavior to organizations, we want leaders to use what we *know* about human beings to create an environment that brings out the best in people, accomplishes organizational goals, and makes the lives of others better.

How Do You Create Community?

Leaders can create a culture of Community by linking people through openness, trust, and compassion.

Missing Link: Openness

For this strand, we want to start by discussing openness because of its foundational role in creating Community. In the story from the beginning of this chapter, we highlighted how limited openness was catastrophic for the final mission of the space shuttle *Columbia*.

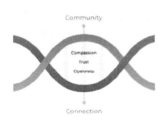

Openness is the foundation for Community. True connection comes through our willingness to allow ourselves to be seen. It takes vulnerability to allow yourself to be seen, and that vulnerability is where human connection is formed.

We define openness as a willingness to be vulnerable by disclosing your awareness of your own experience or what feels true for you. In *The Human Element®*, Dr. Schutz defines openness as self-awareness + self-disclosure. When you're self-aware, you allow yourself to know your own experience. You're able to identify your thoughts and feelings, the stories in your head, your fears and insecurities, your intentions, and what you want. Openness begins with you being open with yourself.

Self-disclosure means choosing to share your experience honestly with others. As humans, we often withhold our true thoughts and feelings, or we share some distorted version of the truth to protect ourselves or control the outcome of the conversation. Openness means choosing to share your self-awareness with someone else, which requires self-acceptance and self-accountability.

Openness Contributes to Connection

Because openness requires vulnerability through sharing your personal thoughts and feelings, it contributes to our human driver of connection.

The opposite of openness, either withholding or distorting your truth, gets in the way of true connection. And yet, research finds that people frequently fail to be open and truthful with one another. Most people overestimate the negative reaction that others will have to them sharing their truth, so they avoid doing so. In some cases, this is because they are confusing openness with "brutal honesty." However, brutal honesty is not openness because brutal honesty lacks self-accountability. Real openness includes being self-accountable, which means that you recognize that your thoughts and feelings are yours to own, and they do not represent an "absolute truth."

If, for example, you believe that somebody is "making you feel" something, that lacks self-accountability. If you believe that somebody else is just intrinsically a jerk, and it's an absolute, universal truth that everybody accepts as fact, then you lack self-awareness.

When people fear the negative consequences of being (brutally) honest, they tend to avoid doing so and often opt to withhold or focus on kindness. But research has shown that asking people to focus intently on kindness in their interaction does not yield the same level of connection as asking them to focus on being honest (Levine et al., 2016).

Openness contributes to connection because it allows you to have difficult and powerful conversations that help you solve important problems together and stay aligned in your intentions. Consider an example from one of our clients. The organization was gearing up for a large growth phase that required acquiring many leads very quickly, and the marketing department responsible was very small. The CEO knew there was a resource constraint, but he also questioned if the leader of this department had the capacity to build her team and get qualified leads as quickly as the organization required. He withheld those concerns, wanting to wait and see if the apparent bottleneck would improve when she had more resources. At the same time, she found herself expending energy, wondering if her performance was being questioned. In coaching, she realized that if she trusted that her CEO would be open with her about any question about her performance, she would feel less anxious and could spend less energy there and more energy on getting things done.

In coaching the CEO, it surfaced that he had a fear about sharing his doubts with this leader. He found himself more cautious with her because he didn't want to upset her or cause her to shut down. This is something that Dr. Will Schutz calls "First truth first." This is a vital part of openness. When you withhold thoughts, feelings, or feedback from somebody, there is a reason (a story in your head) you are choosing to withhold. In this case, the CEO's fear was that she would become upset during the conversation. This is his "first truth." And we call it the "first truth" because it's actually the most important conversation to have.

When he was asked, "How important is it to the success of your organization for you to be fully open with your head of marketing during this growth phase?" He said it was critically important. So instead of jumping into a conversation about resources, or even a conversation about capability, the first open conversation they had was about their ability to have an open conversation. Being more open first helped the two connect as humans and then focus on the task.

Openness from leaders enhances the connection felt by employees. Dr. Adam Grant was invited to work with the Gates Foundation to help them build psychological safety in their culture. He invited Melinda to engage in a creative practice of recording herself sharing aloud the tough comments she received in feedback from employees. When this was shared with employees, one commented, "...she broke through the veneer...and I saw that she was no less of Melinda Gates, but actually, a whole lot more of Melinda Gates." Melinda's openness made it easier for employees to feel connected to her, and they were more willing to reach out to her and return the openness by sharing both positive and negative feedback.

Linking Humans With Openness Creates Community

When all the humans in an organization focus on being open with one another, that collectively creates a culture of Community. A key piece of how we define Community is a sense of liking between the individuals. The FIRO theory asserts that openness between people occurs when there is "liking" and that we are more likely to like those who are open with us. When somebody is truly open with you about their personal thoughts and feelings, they are showing you they value you and believe you have their best interest at heart. One way to think about liking someone is, "I like myself in your presence." If, when I'm around you, I feel good about me, I'll feel that I like you and be more open with you, and you'll be more open with me. The more this happens in a culture, the stronger the sense of Community.

Software Advice, a service company that connects people to software to fit their needs, conducted research and found trust and honesty are key to creating camaraderie and a sense of Community that people value in company culture. They found that while terms like "casual" or "relaxed" came up when asking people to describe their ideal culture, the number one attribute that actually influenced people to want to work for an organization was honesty.[71][72]

And openness can extend the sense of Community even beyond the formal borders of the organization. One client, Nebbia Technology, who was later acquired by New Signature in 2019 and then by Cognizant in 2020, learned the power of openness

---

[71] Erin Osterhaus, "Honesty is the Secret to Success," Blog Post, July 11, 2013, https://cx-journey.com/2013/07/honesty-is-secret-to-success.html.

[72] China Gorman, "It's All About: Trust, Honesty, and Transparency," Great Places to Work, August 12, 2014, https://www.greatplacetowork.com/resources/blog/it-s-all-about-trust-honesty-and-transparency.

in their work with us. They practiced Openness (self-awareness + self-disclosure) within their team and also with their clients. At one of our workshops, a couple of the leaders were excited to report back that they had begun approaching their more challenging conversations with their clients through openness. While sometimes our clients initially think they can only be open (in this way) with others who have learned about openness in the same manner, these leaders practiced openness and found that it led to some of the most productive conversations they had ever had!

Openness can strengthen and expand a sense of Community by showing others that your walls are down and that you are on the same team, working together to solve problems. Openness is a core method for problem-solving. It helps you short-circuit the "story in your head" situation, where you make assumptions about what's going on for other people without finding out what's true for them. Openness builds Community by sharing the real problems you want to solve (like "How can we best work together?") and invites others to join in that problem-solving instead of relying on the story in your head. When you have Community, there is a genuine feeling of being "on the same team" even when you're not "on the same page" because your openness shows that you're on the same side.

Openness, instead of withholding, could have saved lives in the space shuttle *Columbia* tragedy. A willingness to express vulnerability by saying,

"I don't know how we can solve this problem in flight" could have created an opportunity to explore options. Or the concerned engineers being open with senior management in the Shuttle Program about their fears of risking being wrong could have made a difference. Openness creates Community, which helps people problem-solve together, develop better solutions, and feel supported along the way.

At Gallaher Edge, we have created a highly effective tool for structuring difficult conversations. We call it the FRIC Model (Fear, Request, Inquiry, Commitment). It's a simple way to get clear about what you really want from the conversation, as well as an outline to follow during the conversation. To learn more about the concept of openness from The Human Element® and our FRIC Model, check out our Foundations of Openness series on Insider Edge.[73]

To learn more about your own tendencies to be open or avoid openness, head on over to The Missing Links book resources page[74] and take our openness quiz.

---

[73] https://gallaheredge.com/login/

[74] https://gallaheredge.com/themissinglinks

Missing Link: Trust

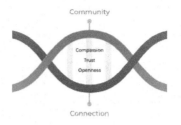

Trust is the next missing link in our Community strand and is a critical way to link individuals to create Community. We define trust as a firm belief that someone has your best interest at heart and has the ability and commitment to do what they said they would do. While it is true that we long for connection with others, it isn't just any type of connection that we want. We want meaningful connection that is characterized above all by trust. In fact, being linked to individuals through low or no trust relationships can actually be draining, so it is important that we specify the presence of this link. When woven into the fabric of the organizational culture, trust strengthens Community and serves as a catalyst for organizational performance.

PricewaterhouseCoopers (PwC) reported that most CEOs believe that a lack of trust will inhibit their organization's ability to grow.[75] Paul Zak and his research team found that high trust organizations

---

[75] PricewaterhouseCoopers, "Redefining Business Success in a Changing World: CEO Survey," January 2016, https://www.pwc.com/gx/en/ceo-survey/2016/landing-page/pwc-19th-annual-global-ceo-survey.pdf.

fare much better than low trust organizations.[76] Comparing high trust to low trust organizations, they found 76 percent higher engagement, 106 percent more energy, 50 percent higher productivity, and 29 percent greater life satisfaction. That's hugely important! Life satisfaction is positively impacted because of trust at work—this is why trust matters.

Trust also reduces negative work experiences, with high trust companies reporting 74 percent less stress, 13 percent fewer sick days, and 40 percent less burnout than low trust companies.

Most simply, trust acts as a social lubricant; it just makes everything easier.

A big part of the ease created by trust has to do with an absence of fear. In our work, people often joke about us singing Kumbaya and doing trust falls in our workshops. While we haven't done this (yet), there is validity in the idea of trust falls! Consider the amount

[76] Paul J. Zak, "The Neuroscience of Trust: Management Behaviors that Foster Employee Engagement," Harvard Business Review, January-February 2017, https://hbr.org/2017/01/the-neuroscience-of-trust.

of fear you would have if you were to allow your body to simply fall backward without having any visual confirmation of what was going to happen to you. Now, imagine that you allow yourself to fall backward, having full faith that people were there to catch you. Picture Lady Gaga crowd-surfing at a concert here; at no point does she question if those hands will reach out to safely stop her from falling.

Now think about this same metaphor in the context of the workplace. What would happen if everybody trusted each other so much that they could metaphorically fall back without looking and trust that others had their backs? This creates a sense of psychological safety.

When psychological safety exists on a team, people can put their energy into problem-solving toward our collective, shared goals. In his best-selling book, *Think Again*, organizational psychologist Dr. Adam Grant describes the work he did with the Gates Foundation to build psychological safety because they knew it was an essential ingredient to empowering people to take bold steps in solving "some of the world's most vexing problems."

Trust also equates to the absence of fear, which means greater tolerance for risk, yielding increased innovation and creativity. And, as humans, we make better decisions when we reduce fear. Fear motivates us to *survive*, but we are focused on helping companies *thrive*. That means leaders want to create environments where high trust and low fear contribute to connection, foster Community, and improve organizational performance.

Trust Fuels Connection

Linking humans through trust contributes to our human driver of connection. If you don't trust somebody you work with, you will have walls up, inhibiting connection. But when trust is present, fear drops, your walls drop, and you can connect with others from a place of authenticity.

This trust contributes to our human driver of connection, even between strangers. In a trust-based game with high interdependence played between strangers,[77] researchers measured the interaction between trust and the hormone oxytocin within each human. Oxytocin is a key hormone not only in our existence but specifically our connection as humans, as it is a facilitator for childbirth and breastfeeding, as previously noted.[78] But it has implications between humans beyond mother and child. When oxytocin is flowing in us, it reduces our fear and increases our trust.

---

[77] Carolyn H. Declerck et al., "A Registered Replication Study on Oxytocin and Trust," Nature Human Behavior 4, (2020): 646-655, https://www.nature.com/articles/s41562-020-0878-x.

[78] Navneet Magon and Sanjay Kalra, "The Orgasmic History of Oxytocin," Indian Journal of Endocrinology and Metabolism no. 3 (September 2011): 156-161, https://www.ncbi.nlm.nih.gov/pmc/articles/PMC3183515.

In this study, researchers found that an intranasal administration of oxytocin increased the generosity, tolerance for uncertainty, and presumably trust between two strangers. The effect was also found in the other direction. The more a stranger demonstrated trust (by sending a larger amount of money, suggesting trust in getting some back), the more oxytocin the trusted participant's brain produced.

This research demonstrates that we have a much greater willingness to help one another when we are in high trust environments. In today's times, organizations are highly interdependent, and a team's ability to collaborate is paramount to their success.

In 2017, Laura hired her first employee at Gallaher Edge, Kayla. Not even six months later, Laura invited Kayla to join her in living, working, and traveling internationally for a twelve-month experience (a remote year). To Laura's  surprise and delight, Kayla accepted with enthusiasm! They had worked together for such a short time, and yet not only did Laura feel willing to invite Kayla to join, Kayla was willing to say yes!

In the short time they had worked together, they built a tremendous sense of trust. Kayla finally felt like she was working in an environment where mistakes are OK (they happen to everybody), where her input mattered (Laura was so happy to have her opinion to factor in when making decisions), and she felt valued. Kayla had a very clear story in her mind that "Laura won't abandon me or let anything bad happen to me" before she was invited to join the remote year experience. And Kayla had earned Laura's trust by going above and beyond, holding meaningful confidences, and demonstrating true care.

The two felt so connected that spending that year apart felt awful! So even though it felt risky to commit to a year abroad without knowing each other that long, their connection was so strong due to the trust they had built, they jumped in with both feet.

Linking Humans With Trust Creates Community

Because trust contributes to connection between humans, at an organization level, trust between humans creates a culture of Community. Without trust between people, fear is high, and individuals tend to protect themselves. They don't have faith that others are looking out for their best interest, or they don't trust that others can get their jobs done in a manner that helps them all succeed.

Humans are intrinsically driven toward mastery. We all want to perform well, so when you're on a team, you want to trust that your team members won't throw you under the bus, and you want to trust that your hard work won't go down the drain based on your teammates' incompetence.

Being part of a team means working toward a shared goal with some amount of interdependence, so if one person is struggling, it can have a ripple effect on the rest of the team. If you trust the people on your team, both competence and character, you are far more likely to ask for help when you need it. You're also more likely to admit when you've made a mistake because your shared trust and sense of Community leads you to put what is in the best interest of the team above your own ego or sense of embarrassment. High levels of trust create an environment of psychological safety, a term originally developed by MIT professors Edgar Schein and Warren Bennis in 1965. As a reminder, psychological safety refers to people's perceptions of the consequences of taking interpersonal risks, and research over the last several decades has shown that it is linked with contributing ideas and actions to a shared enterprise through sharing information, speaking up with ideas, and taking initiative.

One way we work to build trust in organizations is through a structured exercise of self-accountability from The Human Element® program that we explained in chapter 5. It's a powerful exercise partly because each person is only speaking to their own contribution, which means no blame. One client worked through this exercise, going around the circle for about a dozen rounds of self-accountability. Afterward, we asked them how they felt, and they overwhelmingly felt a sense of increased trust. One leader said it was so meaningful to hear others be self-accountable for things he was blaming them for in his head. But because it didn't come out through blame, trust felt higher than ever. Another leader said that he never felt more confident in that team's ability to solve the problem now that they had all come together in this way.

It's a powerful example of how trust creates a sense of Community. The feeling of camaraderie was high, fear was low, and because of the trust they created, they had a sense that they could tackle anything together.

Missing Link: Compassion

The third link in our Community strand is compassion. We define compassion as an understanding of how others feel with a corresponding desire to take action to support.

Community can be fragile, and it needs the proper environment to grow and thrive. In essence, we have been building an incubator for the little egg of Community within your organization. If openness is the foundation and trust is the support structure, then compassion is the roof that provides shelter and protection from the storms of life. OK, we know it's kind of a goofy metaphor, but it works. Everybody is human, so we all have things happen in our lives where we will benefit from the compassion of others rather than feeling judged.

We're all hit by the storms of life, and it's the compassion of others that creates shelter for the Community from those storms and provides us grace while we're going through them. Because we're all human. Otherwise, we'll just put on a fake hard exterior shell to protect ourselves, and true Community will die.

Compassion Contributes to Connection

Compassion is empathy combined with the desire to help. Empathy is defined as the ability to understand and share feelings with another. So, by definition, empathy requires vulnerability. If you are unable or unwilling to access your own feelings, you will not be able to empathize with others. As we articulated while speaking about openness, you must first be open with yourself. Allowing yourself to know and feel your own thoughts, feelings, and overall experience is a crucial part of compassion.

> "Compassion is not a relationship between the healer and the wounded. It's a relationship between equals. Only when we know our own darkness well can we be present with the darkness of others. Compassion becomes real when we recognize our shared humanity."
>
> -Pema Chodron

Compassion is hard for many people because they tend to defend themselves against unpleasant feelings. You have to get past your own defenses to feel compassion for others. Getting past your own defensiveness signals to others that you care about their interests as well as your own, which builds trust.

Compassion is a powerful way to contribute to connection through its ability to reduce defensiveness between two people. Because defensiveness emerges based on a story in your head about what that person must think of you if they treat you that way, compassion works as a powerful reframing tool. Imagine you're in a meeting, and a team member snaps at you when you make a suggestion. A common defensive reaction would be to snap back or perhaps shut down. But if you felt a strong sense of compassion for that person, even without knowing their story, you could set aside the story in your head and recognize that they are in some pain or having difficulty, which is leading to that behavior. Responding with curiosity and compassion is a powerful diffuser.

Research has shown that compassion between coworkers results in them feeling a stronger connection to each other (Powley, 2009). Because compassion requires empathy, and empathy requires listening, it's clear that compassion will contribute positively to our human desire to feel a connection with each other.

When you're on a team where each person is putting the needs of the others first, everybody's needs get met without anybody fighting to get their own needs met. This is a much healthier dynamic than when everybody is out for themselves.

A well-known parable describes a scene where thin, undernourished, sickly people all sit atop a bowl of stew, holding spoons with handles longer than their arms. So, while they can reach their spoons into the stew, they can't get the stew back into their mouths. Another scene looks identical at first glance, except in this one, the people are well-nourished, happy, and healthy, still holding the spoons with the giant handles, unable to reach the stew into their own mouths. The difference, in this parable, is that in this scene, the people feed *each other*.

When each person is only caring for themselves, while it is *possible* for each person to get their needs met, it feels completely different. When there is a true sense of Community and barely a whisper of fear, people can keep their energy focused on one another and their common goal, rather than focusing their energy on making sure they "have enough" for themselves. It becomes a much more powerful use of energy.

Linking Humans With Compassion Creates Community

When team members in an organization are kind to one another and expressing compassion, research shows it doesn't just impact the two people involved but also has a positive impact on the organization's performance culture as a whole (Brody, 1992).[79]

Compassion is related to several positive workplace outcomes, including healthy interpersonal relationships (Dutton and Ragins, 2007), building trust and reciprocation (Clark and Dutton, 2007), less stress, and greater job satisfaction (Fineman, 2000), all of which create a culture of Community.

One client, Jonathan Taylor, a serial entrepreneur, used to tell his teams that their first job is to help the customers, their second job was to help their coworkers, and their third job was to do their own job.

He says, "In addition to the cultural benefits of making our goals clear, it made it easier for managers to understand when we didn't have enough people to help customers or help other employees who were stuck waiting for their peers. It's very simple to see when someone isn't doing their job. You ask why, and they say, 'I'm helping everyone else all the time.'"

---

[79] Madhuleena Roy Chowdhury, "How to Foster Compassion at Work Through Compassionate Leadership," Positive Psychology, June 16, 2021, https://positivepsychology.com/compassion-at-work-leadership.

This means that if you're struggling to get your own job done, instead of a culture of blame, your team will take a look at what's contributing to that in a more comprehensive manner and approach it with shared accountability to solve the problem together.

Picture two people sitting back-to-back, leaning on each other. This configuration requires less energy from each of them to hold a position of sitting up compared to them each sitting up on their own. So, it's much less energy to have the same output. Compassion and a sense of Community create this same phenomenon on teams.

Tying It All Together

A culture of Community can only emerge when all three missing links are present between the humans: openness, trust, and compassion. A beautiful example of this can be found with one of our clients, a medical practice. The staff was dedicated to providing the best care to their patients, and they all wanted to be the best teammates they could be to each other. But despite these positive intentions, there were challenges around how the work would flow when they got really busy. While they each had a tremendous capacity for compassion (after all, they chose a career in medicine to help alleviate people's suffering!), their desire to be good teammates stopped them from being open. Because they didn't want to make their coworkers' jobs harder, when they felt overloaded or backed up, they didn't want to ask anybody for help out of fear of imposing or being seen as a bad teammate. We helped them uncover that they didn't trust that each person could set meaningful boundaries, and that stopped them from being open. For example, if you believed that asking your coworker for help meant she would help you, whether she considered it an imposition or not, you might withhold your request for help. And then she wouldn't know that you needed help.

To help them strengthen their collaboration as a team, we brought together the missing links of openness, compassion, and trust. We helped them cultivate an openness practice, where they each became more open and vulnerable by asking for help when they needed it and also practiced openness around if they had the bandwidth to support or not. The more openness they practiced with each other, the more they built trust. When these two links interacted with their capacity for compassion, a culture of Community emerged where they felt a stronger connection with one another, a sense of camaraderie, and their ability to collaborate effectively significantly improved.

When leaders foster a culture of Community, they have positioned their teams to be ready to tackle the world's biggest challenges, as this Community leads to the development of a culture of Unity.

 [80]

---

[80] https://gallaheredge.com/themissinglinks

Chapter 8

The Fourth Strand: Unity

"There is no unity without accountability."
—Brené Brown

81

A Flawed Structure

Following the space shuttle *Challenger* accident in 1986, NASA created a centralized safety organization at its headquarters to independently monitor safety and hold programs accountable. However, the Shuttle Program had been allowed to organize in whatever way it felt was most effective, which meant that the functions of safety and engineering were grouped under the shuttle program manager.

On the surface, organizing in this way increased the speed and effectiveness of decision-making and communication within organizational units.

---

[81] https://gallaheredge.com/themissinglinks

However, when the organization was put under stress, it meant that leaders in the Shuttle Program were forced to make decisions while balancing schedule and budget concerns with technical and safety concerns.

Leading up to the *Columbia* accident, NASA felt incredible pressure to meet a political mandate of having the International Space Station reach its "Core Complete" configuration by February 19, 2004. To make matters more complicated, because the schedules of the shuttle and the International Space Station were tightly coupled any time changes were needed, there were big impacts as there was so much to figure out in the coordination. All of this was occurring after years of budget cuts and downsizing, and leaders at NASA believed that they had to hit the February 19 launch date to restore their credibility with the White House and Congress, or more cuts would be coming.

This meant there were risks to manage in terms of safety and technical concerns, and there were also perceived risks to the Shuttle Program as a whole in terms of budget and schedule. And the dangers were even more amplified within a culture where "failure is not an option." It is just too easy for the brain to find ways to justify decisions that get them out of the impossible trap they find themselves in—typically by discounting risk.

While so much of culture comes from the self, it would be foolish to discount the impacts of the environment. Even high-performing teams who care deeply about the mission can lack Unity because decision-making is unclear, or the system is designed in such a way that leaders are asked to do the impossible task of simultaneously balancing choices of schedule and budget while also understanding technical and safety risks. NASA's workforce rated the agency as the number one place to work in the Federal Government only months before the *Columbia* tragedy. Employee perceptions of the working environment were positive, and they felt they had a strong Community, yet tragedy occurred shortly after.

Unity Requires Community

The final strand in our Missing Link Culture Model is Unity. Because it requires making numerous decisions, lots of conversations occur in the process of creating Unity. Building Community within your culture is necessary to create true Unity. The missing links of compassion, trust, and openness that interact to create Community are critical to having highly effective conversations.

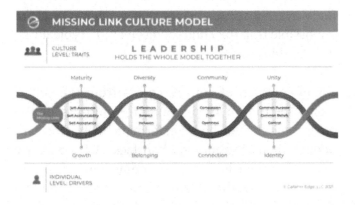

For example, we're confident you've had the experience of being in a meeting where decisions are made, only to have people express their doubts or confusions about the decisions after the meeting ends. Far too often, leaders mistakenly believe that silence means agreement. In critical conversations where leaders are making key decisions about the company's strategy, about who to empower with what authority, and how to design reporting relationships, the ability to practice openness is paramount.

Openness, which can be vulnerable, requires trust between team members. If you don't trust your team to honor your vulnerability when you express confusion over a potential strategic direction, you're less likely to express that confusion, and you may agree to something that you don't quite understand, which does not yield Unity. Or, if you don't trust in the capability of others on the leadership team to contribute in a meaningful way, but you fail to be open about that, you'll be dismissive about their input or ignore their level of inclusion in the conversation, which will not yield Unity.

When humans on a team are linked through compassion, trust, and openness, they have a strong enough connection to have hard conversations, to admit when they don't understand something, to disagree and challenge each other, and have the resilience and stamina to continue the conversations until they have reached alignment. Without Community, any perception of Unity is fragile or artificial. Community is essential for the formation of Unity.

The Power of Unity

We define a culture of Unity as one where individuals work as one with a high degree of alignment around purpose, direction, goals, and behaviors. The Unity strand is most closely aligned with the organizational level of our Inside Out Model, where you SET (strategy, execution, talent) your organization up for success.

Developing a common purpose, common beliefs, shared goals, and other mechanisms of control significantly increase employee engagement. It's far too easy for people in organizations to work at cross-purposes and feel very frustrated when they're struggling to get their work done. When teams are truly on the same page, they have less unhealthy conflict, better relationships, and higher job satisfaction, as they are achieving real results together.

Unity means there is a clear intention and focus, which is essential for driving business results. It's not enough to just hire smart people; if they're not aligned, they'll struggle to get very far. As you recall from chapter 3, "No steam or gas ever drives anything until it is confined. Niagara cannot be turned into light and power until it is tunneled." As a leader, the trait of Unity emerges once you "tunnel" your team by bringing them together through a common purpose, common beliefs, and control.

Tunneling the efforts of your organization means that the system is getting greater output with the same input. Consider the metaphor of pushing a child on a swing. If you push at the right time and in the right direction, a little effort will send the swing higher and higher. If you've ever gotten distracted while doing this, though, you know how different the experience can be if you are out of sync with the system. Not only could it require far more effort to get the same result, but if you're really out of sync, somebody could get hurt! Without Unity, you're more likely to experience burnout and its associated health impacts. But when you have Unity in your culture and are doing more with less, your quality of life and the lives of your employees improves.

[82]

---

[82] https://gallaheredge.com/login/

Linking Unity with Identity

The driver of identity is a fundamental human motivation to feel ownership of ourselves as individuals and how we fit into the world. Identity and self-concept are huge drivers in our beliefs and our behaviors in relation to ourselves and others. So, when an important aspect of your self-concept is shared with others' self-concept, we experience shared identity. This shared identity translates into trust, the willingness to do favors (even for strangers), and cooperative behaviors (Neville & Reicher, 2011; Reicher & Haslam, 2010). Within an organizational context, it translates into greater team alignment and performance.

We feel a strong sense of Unity with our coworkers because we identify with them in some way; in other words, because they are like us. Further-more, we feel a strong sense of connection and commitment to our organization because our definition of who we are is positively influenced by the fact that we work at that company. To illustrate this, let's start with a simple experience that many of us may have had. If you are an avid fan of a particular sports team who has just won a major game or championship and you pass another fan of that same team while you're both wearing one of their jerseys, what are the chances that you'll smile and wave at each other? Does it matter if you've ever met? Now, take it a step further. How likely is it that you'd do a favor for him or her? Research by Michael Platow and others from 1999 shows that shared fandom of a sports team does, in fact, lead people to be more likely to do a favor for strangers (Platow, et al., 1999).

There is a well-researched link between identity and behavior. One's identity serves as an internal compass for choices, including how to act in different environments. For example, if you identify as "a healthy eater," you will be more likely to choose carrots as an afternoon snack over a piece of cake.

However, it is important to note that because we are interested in controlling behaviors to drive results within the Unity strand, this identity-belief link is critical and is therefore one more reason identity is the human driver to which we link Unity. This same research is also why you want to recruit employees whose beliefs are already in alignment with the organization. Changing a belief linked to an individual's identity can be extremely difficult.

From a cultural standpoint, the link between Unity and identity is important because people look to the cues around them to guide not only how to behave but how to feel about themselves. For organizations that want engaged, happy employees, this point can't be overemphasized. From psychology, we know that when researchers measured whether the individual differences between people or the environment had a bigger impact on how people behaved, they found overwhelmingly that the environment had a much bigger impact. The Stanford Prison Experiment was one of the most famous studies to demonstrate how much the environment could impact how humans behave. Participants entered the experiment as healthy, normal college students, but when asked to embody the identity of a guard or a prisoner, the setting of the study transformed them into cruel "guards" treating other humans inhumanely or into powerless "prisoners" behaving like zombies obeying the guards. People look to their environment for cues about how they're meant to behave, so you'll want to be intentional about designing the environment to create a unified organization.

How Do You Create Unity?

Leaders can develop the emergent trait of Unity in their cultures by tapping into employees' drive for identity through linking people together through common purpose, common beliefs, and control.

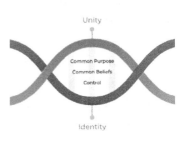

Missing Link: Common Purpose

We define common purpose as a compelling reason for the existence of your organization that inspires people to join your cause of making the world a better place.

A common purpose in an organization is a high-level reason that the company exists. This reason is not financial. Yes, every business needs to earn money to sustain itself, but that's not the common purpose we are referring to. Simon Sinek talked about the center of "The Golden Circle" in his viral TEDx talk from 2009. It's your "why"—a cause or a belief—or colloquially, why you get out of bed in the morning. It's powerful because it rises above the "what" and the "how" of any business and allows people to realize that they care about the same thing—common purpose. When working with our clients to help them clarify their common purpose, we tell them that when it is written well, it won't give anybody any idea about *what* the company does; it simply shines a light on a cause the people believe in.

Common Purpose Feeds the Driver of Identity

A common purpose fuels our individual driver for identity. Research by Kendall Brock highlights a strong relationship between identity and purpose even in adolescents, such that they influence each other in a reciprocal manner. Kendall describes, "Development of purpose supports the development of identity, and the development of identity reinforces purposeful commitments." When we, as humans, feel a sense of purpose, it shapes how we see ourselves. Simultaneously, how we see ourselves (our identity) guides what purpose we find meaningful.

At Gallaher Edge, our purpose is to evolve humanity. This statement inspires us. It triggers a physiological reaction from within that includes a mixture of pride, excitement, and drive.

We light up when we speak about this with clients because it connects with our core identities. Specifically, helping people become more self-aware creates more intentional connections between people, which changes how we feel about ourselves (i.e., self-acceptance) and each other. Then, those people pass those beliefs (of self-acceptance, for example) down to their children, creating a positive cascade throughout the generations, which genuinely contributes to the positive evolution of our species.

This is a big idea. This is a grandiose purpose. And it feels personal to each of us. It is a part of how we define ourselves as individuals. It is not just a job we do, but a movement we contribute to that we believe helps others and improves their lives. It is how we give back—both by helping individuals transform at the Self level and also transforming the organizations where they spend so much of their lives. This common purpose creates a personal connection between the organization as a whole and us.

A common purpose is therefore also a powerful tool for recruitment and retention of top talent because it helps you attract the human beings who genuinely care about the same thing that you do and who feel similarly inspired by how they can contribute to a better world.

Linking Humans With Common Purpose Creates Unity

In an organization, intergroup competition frequently exists, where teams find themselves engaged in turf wars, feeling sentiments of "Us versus Them," or sanctioned off in silos, without identifying strongly with one another. Sometimes their identity as a team feels strengthened by positing other teams as the "other." This is counter to creating a culture of Unity. However, a common purpose combats this tendency and contributes to the emergent trait of Unity.

In their much-cited work on identity in organizations, Ashforth and Mael explain, "Just as a strong group identity unifies group members, so too should a strong organizational identity unify organizational members."[83] Developing a common purpose—a high-level "why" the organization exists—serves to bring people together across the organization. Ashforth

---

[83] Blake E. Ashforth and Fred A. Mael, "Alumni and Their Alma Mater: A Partial Test of the Reformulated Model of Organizational Identification," Journal of Organizational Behavior 13(2) (March 1992): 103-123.

and Mael describe this kind of organizational identification as a feeling of "oneness."

A common purpose con-
tributes to Unity because
it increases the trust between the team members.
When you have established
a clear common purpose,
there is at least one critically important interest
that you can always trust

is shared, which brings people closer together. The common purpose serves as a powerful anchor and criterion for decisions in your organization, from big to small. This common purpose, as an anchor, creates a foundation for healthy conflict, which also improves decision-making.

For example, sometimes Unity is challenged when an organization is looking to grow and innovate. A desire to figure out how to focus and say "no" to opportunities while still taking strategic risks to stay ahead of the market can be a source of much conflict.

One of our clients originally had their purpose rooted in the idea that they wanted to help level the playing field for small businesses. When leaders at the organization were approached by a large company, they considered for some time if they wanted to work with that organization. As they talked about it and thought it through, they saw that to do so would be disruptive to their operations as they had been designed up to that point. Even the process to prepare themselves to demonstrate to this company that they could fulfill their request was pulling a lot of time and energy away from their core business. It was a white whale.

They felt the temptation, as all leaders do at one point or another, to move toward the opportunity because if it were to happen, it could have an exponential impact on their revenue but that was only if it actually came to be.

They decided that this opportunity was detracting too much from their core purpose, and while it was not necessarily an easy decision to make, they got through the healthy conflict and decided for themselves that they would pass on the opportunity and stay focused on the path they had laid out for themselves. Their common purpose served as a powerful anchor to root them in what they cared about in the beginning—the thing that inspired them to start the company in the first place.

Common purpose between team members creates a broader sense of clarity and Unity for what the future can hold. In *Start with Why*, Simon Sinek highlights Kodak as a powerful example of the absence of a purpose statement. If Kodak had clarified for themselves, internally, that they exist to connect people to their memories, or that they exist to capture moments and memories, they likely would have succeeded in evolving into the digital era of pictures, instead of clinging to *what* they do—develop cameras and film.

Missing Link: Common Beliefs

The next missing link for connecting employees' Identity to create Unity is common beliefs. We define common beliefs as a shared world view that defines how people will behave toward one another.

What we believe about ourselves and the world will dictate our behaviors. For example, if, on the one hand, you believe that a dog is friendly, you're more likely to engage in the behavior of petting that dog. On the other hand, if you believe that dogs are dangerous, you're not likely to put your hand near its face! This all seems fairly straightforward, but what we don't often see is the subtle way our beliefs influence the way we see and interact with the world, creating a self-sealing bubble of our own "reality."

What we actually see and perceive from the world is more a function of what we believe than it is an objective observation of reality.

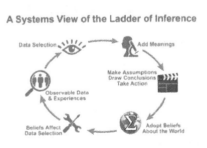

A Systems View of the Ladder of Inference

Seeing isn't believing; believing is seeing. To illustrate this, we will revisit the Ladder of Inference we discussed in chapter 6. Because our brains can't process the overwhelming amount of stimulus that comes at us every second, we must make millions of subconscious choices about which data are most important and which are irrelevant. These choices are based on the model of the world we've created from our beliefs—our mental model.

But data alone aren't actionable, so we take this incomplete dataset and add meaning to the data based on our beliefs and in accordance with our mental model. Finally, to fill in any remaining holes, we make assumptions and then draw our conclusions. Based on these conclusions, we then take action. The figure on the previous page illustrates how this process acts as a feedback loop where we tend to select data and take actions that confirm our beliefs in a reinforcing way over time. Beliefs actually "defend themselves," which makes it very difficult to recognize our own mental models and change them.

Let's reexamine that dog example. This time, suppose that you decided to get a family pet and your Gen Z-er convinced you it was your social responsibility to rescue a dog. This works out great, and he's a wonderful dog—until you give him a bone. Then he quickly retreats into a corner, growls, and snaps at anyone who comes near him.

Here's where your belief system influences things. For simplicity, let's say that you can have one of two basic belief systems: good dog or bad dog. The bad dog belief system says, "He's a bad dog and is behaving in a bad way and should be punished." So, you scold him, call him a bad dog, and take the bone away from him.

Now, if we zoom out and take a systems view of this, we'll realize that the dog is behaving this way because he was in a very different environment before he was rescued. He learned that whenever he had something nice, someone would try to take it away from him, so he had to try to protect it. If we walk through this situation using the systems view of the ladder of inference above, what do you notice?

The "bad dog" belief system creates a self-reinforcing mental model for both you and the dog. The dog's belief that every time he gets a bone, someone tries to take it away is confirmed, so he leans harder into his belief that he must fight to protect it. Meanwhile, you feel more justified in your belief that he is a bad dog and doesn't deserve to have a bone and should be punished.

There is an alternative, however. You could realize that the dog's behavior is not a result of some fixed character flaw but the product of a belief he has based on past experiences. This belief system sees him as a "good dog" who has had a rough life and needs to learn how to respond differently in his new environment. Your job will be to patiently retrain his mental model.

Similarly, as humans, our past experiences shape our beliefs and our behavior, which lead to results. In your organization, you want to have specific results that you *intend* to have, so you want to be *intentional* about behaviors and beliefs. While you may not be able to control the experiences people have had in the past, you can be intentional about the experiences you create for them today. Specifically, you can design experiences that are likely to create the desired beliefs that underlie the desired behaviors within your organizational culture.

In our chapter on Diversity, we explained the importance of intentionally including different ideas and the organizational benefits such as creativity and innovation and better serving your customers. Our goal is not for employees in an organization to share the same beliefs about *everything* but rather, there are key beliefs we want to intentionally make common amongst employees to drive the desired behaviors.

For example, in an organizational context, if you believe that you will be criticized or belittled if you bring up a half-baked thought in a meeting, you're more likely to withhold your thoughts and ideas unless you think they're fairly bulletproof. On the other hand, if you believe that other members of your team will nod encouragingly while you share your half-baked thought and jump in with their own partially formed thoughts to create a powerful snowballing brainstorming session, you're far more likely to get that ball rolling!

Common Beliefs Fuel Identity

At Gallaher Edge, one of our core values is Progress Over Perfection, and it's meant to drive exactly that! Partial ideas and incomplete thoughts spark other thoughts and let us move ideas forward without analysis paralysis or the practice of procrastination.

And core values are central to what we're talking about when we talk about common beliefs. We agree with Patrick Lencioni about the importance of having three to five core values to drive behavior in your organization. We also appreciate how he distinguishes between core values, aspirational values, and permission to play values. Core values are the unmistakable drivers of your culture *today*— not in the future (aspirational)—and they are unique to you and go a level beyond the essentials that every organization needs (e.g., honesty, teamwork).

84

---

84 https://gallaheredge.com/themissinglinks

As an executive team, taking the time to become fully aligned on what your core values are means uncovering your collective beliefs about the world and identifying how those beliefs translate into behavior. In the earlier example, a belief that progress is better than perfection will lead to behaviors of taking the initiative, offering ideas, taking more risks, and failing forward.

For Laura specifically, this core value required reframing some deep-seated beliefs she had since childhood. Her beliefs were tied to her identity and her feelings of self-worth. She had strong perfectionist tendencies. Those perfectionist tendencies would lead her to procrastinate on really important projects, delay launching things because they "weren't ready yet" and led her to be more emotionally sensitive to criticism. Once she would finally put something out there, something that felt less than perfect was deeply painful and would trigger defensive tendencies.

So, to set a core value, as an organization of "progress over perfection," meant she made a fundamental shift in her beliefs about the world and her beliefs about herself. Now, she believes that perfection is a myth and there will always be a way to improve upon something, so that's no reason to not share it with others to learn and gather feedback. This also meant that she shifted her beliefs around feedback being *useful* instead of being *scary*. You can't change your governing beliefs without changing yourself.

Research has shown that organizational values actually resonate more strongly with employees when given a chance to clarify their own personal values and create linkages between their personal values and the organization's values. Leaders can use common beliefs or core values to contribute positively to an individual's identity, as it is strengthened through connecting with the organizational environment.

Linking Humans Through Common Beliefs Creates Unity

As humans, our beliefs are created using theories and judgments based on selected facts and personal subjective experiences, which is why it is so important to be explicit about what you choose to believe as a company.

Unity emerges from a clear set of common beliefs because it builds trust. Southwest Airlines is known for its culture, and its leadership stands behind it. One of their core values is fun, and their flight attendants often use humor during the safety briefing to bring that value to life. When one passenger complained to corporate about this behavior, the CEO famously wrote, "We will miss you." Imagine how comforted that flight attendant must have been to know that leaders in the organization supported her so fully. This adherence to core values and a willingness to be punished (i.e., losing a customer) to stay aligned to them creates Unity by getting people on the same page and upholding trust.

When your core values drive the behavior of the leaders in the organization, you create the environment for the rest of the team. Humans constantly look to our external environment for cues about what is ok or not ok. Think of a simple example of one's behavior at a rock concert versus one's behavior at a library. The same exact behavior of jumping around and singing loudly off-key is acceptable at a rock concert (right?? I hope so, it's what I do) but would be wildly out of place, disruptive, and "not OK" in a library.

For their book, *Built to Last,* Jim Collins and Jerry Porras studied eighteen organizations that have stood the test of time and found that nearly all had developed clear ideologies, including core values that were meaningful. One of these organizations, The Walt Disney Company, does an extraordinary job of creating an identity for its employees, known as Cast Members. Their use of the four keys prioritized as safety, courtesy, show, and efficiency are well understood and lived by all the Cast Members, which creates a clear sense of Unity between them. They understand how to behave with one another and the guests and collaborate to create a great experience for guests and each other. Clear expectations of behavior enable teams to work together in Unity toward their goals. And while these values often stand the test of time, it's useful to surface and validate your assumptions.

Sometimes, as in the *Columbia* accident, what seems like a positive organizational value can actually work against you. The historical can-do attitude of NASA, where failure is not an option, actually has a dark side when extreme schedule and budget pressures are applied. The CAIB report noted, "When workers are asked to find days of margin, they work furiously to do so and are praised for each extra day they find. But those same people (and this same culture) have difficulty admitting that something *can't* or *shouldn't* be done, that the margin has been cut too much, or that resources are being stretched too thin. No one at NASA wants to be the one to stand up and say, "We can't make that date.""

Beliefs will defend themselves unconsciously with confirmation bias and our human desire to feel "right." While this can be helpful and reinforcing in strengthening core values that are working well for your organization, it's also important to make sure that they never just sit on a shelf. Revisit them each year to make sure they still feel true for you and they are taking the organization in the direction you want to go. Even Disney, who has held onto their four keys for over sixty years, in light of the antiracism movement that gained momentum in 2020, announced it was adding a fifth key: inclusion.

Values work when you work them. Values also work when you align them to your talent management processes. Unity is created when these common beliefs are key to your talent acquisition process—everything from recruitment to selection and onboarding. Laura worked for The Walt Disney Company and can attest that they did an outstanding job at bringing all different types of cast members together with shared beliefs. Whether a cast member worked in food and beverage in the parks or worked in corporate human resources, the same common beliefs were shared, creating a strong sense of Unity. Besides hiring around core values, to maintain Unity in your culture, be willing to fire around them as well. If an employee is unwilling to modify their behavior in alignment with core values, letting that employee go actually strengthens the bonds between the people who remain.

And that brings us to the final link in our Unity strand, control.

Missing Link: Control

The final link between the individuals in your organization that produces the trait of Unity is control. We define control as the boundaries and mechanisms which determine how the organization functions and achieves its goals. A critical component of the control link is alignment. For a system to be aligned, a single common point of reference must be used for that alignment: your competitive strategy. An effective culture supports the strategy, and we use this as the alignment point for all of the control functions as well as a sanity check on behaviors.

The word control brings up a lot for people. Many people think "command and control" or immediately think about coercion, manipulation, and other negative forms of influence. But the word control by itself does not have a positive or negative valence. And when you step back, you can probably think of several examples where control is very welcomed. Perhaps you'd appreciate it if your pilots were in control of the airplane. You'd probably also appreciate it if your surgeon was in control of your operation.

Whatever association you have with the word control is useful to know, so before you let us talk you out of what you think about it—let yourself know your own story about control. If, for example, you immediately associate control with feeling stepped on because in the past you had a boss that micromanaged you and wouldn't let you make decisions for yourself, then now, in a position of leadership, you might feel afraid to make decisions that affect your employees. Or perhaps you feel comfortable making decisions for others but rebel against any decision that others try to make for you.

There is no real issue with your behavioral preferences around control—the work of The Human Element® emphasizes that trouble only arises when you become rigid around your preferences. And the stronger your emotional reaction is to the word control, the greater the likelihood of you developing rigidities in your control behavior, rendering you less effective.

In the context of culture, control gives your organization a sense of direction, clarity around goals, and a shared understanding of how people work together to get things done.

Organization design is the primary way we recommend linking humans together through control. When we say "organization design," we are talking about far more than just an organizational chart. We are referring to aligning everything about how work flows through your organization (decision-making authorities, strategic processes, key performance indicators, and reporting relationships) to your competitive strategy. Imagine, for a moment, an organization that has no control over these key components. Sounds chaotic, right? This is the value of control.

Control Contributes to Identity

Another way to think about control is as a set of boundaries. Many of us are familiar with the idea of having boundaries to create healthy interpersonal relationships. Boundaries build trust and let people know what is OK and not OK. When somebody is willing to tell you "no," you are far more likely to trust and believe them when they tell you "yes."

When they are taking responsibility for themselves, then you don't have to.

And boundaries can be very helpful in clarifying and contributing to our individual identities. Consider a study from the Journal of Cognition and Development[85] that examined children's behavior in two settings. While both settings were a playground, one playground had a fence that set the boundary for the children to stay within, while the other playground lacked a fence and was open space. In the condition without a fence or boundaries, the children clustered around the teacher and barely strayed, even to play on the equipment. They felt unsure of themselves and were overly reliant on the teacher's presence to guide their every move. In the condition with the fence, children were far more likely to cover more ground, explore, and play in a way that felt safe because they knew what their boundary was. They no longer felt the need to stay close to the teacher to stay safe. They felt more sure of themselves and had a stronger sense of identity.

If you can imagine this in the context of an organization, think about a leadership team who hovers close to the CEO, constantly wanting to ask what path to take to solve problems. When decisions run through the leader at the top, it forms

[85] Penney Nichols-Whitehead and Jodie M. Plumert, "The Influence of Boundaries on Young Children's Searching and Gathering," Journal of Cognition and Development 2 (4) (2001): 367-388.

a bottleneck that stifles the organization's growth, inhibits creativity, and creates frustration and learned helplessness from the leaders.

Role ambiguity is defined as the extent to which one's work responsibilities and authority are unclear, and research has shown that it is correlated with multiple negative outcomes, including poor self-image. Even a highly confident person could struggle with their identity if they're in an organization that lacks clear mechanisms of control.

In contrast, now imagine a leadership team that is clear about goals and direction, empowered to make decisions on their own, and able to create solutions that fit within the boundaries the team has agreed upon. The CEO is then freed up to contribute to solving the hardest problems, thinking strategically about the future of the organization, and developing the leadership capacity of her team.

This was the case with one of our clients, who found that after completing our organization design process, she felt freer and more confident in her own identity as a people-focused leader who did not need to be in the weeds of the decisions being made by all of the executives on the team.

 [86]

---

[86] https://gallaheredge.com/themissinglinks

Linking Humans Through Control Creates Unity

When humans understand their roles and how they are meant to work together, it increases trust and accountability and reduces unhealthy conflict.

Remember, creating clarity on the competitive strategy is the first step to creating control in an organization. If some employees think that the main strategy is to deliver products quickly even if they have a lot of bugs, and others think the strategy is to prioritize quality with minimal product launches, the organization will metaphorically spin in circles. In-fighting will occur within and across teams, as they have wildly different ideas about what they are supposed to be doing. Role ambiguity has a negative impact on Unity as it is associated with interpersonal conflict and a propensity for people to leave the organization. Criticisms will build as it will be harder to differentiate true gaps in competence from misalignment on "the best" approach.

In some cases, if the CEO thinks the strategy is clear but hasn't made the time to align the executive team and the rest of the organization around that strategy, he blames the leadership team, questioning their ability to take the company to the next level, or even firing people for "poor performance."

To illustrate how unfortunate this is, we use the met-aphor of a car. If your strategy in using your car to achieve your future vision includes hauling heavy loads up a mountain, you'll develop design criteria for what looks a lot like a dump truck.

If your strategy is to pull 3 G's rounding a corner at 100 mph, you will develop design criteria for what looks like a race car.

There is nothing inherently superior or inferior about a dump truck to a race car; they are simply different vehicles designed to do different things. But it's critical that you align the design of the vehicle with its purpose. Imagine a leader beating up on the driver of the dump truck when the truck fails to pull 3 G's while rounding the corner at 100 mph— that would be crazy, right?

But we see this happen in organizations all the time. Leadership teams at the top are doing their best to enhance the performance of the organization, and they want to point to things like "accountability" to make a difference when they haven't designed the organization to execute the strategy. Accountability is important, but it must be designed on the front end, not just demanded after things go wrong.

Creating control in the organization means replacing role ambiguity with role clarity, which is correlated with greater organizational accountability and improved teamwork (i.e., Unity).

Returning to the example that opened the chapter, this is exactly the type of organizational design that we performed at KSC. It was one of the largest organizational changes ever made at KSC, and the entire center was restructured to create independent engineering and safety organizations. These organizations not only had separate management and reporting structures but also had independent budget authority apart from the programs. This established an independent technical authority for safety and engineering with equal voice, authority, and representation while eliminating conflicts of interest that create impossible workplace situations.

Tying It All Together

The process of organization design is a powerful and important element of organizational culture.

 [87]

When this design is done factoring in all of the elements of Unity—the common purpose, the common beliefs, and the strategy to achieve that future vision—you're not describing an organization that is highly bureaucratic; you are simply describing a dump truck that is *really good* at hauling heavy loads or a race car that is *really good* at going *really fast!* The combination of these missing links creates the emergent property of Unity.

---

[87] https://gallaheredge.com/themissinglinks

PART THREE

Scan here to access free additional content [88]

Chapter 9

Leadership From the Inside Out

"The only thing of real importance that leaders do is to create and manage culture.
If you do not manage culture, it manages you, and you may not even be aware of the extent to which this is happening."
—Edgar Schein

89

Leadership That Fuels Growth

We met Suneera Madhani, CEO of Stax by Fattmerchant, when she was part of a start-up accelerator called Starter Studio in Orlando, Florida. Her leadership ability was clear early in the development of her company, Stax. She and her brother, Sal, joined with a clear vision of what their company could become, and they knew they needed more talent to get it done. Over the course of the twelve-week accelerator, she conducted the

---

89 https://gallaheredge.com/themissinglinks

first "in-accelerator" acquisition of another start-up before the program even ended.

That is one of the first things about her leadership that is so powerful. She knows how critical it is to surround herself with talented, driven, intelligent people and empower them to get things done.

While we had the pleasure of mentoring and coaching her team while they were in the accelerator, she didn't officially hire us until the team had hit $1 million in annual recurring revenue (ARR) and was past the twenty-employee mark.

Suneera had intentionally focused on building her culture from the start of her company, and as they grew, she knew the value of investing. She knew that every new level of the organization's growth required a new level of leadership and was always ready to grow from the inside out. One thing that makes her a great leader is that she was always willing to look inward, first and foremost. And she knew that once Stax hit a certain size, she couldn't carry the full load of leadership.

She decided to invest in the growth of the leaders she had put in place within the organization with our workshops and coaching. The executive team at Stax fully bought into the critical importance of team cohesion when it came to the performance of the organization. They built self-acceptance through practices like "taking credit" (each leader acknowledging themselves for the progress they're making, rather than always focusing on the gap), focusing on the journey and sharing vulnerable experiences as a team. They built self-awareness through open, real, raw feedback sessions to each other as a team and exploring their self-concept through psychological instruments. And they enhanced their self-accountability by creating collaboration contracts to recenter themselves when their defenses were triggered and structured exercises to openly explore "what happened" instead of "who to blame" when it came to solving problems. Their work with us helped them accelerate their growth to become more mature leaders with higher self-acceptance, self-awareness, and self-accountability.

But dedicated time with the leadership team to grow their self-awareness and skills was not enough. Another thing we led Suneera and her team through was establishing core values. And she did not just "set it and let it;" she revisited their core values regularly, and they asked themselves if the core values felt true and how those values were felt and understood by the team. They also did regular checks across the workforce to ask themselves, "Who, in this organization, is regularly misaligned with these core values?" They were proactive in giving feedback and providing people with an opportunity to develop and grow into the values but were also decisive when people did not show enough progress. Being willing to let go of employees for lack of culture fit is one of the strengths of the leadership team at Stax.

As they continued to grow, we worked with them to put more dedicated time into intentionally designing their organization. They made important calls about decision-making in their organization to empower people to get things done at their level and allow the leaders to focus their energy on more and more strategic thinking. They clarified reporting relationships and strengthened each of their leadership teams' alignment, so they were on the same page about what it meant to put the team over self. And they have never forgotten the power of having fun to align with their core value of creating joy. In one of our most recent executive meetings with the team, before we started, the CEO called one of their employees into the conference room as he was walking by, just arriving at the office. When he came in the room, she started clapping, and then the whole team jumped in and clapped and cheered for him—just for fun. Then she announced: "Have a great day!" Just because. How's that for creating an experience for an employee?

Why Does Leadership Matter?

Leadership is an incredibly expansive topic, and it would undoubtedly take more than a single chapter to address it adequately. However, it plays such a pivotal role within the context of organizational culture that we felt the need to discuss it here. So, while we have a lot to say on this topic and may likely write our own book on the subject in the future, we will attempt to remain narrowly focused. Specifically, we are focusing on the role that leadership plays in creating, managing, and changing culture.

> **"Leaders create culture.**
> **It is their responsibility to change it."**
>
> **—The CAIB Report**

Leaders create the culture, and your organization's leadership serves as the engine for your culture change. We would argue that the primary function of leadership is to inspire and lead change. This distinguishes leadership from management. And as Edgar Schein said, leaders' truly important work comes from their impact on creating and managing the company's culture.

Leaders are so influential in shaping the culture that they actually do so through both their action and their inaction. If you are a leader, it doesn't really matter whether or not you *want* to create your organization's culture. You are doing it. Everything that you do, don't do, say, and don't say sends a message that the employees in the organization interpret as a signal (or experience) that they add meaning to and use to shape their beliefs about the organization. While this can sound overwhelming, and it is, we can sort how leaders create the culture into two basic areas: they set the standards for behavior and they design the organization.

Leaders Set the Standards for Behavior

The first way leaders create the culture is by setting the standards of behavior. As we've discussed, people's common behaviors ultimately define the organization's culture. So, when leaders define the standards of behavior, they are establishing cultural norms. The extent to which this shapes the culture depends on the extent to which the behaviors are enforced and adhered to.

We worked with one company that was growing rapidly through acquisition. The CEO's strategy was to expand its operations to cover most of the east coast by acquiring geographically positioned competitors in strategically key areas. He knew that he would need the capability to integrate these new companies into his and wanted our help to create a strong, well-defined culture to support his acquisition strategy.

To his surprise, when we began working with him, he discovered that his company did not have a single intentional core value. All of their values and cultural norms were accidental and had evolved over time based largely on the personality of the previous leadership. As he studied the behaviors of his organization, it was clear to him that they weren't aligned with his strategy and wouldn't support the new organization he was trying to create.

The most basic way for leaders to set the behavioral standards is to define and communicate them to the organization.

If you are a leader, then you are doing this for your organization, whether it is intentional or not. Many leaders take steps to define behaviors for the organization and directly communicate them to the workforce. However, this is not the only way that employees get this communication. They also determine the standards of behavior based on what is rewarded and what is punished within the organization. Additionally, they infer it from your other communications and what things you emphasize and praise.

One client took the time to create their organizational values and an employee recognition program to support them. Several months in, however, one of the executives noted that they did not recognize the values equally. One value of "grit" was being rewarded disproportionately and sending a message to the workforce that "If you're not working evenings and weekends, we won't acknowledge your contribution." After this realization, they made an intentional push to seek behaviors that aligned with other core values.

Model the Behaviors You Want

The timeless saying is still true: actions speak louder than words.

Leaders set the standards for behavior by modeling the behavior they desire. Again, this may either be intentional or unintentional. Regardless, employees see their leaders' behavior as a strong signal telling them what behaviors are acceptable and rewarded. The implicit message is that if you want to advance to a leadership level or make it to the executive ranks, you should behave in that way. Furthermore, we all know that insisting people to "do as I say, not as I do" is ineffective. More than that, it undermines credibility and trust as a leader.

A word of caution: not all of these examples have to come from a bad place. If you, as a leader, are working sixty-plus hours a week and taking work home on the weekend while sending emails at all hours, don't be surprised when your employees don't take your speeches about work-life balance seriously. When you see signs of burnout in your organization, look in the mirror first.

Don't Let Fear Hold You Hostage

It is imperative that leaders understand that, whether it is their own behavior or that of an employee, the worst behavior allowed determines the organization's culture. It is tempting to think that the culture can be defined by an average instead. This provides a convenient escape for leaders to claim that most of the organization behaves a certain way or lives a certain value, so on average, this is true of the organization. But organizational culture doesn't work that way.

This doesn't mean that the organization has to be perfect in its behavior or in living a value. We are talking about when a behavior is acknowledged and accepted by leadership. In this case, that standard of acceptance is what defines the culture.

As an example, we worked with a company that felt strongly about creating a culture where everyone enjoyed working together. They felt so strongly that they proposed a core value of "no assholes" (their words, not ours). Although this was said jokingly, everyone on the leadership team got very excited about the basic idea. The CEO wanted something along these lines to be a core value and was pushing for agreement.

As we were scanning the room, we noticed some reluctance from a couple of executives and probed them about it. Exasperated, one leader burst out, "What about Charlie?" Suddenly, the mood in the room completely flipped. It was as if the energy was magically sucked out of every individual; they all got quiet, nervously looking at the table and playing with their pen or shuffling their papers.

Charlie was the company's chief software architect, and the CEO considered him to be essential to the success of their product and irreplaceable. He was also exhibiting toxic behaviors like arrogance, rudeness, and he created intense conflict with nearly every employee he worked with. Any guesses why he wasn't invited to this meeting?

Every member of the executive team thought that Charlie should be let go, except the CEO, who was operating out of fear. The leadership team concluded that it couldn't possibly have a core value along the lines of "no assholes" as long as Charlie was on the team. Doing so would cause them to lose credibility as leaders and invalidate the worth of the values they were working so hard to establish.

As a side note, we worked with the CEO to coach him on dealing with Charlie. We don't believe that any employee should be irreplaceable, and no company should let itself be held hostage by fear. It wasn't a quick or easy process. The CEO went so far as to create an office in another city and move Charlie there as the only employee in an attempt to keep his technical knowledge while effectively isolating him from all human contact with the rest of the company. Finally, when Charlie chose not to change his behaviors after plenty of feedback and coaching, he was let go. To the surprise of no one but the CEO, company performance and innovation increased after his departure.

The moral of this story is that leaders must be willing to be punished for upholding the culture. When they let fear stop them from enforcing the standards of behavior, the culture suffers. This fear can come from a variety of sources. It can come from a fear of how they will be seen as a leader, from how an important customer or stakeholder will react, or as in the example above, from fear of losing a critical asset. However, as stated earlier, when leaders fail to take action, the culture ultimately drops to the worst behavior allowed.

Leaders Design the Organization

The other way leaders create and manage culture is through the organization's design. At this point, you should have a good understanding of what we mean by organizational design. Leaders are the ones who are ultimately responsible for this design and the associated design choices.

The way you design the organization exerts an enormous influence on the culture. It does this primarily through the experiences it creates for employees and how it contributes to the environment and how employees feel about themselves while at work.

Environment plays a huge role. Author and organizational psychologist Dr. Benjamin Hardy describes the importance of environment in his book, *Willpower Doesn't Work*. "Without the ability to change our environment, we *wouldn't* be able to change. To change one is to change the other." As a leader, being intentional about the environment you create is essential to inviting the behavior you wish to see in your organization's culture. Take our Dirty Dozen assessment to reflect on your organization's environment.

As you recall, organizations are complex adaptive systems. The behavior of these systems emerges from the systemic structure—in this case, the policies, processes, decision mechanisms, etc.

Consider our old childhood friend, the Slinky. Imagine I'm holding Slinky by one end and letting the rest of him hang motionless below my hand. If I move my hand quickly up and back down two times within a four-inch range, what will Slinky do? The bottom part of the Slinky will oscillate wildly up and down by much more than four inches and for much longer than I moved my hand.

OK, that was the easy part; now, here's the test. Why did the Slinky behave the way it did (oscillate wildly for a long time)?

The average person off the street will probably say it behaved that way because I moved my hand. But you've been paying attention as we've been

---

discussing systems theory, and you know better than to bite on this simple answer, right?

What if I had been holding a stick instead of a Slinky and had made the exact same motion with my hand? Would the stick have behaved the same way? Of course not! The bottom of the stick would have moved up and down by four inches twice and then immediately stopped. So, if your answer to my first question was that Slinky's behavior was because of me moving my hand, why didn't the same movement of my hand produce the same behavior in the stick?

A system's structure determines its behavior. You can see from this example that the fact that the slinky is made of a thin metal wire wound in a spiral form contributes greatly to its behavior. Different materials combined in different shapes produce different behaviors.

Design the System Structure

The same is true for organizations. Different policies, processes, and decision mechanisms combined in different organizational structures produce different organizational behaviors. And, as we've been discussing, this creates different organizational environments for employees to work in. These different organizational environments have different effects on how employees feel about themselves while they are at work, which heavily influences their beliefs about the organization and their behaviors, i.e., the culture.

We've already given several examples of how this works within organizations, but we will offer one more here to help bring the point back to the business setting. The process or system an organization uses to provide employees feedback is a powerful element of system design. The interaction between a leader and an employee is an important experience in shaping that individual's beliefs about the company. It can also profoundly affect how that employee feels about herself at work. Suppose a leader does not take it seriously and devote ample time to providing meaningful, actionable feedback aligned to the employee's individual career goals. In that case, the employee may have a negative experience.

Consider the example from chapter 7 where the CEO was withholding feedback from one of his executives because he feared she was under too much pressure for him to be open with her. She experienced higher anxiety due to uncertainty without getting clear feedback. She felt less significant when she felt her CEO wasn't giving her as much time and attention. And she feared feeling incompetent when she didn't know where she stood with her performance. She could have even felt unlikable if she perceived that he avoided her because he didn't like her.

Any or all of these can trigger defenses and lead to a variety of negative beliefs about the company, such as, "They don't care about me as a person," "They don't care about my growth," or "There's no future for me here." If these beliefs become commonly held, they become a part of the culture. Once she trusted that feedback would be delivered in a timely manner, it made her more comfortable in the absence of that feedback, and she could squash those prior fears and beliefs.

Design Employee Experiences

Leaders are constantly creating and influencing the culture through the experiences they create for employees. These experiences come through the design of the organization, as we just discussed. They also come through a virtually continuous stream of ad hoc interactions with leaders and the organization.

These include all forms of communication, from emails to formal company addresses and even casual random encounters. It also includes the visual cues that the company creates for employees, such as the office layout, swag, décor, and other factors affecting the work environment. Leaders also intentionally create experiences intended to boost morale and create a culture, such as holiday parties, casual Fridays, free lunches, or even the ping pong table we like to joke about.

Being intentional and clear is important. One client had a game room in their office, with (of course) a ping pong table, an arcade-style game, and more. But the leadership team did not talk through the idea of a game room and why they wanted to have it. They were not aligned on whether it was an effective choice and what it even meant for it to be effective.

As a result, employees in the organization had different opinions as to why the game room was there and how they felt about it. Some felt it was awesome, and they loved that they were being treated like adults who could manage their own time and play if they wanted to. Others had a more cynical view that the game room was meant only to keep them at the office longer so the CEO could get more work out of them.

If the leadership team was intentional, clear, and aligned on having a game room and the why behind it, they likely would have created more common beliefs between employees.

By intentionally designing the organization and the continual flow of experiences they expose their employees to, leaders create and manage the culture. Employees constantly add meaning to this flood of signals and form beliefs about the organization and themselves within the organization.

Unfortunately, these may not always be the beliefs you would like them to have. This is one reason that managing organizational culture can be so challenging: We can't directly control the resulting belief, only the experience. But one thing is certain, you will drastically improve your chances of creating the culture you want if you intentionally design your culture rather than just hoping for the best.

The Power of Intentional Culture

Now that we have established that if you are a leader, you are creating your organization's culture, we want to discuss how you can use this to intentionally create the culture you want. But who are these leaders that successfully create and manage culture? What is it that they know that other leaders seemingly don't?

Know Your Power

First, these leaders are acutely aware of their impact on the organizational environment. You have a tremendous effect on this, which determines how it feels to work in your company. And while it may seem like employees are reacting to how they feel about aspects of the environment, it is really how individuals feel about themselves that drives their behavior.

As a leader, your goal is to create an organizational atmosphere in which people feel positive about themselves. This translates directly into productivity.

---

[91] https://gallaheredge.com/login/

When employees feel good about themselves at work, their concentration on tasks and jobs increases, as does motivation, enthusiasm, and energy in their work. They volunteer more for assignments and have a stronger sense of responsibility for results and outcomes. Additionally, they tend to have a more positive outlook and focus on problem-solving rather than blaming when things go wrong.

A quick glance through the business news will tell you that organizational atmospheres like this don't happen by accident. We've already discussed the myriad of ways you are creating this atmosphere which can affect how employees feel about themselves while they are at work. The question becomes, how much forethought and intentionality did you put into those messages and whether they would create the above-described atmosphere or destroy it? Are you intentional about everything you do to create experiences of inclusion, control, and openness for your employees that support their significance, competence, and likability?

Know Your Culture's Importance

"...culture isn't just one aspect of the game —it is the game."

—Louis V. Gerstner Jr., former chairman and CEO of IBM

Second, leaders who are effective at creating and managing culture are intentional about creating it because they understand the importance of culture. They recognize that it has the power to determine their success as a leader and as an organization. They have concluded, as Lou Gerstner Jr., chairman and CEO of IBM, did, "that culture isn't just one aspect of the game—it is the game."

Because of this, they are willing to invest the time and resources necessary to make culture a priority for themselves, their staff, and their entire organization.

Know All Things Grow

Third, these leaders also possess a growth mindset. They don't see the capabilities of individuals or their organization as fixed. Rather, they believe that both can grow and improve with the proper support. Because of this, they believe in the importance of developing themselves and others. They recognize that their own capability serves as a lid for their organization, and for it to continue growing, they must continue growing themselves, like the leadership team at Stax. They lead by example in their own development and ask the leaders that report to them to do likewise. Growth is a journey without a destination, so no leader is ever "done."

These leaders understand the return on investment (ROI) and intrinsic value of personal growth and investing in culture. This commitment to investing in self-development, as well as the development of others, lays the groundwork for intentionally managing the culture. Since organizational culture starts with the Self at its core, it is impossible to work on the culture without working on the self. And, as we will see, work on the Self is a necessary foundation for intentionally designing your culture.

So, are you one of these rare leaders who recognizes your impact on the environment, understands the importance of culture, and believes in developing yourself and others? If so, how do you take the next step and create an intentional culture in your organization? By intentionally setting the standards of behavior and intentionally designing your organization.

Be Intentional With the Behavior Standards You Set

Leaders want to manage and shape the culture to ensure that it aligns with their strategy and produces the environment and results that they desire. To do this, you will first want to be very clear about what results you are looking for and what executing your strategy looks like. Then you will want to determine what critical behaviors are required to produce those results and what critical behaviors are required to execute your strategy.

You want to be clear about the organizational environment you want to create and what behaviors are key contributors to producing that environment. Once you have done this analysis, you will have a list of critical behaviors for your culture that you can intentionally design for.

Once again, we will begin our discussion of intentional culture by focusing on creating behavioral standards. This is clearly a leader's role, but sadly not all leaders embrace it. Doing so requires intentionally setting standards of behavior, communicating them, and modeling them.

Talk the Talk

One of the primary ways that leaders can communicate behaviors is through company values. If done properly, these can be highly effective at establishing standards of behavior for the organization.

Another great way that is shockingly simple is just to tell people how you expect them to behave. And while this sounds simple, it requires you to have clarity for yourself before you can create clarity for others. Being clear and direct in your communication in this manner can do wonders!

The leaders at Stax worked internally as a team to clarify the messaging behind their core values. They thought through the different interpretations and shared with the workforce that the values represent a three-pronged stool. Each employee was expected to use all three as a decision-making filter when using the values to guide their choices. It's not just enough to GSD (get s*** done); they're also expected to "create joy" and put "team over self." The leaders ran through different examples of situations they had faced to see if those three values created clarity when combined and found they did. This was a key part of how they were communicated throughout the workforce.

Walk the Walk

But actions still speak louder than words. So how you behave as a leader sends a powerful message. And how you react and respond to both internal and external events will influence employee beliefs and behaviors as well. This includes whether you tolerate poor behavior from an employee internally or remain silent on an important social issue externally. Remember, everything you do and everything you don't do affects the culture.

One of our clients made a decision that felt hard at the time to let go of an employee who had been a part of the organization for a long time and was well-liked. Her role required her to maintain a high degree of confidentiality, but she violated that agreement when she shared too much with others in the organization. Much of the workforce was upset by the decision, but the leadership team knew that to protect the integrity of the role and the culture, they couldn't tolerate that behavior.

Ultimately, even when we talk about performance as a leader, effectiveness comes back to our Self Model. We would say *especially* when talking about performance as a leader!

Who you are as a leader and how you show up with your employees forms the heart of how you walk the walk. And engaging in this walk in a fully authentic way is a two-way street. This is where you will want to employ your twin superpowers of listening and curiosity to unlock genuine exchange of ideas, honest questioning and even challenging of the status quo and deeper understanding. Being vulnerable is required for authenticity and trust.

The personal capacities of self-acceptance, self-awareness, and self-accountability are all crucial to enabling leaders to walk the tightrope of managing conflicting priorities and styles. These capacities contribute to leaders' resilience when the organization is facing challenges, which inspires people to follow. True leadership is permission-based, and these capacities help leaders garner the trust required to gain willing followers. When leaders focus on growing their Maturity and develop high levels of this trait, they can respond to the daily challenges in ways that will enable them to continually reinforce the standards of behavior they have intentionally set for their organization.

Be Intentional With the Design of Your Organization

Beyond just communicating and living the critical behaviors, you will also want to ensure that you intentionally design your organization to produce the behaviors and resulting culture you desire. As humans, our environment heavily influences our behavior, which often happens subconsciously.

Just think back to our example about how you naturally behave when you walk into a library compared with a sporting event or rock concert. The combination of social norms, behavioral cues from those around us, design and layout of the physical environment, signs and visual information, strategy (or purpose) of the event, and potentially even the timing or our dress affect how each venue feels and how we behave. As the leader, you get to set the rules and create the environment that produces this influence on your people.

Culture Design is a Team Sport

When designing your organization for critical behaviors, the process is involved, thorough, iterative, and continuous. It is your job to own this

---

92 https://gallaheredge.com/themissinglinks

process as a leader, but it is not your job to do this alone. Designing your organization to create the culture you want is a crowdsourced activity. You will want the entire organization's support; seeking constant feedback from everyone in the organization will make this much more manageable.

Since you have already been clear about the critical behaviors you desire, you now invite the organization to identify areas where the organizational system may unintentionally discourage those behaviors. Creating culture isn't just about telling people what you want; it's asking a lot of questions and engaging in active listening.

This in and of itself is an organizational capability that will take time to develop. Still, once you demonstrate a willingness to listen and make changes, you will find that people will be happy to point out where they feel conflict between what you are asking them to do and what they feel pressured by the organizational system to do. No one likes being in that situation.

Continuously Assess the System

Intentional culture design involves critically assessing the existing organizational design to ensure that it maximally encourages the critical behaviors. The same critical analysis is applied whenever new processes, policies, or systems are created or introduced. Similarly, any changes or modifications include a step to ask what effect the changes have on critical behaviors. As a leader, it is your job to ensure these questions are asked and that the behaviors are included as design criteria.

The leaders at Stax continuously hired bright, talented employees who took a lot of initiative and were very dedicated to achieving results for the organization. An unintended outcome of this was that there were often multiple big projects happening, each of which felt like the highest priority for their respective departments. But those projects required interdepartmental collaboration, so the team would sometimes work at cross-purposes, even with the best intention. The executive team came together to create a singular priority for the organization that touched nearly every department to remove the confusion and friction in the system and were thrilled with how quickly they were able to move the needle on an incredibly important initiative.

You want to learn to think in terms of employee experiences and what experiences you are creating for employees through the design of the system. As stated earlier, work collaboratively with them to understand these experiences and what beliefs you are cocreating as a result of those experiences.

These beliefs are what drive the behaviors, so understanding the entire chain from experience to behavior is extremely valuable. The dial that you can most easily turn is the design element of a process, policy, or system. If you understand how to change this so that it changes the employee experience to ultimately produce the desired behavior (or even removes a barrier to that behavior), you can manage your culture.

Intentionally Creating the Missing Links

We have been focusing heavily on behaviors to this point because they are more tangible, and there is a clear, direct link between leadership and employee behavior. Behaviors also become synonymous with culture when they are widely held and become the commonly accepted way things are done within the organization.

However, to create and manage culture, it is necessary to intentionally design and build an organization that establishes the Missing Links between employees so the cultural traits of Maturity, Diversity, Community, and Unity emerge. Implementing the Missing Link Culture Model will ensure an effective organizational culture, which is the foundational basis for everything else. Take your Missing Link Quick Assessment today on the resources page for a free report. Once this Culture Model is in place, you can focus on aligning specific behaviors as described above.

While the Missing Link Model is general in its application, leaders can tailor the links to match the organization's specific DNA. We provide an in-depth example of this with safety in chapter 12. So, while the theory and power of the connections are universally applicable, how they ultimately manifest themselves in a specific organization can vary. What openness looks like in one organization may differ greatly from what it looks like in another. Some organizations are designed to be more business-like, while others are more sociable, and that's fine.

We like to extend our DNA metaphor to its limits and say that the model's links are like the genotype, but the observable behaviors in the organization are like the phenotype. In this example, all people have a gene for eye color (genotype), but that eye color can be expressed as blue or brown on an individual (phenotype). If you are a geneticist, please forgive us for oversimplifying and slightly perverting the science to make this analogy work.

As organizations do the work of creating connections, these differences will naturally emerge. This is especially true if leaders have done the work (on their own or with consultants like us) to identify their critical behaviors and focus on strategic align-

---

ment. Primarily, the work of aligning the critical behaviors to the organization design is found within the Unity strand. This is where we find our connection to strategy and the links of common beliefs and control.

When leaders follow our culture and organizational design steps while intentionally designing for critical behaviors, the result will be an organizational culture that is both highly effective and promotes behaviors specific to the organization's unique needs.

You Can Do It!

Leadership is a big job. While it may be true that a few leaders get ample pay and recognition, we think the vast majority sacrifice for the position. Expectations for leaders continue to rise while the challenges associated with meeting those expectations continue to grow. The pace of change is increasing and coming from seemingly every direction, while customer demands grow ever higher and competition becomes ever fiercer.

The best hope available to leaders is to design an organization and culture optimized to perform the way they need it to perform. This is like our race car versus dump truck example from chapter 8 about the Unity strand. If you're driving an organization designed for a different mission, you're in for a rough time!

The great news is that as a leader, your organization's design and culture are up to you. Leadership is what holds the Missing Link Model together. You can choose to be intentional about creating and managing your organization's culture. You can choose to be intentional about establishing, communicating, and modeling standards of behavior for your employees. You can choose to invest in developing yourself, the leaders who report to you, and your organization. You can choose to intentionally design your organization around the Missing Link Model and build in the critical behaviors necessary for your success.

See, you're swimming in a sea of choices! All you have to do is choose. Choose to be intentional. Choose to lead!

 94

Chapter 10

Assessing the Organization

"Forgive yourself for not knowing what you didn't know before you learned it."
—Maya Angelou

 95

When Surveys Attack

From the beginning of the organizational assessment process, Jeff worked with us to be very intentional. As the president of a large insurance broker spread across the country with different types of employees (salaried and independent contractors), he was aware that not everybody experienced this company the same way. We were working with him to set up the custom demographic variables for our Missing Link Culture Survey, which measures the opinions and experiences of the workforce. Jeff developed hypotheses and questions about what differences might be meaningful, such as: Is there a difference

---

95 https://gallaheredge.com/themissinglinks

between how sales leaders and operations leaders experience the culture? He also realized that with different regional presidents, there were different leadership styles, and subcultures had likely been forming.

When the survey was administered, the workforce participated heartily with a response rate of 80 percent. While overall, the scores reflected a positive perception of the culture, there were areas that could be improved, as we always see in our surveys. The data highlighted that not everybody saw the organization the same way. For example, the operations leaders believed that people could get away with misaligning from culture, but the sales leaders didn't see it that way. Additionally, while senior leaders usually tend to rate the organization higher than the rest of the company, the board was honest with themselves and rated their own trait of Unity lower than the rest of the respondents.

We had been taking the board through our Growing Leaders from the Inside Out (GLIO) program, which helped them learn about defensiveness. Our engagement was designed such that they would learn how to identify their own defensiveness before we went through the survey results because, in our experience, survey results almost always triggered at least a little defensiveness from leadership teams. When leaders who care deeply about the company learn that some people feel like they're not doing well in some areas, survey results like these can trigger their insecurities. This board was no different. As we talked through certain results, defenses were triggered, and the board seemed to fall on one of two sides. They were either an advocate for the company's culture—because it was great—or they started pushing more on how the data suggested they had room for improvement. Some were inclined to overfocus on the negative and felt it was an "indictment," whereas others were quick to point to one of the most remarkable results of the survey: the number of people who answered "nothing" when we asked them what they *didn't* like about the culture (350).

We directed their focus on the "and." There are many great things about the company—AND—there will always be things to improve. In the workshop session that followed the survey debrief, we invited them to reflect on at least one thing from the survey meeting that triggered defensiveness in them and what the story was in their head that triggered the defensiveness. It served as a great real-life example of how defenses are still triggered even when we understand what defenses are and how they work. It also helped each of them see how they could internalize the survey results differently.

Following our GLIO workshop with them, we sat down with the president and outlined a front-loaded, three-year plan to help the culture grow in alignment with their vision and future direction. We connected each piece of the agreement back to their survey results. We met with the board to design the communication plan back to the workforce, which we did first in a meeting about the survey results, and then again in a kickoff meeting about the workshop series for leaders and individual contributors.

We took every employee through a workshop focused on self-acceptance, openness, and inclusion (the lowest scores on the survey). Our focus with the board during the whole first year was on our Uniting Leaders from the Inside Out because the board had rated the Unity of the organization lower than the rest of the company. From where they sat, they could see how there were divides and rifts in understanding future vision and strategy, so we guided them through that process together as well. Finally, the president included an annual resurvey effort in our engagement so they could assess their progress against the baseline. The leaders in this organization knew that their culture really could be their competitive edge, so they committed to the continual improvement and measurement of that culture.

To Assess or Not to Assess, That Is the Question...

If you have chosen to be intentional about your culture, one of the first steps you will want to take is to assess your organization. This is critical to your success in managing your culture for two primary reasons. First, it provides a baseline measurement for where your organization's culture currently is. This baseline will allow you to know whether the things you are doing to improve or sustain your culture are actually working over time. Without this ability to measure change over time, it can be difficult to detect slow incremental changes in the organizational environment. This is what happened with the acceptance of foam shedding leading up to the *Columbia* accident. Because small pieces of foam came off the external tank on every launch, engineers began to accept the condition as normal. As a result, NASA began to accept more and more risk without consciously evaluating its decision to do so. The technical term for this is normalization of deviance. What makes it scary is that this is an inherent part of our psychology.

We see this phenomenon in many areas of human behavior. Large, sudden changes are easy to detect and correct, but we are often blind to slow, incremental ones. One example of this is the "slippery-slope effect." Major scandals like the one at Enron don't start

off with transactions in the billions of dollars. They typically start small and continue to build. The notorious fraudster Bernie Madoff told *Vanity Fair* that, "It starts out with you taking a little bit, maybe a few hundred, a few thousand. You get comfortable with that, and before you know it, it snowballs into something big." For Bernie, "something big" was $18 billion.

If you aren't concerned with the slippery-slope effect of employees stealing pens, what about the all-too-common condition of accepting lower standards of performance? This is another form of normalization of deviance where the bar for expected performance is slowly lowered over time. Each time it is lowered, the new low becomes the new standard. If this situation is allowed to persist over a long time, it will result in serious performance or quality issues. This organizational behavior is so common, Peter Senge even includes it as one of his eight system archetypes in *The Fifth Discipline*. Humans are poor at detecting slow changes in the behavior of complex systems due to our tendency to normalize conditions. The consequence is that we fail to notice culture creep because we are always creating a "new normal."

Without measurement of some sort, it is difficult to claim that you actually have the ability to assert control over something. Control requires a feedback loop where you are making changes in response to some action of the system. Whether we are talking about a thermostat or a human driving a car, the ability to either measure the temperature or see the road is a key requirement for controlling those systems. As quality and performance improvement guru H. James Harrington said,

> "Measurement is the first step that leads to control and eventually to improvement. If you can't measure something, you can't understand it. If you can't understand it, you can't control it. If you can't control it, you can't improve it."

So, if your goal is to manage your culture, then plan on measuring it.

Second, a good assessment will enable you to evaluate the organization from multiple angles. Organizational culture is created from the inside out. You will want to assess your organization at the self, team, and organizational levels to understand how each is contributing to your emergent culture. At the Self level, it is important to understand how employees see and feel about themselves within the organizational environment. They can provide valuable insights into how they perceive the organization and the experiences you are creating. Regardless of your intent, this is an area where perception is reality—at least for them. If the experiences you are creating aren't producing the beliefs and behaviors you desire, it is important to understand that.

At the team level, it is important to get information about how the relationships between employees are working to produce your culture. This is where the missing links are in action, so knowing how employees are experiencing and relating to other employees is critical to understanding how the cultural traits emerge. Additionally, organizations are typically dependent on the effective functioning of their teams for their success. Understanding how employees perceive the success and health of your teams will be an important factor in managing your company culture.

Finally, at the organizational level, it is important to understand how effectively and efficiently the organization is functioning as a system. How are the various subsystems working to produce the products and execute the strategy? You will want to know if any of these are misaligned with your strategy or if they are creating negative experiences for your employees and hurting your company culture. These organizational systems are similar to mechanical systems. Over time, they naturally succumb to the effects of entropy or the wear and tear of daily use. As the organization adapts to the ever-changing external environment, these small adaptations cause small misalignments within the subsystems that grow over time.

For this reason, as well as the ability to measure how the culture is evolving over time, it is critical to assess your organization regularly. We recommend developing an organizational habit around assessment. Organizations can create routines for assessment that align them with specific events within the organizational calendar and take place at a set time each year. By doing this, companies remove the question of "if" they will perform an assessment and accustom employees to their occurrence. If companies regularly follow through by acting on the feedback they receive, it builds trust in the process and decreases employee resistance. The assessment itself becomes a part of the organizational culture, and employees accept it as how the company continuously improves.

How to Assess Your Organization

To assess your organization, you will certainly want to evaluate it against the traits of an effective organization. You will want to know how Maturity, Diversity, Community, and Unity emerge within your organization. However, these are emergent traits, and as you recall, we can't work directly on them. To understand your culture and what is contributing to those emergent traits, it will be important to also assess the missing links. Gathering feedback from employees about each of the missing links will enable you to have much greater insight into what steps to take to manage your culture. You will also want to assess the individual drivers to understand the strength of the connections with employees and how well your company allows them to satisfy those drivers.

There is both art and a fair amount of science involved in creating an effective survey. If you are going to take the time and resources to perform the assessment, you will want to know that the tool you are using is reliable. You want to know that you are measuring what you think you are measuring, which depends on the design of the questions and the design of the overall survey. While there can be value in just asking your employees some basic questions, to measure the overall culture in a way that provides meaningful insight into what action steps to take requires a more sophisticated assessment. If you develop your own survey, ensure you solicit the support of individuals trained in the science of survey development.

At Gallaher Edge, we have developed a comprehensive organizational survey aligned to the Missing Links Culture Model, which has been rigorously validated by an independent third party and proven to be effective at measuring organizational culture. This assessment provides information about each emergent trait, the missing links, and each strand's individual drivers. It also provides additional information about the leadership capacity, the organization's ability to adapt, and execution measures about the organizational system. We also designed it to produce views of these characteristics from the self, team, and organizational levels. This is the assessment we used with the company in our opening story, and it is a much more in-depth assessment than the free version we provided earlier. If this is something that would benefit your company, you can learn more by going to https://gallaheredge.com/applymissinglink or scanning the QR code below.

96

But how you assess your organization isn't just about what questions you ask or how you crunch the numbers. There are attitudes, behaviors, and practices essential to a successful assessment program. Even if you have the best assessment in the world, that doesn't guarantee you will get the information, or more importantly, the results you want from conducting the assessment. As you assess your organization, you can apply the traits of an effective organization to the assessment process to serve as a guide.

---

96 https://gallaheredge.com/applymissinglink

The First Strand: Maturity

Once again, Maturity turns out to be foundational to the success of the process. Bringing together self-acceptance, self-awareness, and self-accountability as you assess your organization will enable you to solicit, hear and act on honest feedback. For the process to be effective, you must take all three of these steps. While the Self Model always works in concert, the three steps can be primarily aligned with one of the three components of the model.

First, the individuals in your organization must be willing to provide you with open and honest feedback. This step is rooted in self-awareness. Obviously, they can only provide feedback if they are aware of it themselves, so their Maturity will be important to enable them to become aware of their feedback and share it with you. They will only do this if they trust your response to the feedback, which is dependent on a high level of Maturity on your part. Your self-awareness will be important to monitor your response and how it is affecting those providing feedback. Additionally, you will want to normalize the idea of providing feedback as an organizational practice. This practice includes providing feedback in all directions, so the idea of employees telling leaders what they are thinking or feeling will be a routine event.

Second, you will want the ability to actually hear the feedback. Hearing feedback is heavily supported by self-acceptance. When we have high levels of self-acceptance, we can hear constructive feedback without becoming defensive. There are two components to hearing. The  first, as mentioned above, is the ability to respond to the feedback in a way that encourages continued open dialogue. We conducted an organizational assessment for a sports organization, and when we delivered the results to the president of the organization, he actually yelled at us over the results! His defenses were so triggered by the information that he responded loudly and aggressively. Fortunately, we are professionals, and we recognized that his defenses were really about his fears concerning what he felt the data said about him and had nothing to do with us (but it still got our heart rates up in the moment!). But if we had been employees in his organization, the likelihood we would have ever provided him with feedback in the future would have been very slim.

The other aspect of hearing feedback is to internalize it—to truly listen to the feedback and not just let it bounce off your eardrums. Again, this can be a form of defensiveness. Although not as violent, it can be just as detrimental to your ability to assess your organization. When you ignore the feedback provided or rationalize it away, the feedback's effectiveness is essentially neutralized. We worked with another company struggling with internal issues for years that had stifled their growth. When we presented them with the results of our assessment and recommendations, the CEO responded, "Yeah, we know that. You're not telling us anything new." This is a defense mechanism. Saying "I'm aware of that, leave me alone" is just another way to avoid having to deal with something you don't want to deal with. Stephen R. Covey said, "To know and not to do is not to know." If they truly "knew," they would have been doing something about the problems rather than allowing them to continue for years.

The third and final step is to act on the feedback you receive. This step aligns with self-accountability and requires the ability to believe change is possible and within your control. It also requires the courage to lead your organization in making these changes. It sounds absurdly obvious, but if you don't take any action based on your assessment, the whole exercise was pointless. In making this statement, we are assuming that your organization has opportunities for improvement and you received actionable constructive feedback. We have never seen a perfect organization. This is a very important point for assessments: The whole purpose of an assessment is to improve the organization. It isn't to collect interesting data; it's to do something. This is important to remember when interpreting the results as well. Sometimes clients want to obsess over statistical nuances or dig into the theoretical underpinnings of the assessment questions. While some individuals may be data and organizational theory geeks, this is typically a sneaky form of defensiveness. Subconsciously believing that a good offense is the best defense, some clients will attack the questions rather than focus on themselves or their organization. In every case we can think of, the specific nuance or concern didn't matter. The real question for you to ask yourself when presented with the feedback is, "What is this telling me, and what action can I take?"

Because the organization is a complex adaptive system, there is an important feedback loop at play here that we don't want to ignore. Acting on the feedback serves to reinforce the beliefs of the individuals who provide the feedback. When you act on their feedback, it reinforces the belief that they were heard and that their feedback is desired and valued. These are beliefs you want people to hold if you desire their open input. For this reason, we believe it is important to be open throughout the assessment process and let individuals know where you are in the assessment process as you are going through it. Once you have analyzed the results, be open about what you found and what you intend to do. You will almost certainly want to include them in the process of understanding the data and determining solutions, so bringing the organization along with you on the assessment journey is the best approach.

The Second Strand: Diversity

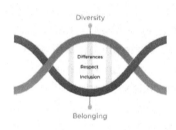

Diversity is critically important in the assessment process. Because we are dealing with a complex adaptive system, it is impossible for a single viewpoint to appreciate the state of the system. Understanding the system and the factors affecting its behavior requires a multifaceted view. For this reason, you must get input from multiple sources of feedback. You want your assessment to view the organization from as many angles as possible to help create a complete picture.

This isn't just about different physical views of your organization. While where a person "sits"—what department, function, or level of the organization they are in—plays a significant part in shaping their view, there is much more to it than that. We are also talking about different mental views of your organization. As we discussed with the systems view of the ladder of inference in chapter 8, what an individual sees is heavily affected by their mental model of the world and what they believe. Their beliefs and mental model are in turn shaped by the sum of their experiences. So, people with different backgrounds, cultures, genders, and ethnicities will bring with them different experiences and mental models. Ensuring that your assessment includes this level of Diversity will gain a more complete picture of your organization. People with similar mental models may suffer from similar blind spots. A diverse group of respondents will help avoid common blind spots while also ensuring that you create an organization that is welcoming to everyone.

One final argument for Diversity in your assessment is that when you solicit feedback from someone in your organization about your organiza-

A Systems View of the Ladder of Inference

tion, you are getting input from someone who is a part of the system. It is incredibly difficult to measure a system you are a part of. Any feedback you get from an individual will be inherently biased to some degree by the fact that they are themselves a part of the system they are commenting on. Maturity and self-awareness, as described above, can help with this, but we can never fully erase it. This is why we want to average responses over a large, diverse pool of respondents. Our goal is to minimize individual bias and blind spots while looking for common trends that emerge from the larger group.

To ensure you are getting the best possible view of your organization, ensure that you have considered Diversity. Some common factors to consider include levels of leadership, departments, functions, tenure, race/national origin, gender, and age. There may be additional factors that are meaningful to your specific organization. You will want to build these variables into the data collection for your assessment. Unless you do this upfront, you won't be able to analyze the results along these dimensions later. Analysis along these dimensions allows you to ensure that you have gotten full representation from each demographic.

Additionally, it will enable you to understand how different groups within your organization experience your culture differently. We are intently interested in the experiences we are creating for employees and how we can design those to produce the beliefs and behaviors we want. So, knowing if there are differences in how employees experience the organization is critical. Your experience as a leader may be very different from others in the organization. To illustrate this, imagine a tree full of monkeys perched on limbs at various heights. The monkeys at the top look down and see a bunch of smiling faces looking up at them. However, the monkeys at the bottom of the tree see something very different when they look up...

Remember, the goal of the assessment is to improve your organization. If you aren't getting a complete picture, it's unlikely that you will be able to define the problem accurately. Accurately defining the problem is essential to developing an effective solution. Albert Einstein reportedly said if he only had one hour to solve a problem, he would "...spend fifty-five minutes defining the problem and the remaining five minutes solving it." After all, what good is the perfect solution to the wrong problem?

The Third Strand: Community

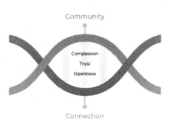

An effective assessment process will also consider Community. Leaders have a wonderful opportunity to build trust with their employees through the assessment process. Unfortunately, the opposite can also happen, and leaders can destroy trust if they neglect this strand. With intention and follow-through, leaders can easily design the process to avoid disaster and serve as a positive experience for employees. As we've mentioned before, you should view the assessment process as a culture-building experience for employees and something that is designed into the organizational norms.

In addition to focusing on trust, you will also want to build compassion into your assessment process. You can best do this by honoring the perspectives of respondents. Admittedly, there is some overlap with our discussion on Maturity. The nuance here is that we are focusing on how we can build trust and a stronger sense of Community through honoring their perspectives. This involves responding in a way that clearly demonstrates respect for their opinion and a clear appreciation for their willingness to provide feedback. You don't have to agree with their perspective to honor it. Practice active listening as you receive and respond to the feedback. And remember to say, "thank you!"

Practicing openness throughout the process will increase trust while keeping people informed of the progress and honoring their perspectives. Regular updates on where you are in the process and when you expect to communicate back your findings will assure everyone that their input is considered and hasn't just gone into a black hole. It is important to openly share the assessment results, both the good and the bad. There's really no reason to hide this information; after all, they are the ones who provided it, so they already know what it says.

Just providing the organization with the results isn't enough. You also want to be open and clear about what you learned and what actions you intend to take as a result. It is also a good practice to be open and clear about what steps you don't intend to take and why. Just because something emerges as a theme in the assessment, you don't have to take action on it. At least not the action requested in the responses. Your action may be to educate the organization on a particular topic, issue, or set of constraints. The communication about the impact of the assessment and actions you are taking is not a one-time event. You will want to continually remind the organization of how you are using their feedback to guide decisions and improve the organization. Track the actions you have taken and report back to everyone on their status and completion. This builds trust in the process and increases the assessment's perceived value and participation.

Use the data you've collected to improve the organization. This is the primary point of conducting the assessment in the first place. It's also the only way to realize a return on your investment. Assessing your organization takes time and money and draws on the goodwill of your employees. If you don't intend to use the feedback you gather to improve the organization, you will be better off not assessing the organization. By using the data to improve the organization, you are justifying the expense and overhead. You are also ensuring a net positive gain in goodwill from your workforce rather than a debit. To help ensure you have the capacity to make these improvements, plan for this effort in advance as part of your overall planning for the assessment. Be intentional about building in the time and resources for the full assessment lifecycle, including implementing recommendations.

The Fourth Strand: Unity

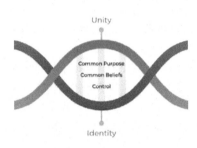

The final trait to consider when developing your assessment plan is Unity. By leveraging Unity in your assessment process, you can rally your organization to support the effort and ensure that you maximize its effectiveness. Since the assessment's fundamental purpose is to improve your organization, there is a strong inherent link to a common purpose. To motivate people to engage in the assessment, link it with the common purpose you all share. As we've already discussed, purpose is a powerful intrinsic motivator. While it may seem obvious, intentionally tie appeals for participation to the fact that improving your organization will better enable you to live your purpose. It is often the implication of the result that is a greater motivator than the result itself. So, while improvement for its own sake is noble, improvement for the sake of your higher purpose is inspirational.

We also want to leverage the power of common beliefs. Work to create the organizational norm and shared belief that assessment is an important part of how your company grows and achieves success. Although we doubt many companies have a core value of "Assess!" it is still possible to employ common beliefs. You can do this by being intentional about the beliefs you want employees to hold concerning assessment and then ensuring you create the experiences that support those beliefs. Many of these experiences have already been discussed, such as how you react, openly sharing data, honoring perspectives, taking action on the results, and communicating progress and completion of actions. Perhaps others would be beneficial to your organization. You will certainly want to ensure leadership communications strongly enforce the desired beliefs as well. We want employees to normalize the assessment process and the idea of providing feedback to their leaders. With intention and consistency, you can achieve this goal.

Once this normalization is accomplished, assessing, growing, improving, and providing feedback will become part of the organization's identity. Employees will see this process as a part of "who we are." Once your assessment program reaches this point, it will be much easier to solicit open feedback and implement improvements. Employees will know what to expect and when to expect it. And because assessment is now a part of their identity, resistance to conducting the assessment will be virtually eliminated. We want to see it as a normal and positive part of how the organization operates.

The Key to Greatness

> "It is not enough to do your best. You must know
> what to do and then do your best."
> —W. Edwards Deming

Assessment is an essential element of culture management. You can't manage what you don't control, and you can't control without feedback. Just like you wouldn't try to drive your car blindfolded, you don't want to try managing your culture without seeing how it is responding. If you take your culture and your ability to manage it seriously, you should also take your assessment program seriously. Ensure that you use a valid assessment tool that provides you with actionable insights into real issues. Intentionally design your entire program to produce the results you want. These results include sustaining and improving your culture over time. They also include producing the desired beliefs and behaviors in employees, so the assessment process itself strengthens your culture. The Missing Link Culture Model can guide you through this process, ensuring that you increase Maturity, leverage Diversity, build Community, and produce Unity. Assessment is not something that is done on a whim or with little thought or planning. It is an important part of how great companies become and stay great.

 [97]

---

[97] https://gallaheredge.com/themissinglinks#register

Chapter 11

Growing Your Organization's Capacity to Adapt

"Today, our very survival depends on our ability to stay awake, to adjust to new ideas, to remain vigilant and to face the challenge of change."
—Martin Luther King, Jr.

[98]

Growing Pains

Gregg was a remarkably compassionate leader who we met when we were looking to connect with business owners in the technology industry in Orlando. He expressed interest in learning about our services because he had just experienced his first major setback in his role as CEO of two companies, Envy Labs and Code School (now Pluralsight): layoffs. They laid off a small number of people, but it was a painful experience because up until that point, they had seen such great success and growth. It was

---

[98] https://gallaheredge.com/themissinglinks

particularly painful because Gregg was such a caring leader, and he took it hard because he felt like it was a failure on his part that led to a potentially large impact on these people's lives.

Code School had emerged as its own organization after a product (an online course to teach programming) gained tremendous popularity, which developed a larger spin-off set of products, and eventually, its own company. But as a very cool start-up organization that was growing fast and provided lots of cool perks, it broke away from many traditional ideas of what it meant to be a company, including clear roles and responsibilities.

We conducted an organizational assessment, including talking personally to each individual (about thirty people at the time) to learn what they loved most about the culture and what their pain points were.

In assessing the organization, we learned that when Code School emerged as its own entity, it took a lot of Gregg's focus away from Envy Labs. As a very trusting leader who felt confident in the team, he didn't realize (until it felt too late) that he hadn't positioned the other leaders to succeed in the same ways he was, and as revenue dropped, he had to make cuts.

There were many shared resources between the two entities. Without clear lines, the growing confusion and context switching was having a negative impact on the overall effectiveness of the organization. But the layoffs were a major wake-up call for the leadership team. One of their biggest fears was losing the things they loved about their culture, like being different, being flexible, and trusting their people. This had become a part of their identity. Additionally, as the organization grew, leaders emerged, but they faced the common challenge seen by many growing companies of straddling the role of leader and individual contributor.

We worked with the leadership team to create a new concept of what the culture looked like that held onto the things they loved most while also creating the structure within which each person could thrive with reduced confusion. You may recall the playground study from the Unity chapter, highlighting how valuable it is to create boundaries for people to feel free and empowered.

We coached the leaders and used assessments to help each person understand how they could reconceptualize what it means to be "competent." Competence as an individual contributor is about accomplishing tasks but shifting into a leadership role looks at competence through the lens of effectively influencing and coaching humans, which can be two very different skill sets!

The leadership team worked hard to grow as people and shift their mindsets, so they could more effectively empower their talented workforce. Within eighteen months of our first engagement, Code School was acquired by Pluralsight for $36 million. This was an impressive accomplishment of which Gregg could feel quite proud. He was so impressed with the impact of the work that he began learning how he, himself, could be a practitioner in a similar field. From a programmer to a CEO to a Licensed Human Element® practitioner—if that is not an impressive story of adapting, we don't know what is!

Maximizing Your Organization's Capacity to Adapt

We have argued that as a leader, one of your primary functions is to lead change within your organization. This is a critical function for leaders because change is an ongoing process, which is why we call it evolution. Organizational change is the organization adapting in response to changes in its environment. So, it is in your best interest as a leader to maximize your organization's capacity to adapt to this change. The greater this capacity, the easier your job will be!

The complex environment companies operate in today is constantly changing with new technologies transforming the competitive landscape and competitors working tirelessly to undermine your strategic position. For any company to maintain long-term financial success, it must be able to adapt faster than the environment. It's like trying to walk up a down escalator: if you aren't climbing faster than the steps are descending, you're never going to reach your destination! How often your company must change, to what degree it must change, and how quickly it must change are all dependent on the market within which you operate. We summarize this by saying that

> *the internal capacity for change must be greater than the external rate and magnitude of change.*

Otherwise, your company will always be playing catch-up and will eventually fail or be taken over.

According to a 2018 study by Gartner,[99] it doesn't appear that the pace of change will be slowing down anytime soon. They report that the average organization has already undergone five enterprise changes in the past three years and that 73 percent of organizations expect more change initiatives in the next few years. This same study also reported that 42 percent of CEOs with digital transformations

---

[99] Gartner, "Managing Organizational Change: How HR Can Deliver on Complex Organizational Change Management Initiatives," Accessed August 9, 2021, https://www.gartner.com/en/human-resources/insights/organizational-change-management.

underway expected to undergo deep culture change by 2020, and 46 percent of CIOs said that culture change was their most significant barrier to success. The ability to successfully manage change is a critical capability for leaders and a critical capacity for organizations.

When COVID-19 spread across our globe, it created a pandemic unlike any known by most of the working world. We felt the impact of lost lives and significant shifts in how we live and work. This unprecedented time shone a light on organizations' capacities to adapt and evolve. Leaders in organizations had to reinvent the way they worked and delivered services to survive. And the need to adapt didn't end with the discovery of a vaccine. As we emerged from the shutdown, the shifts continued as we sought to create our new normal. The pandemic highlights how companies must be prepared to adapt at a moment's notice to changes coming from sources far outside their typical market focus. The importance of adapting quickly to any challenge is a requirement for survival.

Our roadmap's final dimension for an effective culture is the capacity to change efficiently. This capacity enables companies to recognize the need for change (preferably early) and execute the desired change (preferably quickly). One important point to make on adaptation capacity is that companies should undertake change for a reason and with a specific end state in mind. Some companies become enamored with the idea of change or adaptability as the hallmark of a great company and overfocus on this capability. This is especially true in the high-tech industry, where the rate of change can be dizzying. However, if not managed intentionally, change can become a disruptive force that creates shiny object syndrome and stunts forward progress.

Because of the interdependent nature of culture and strategic alignment, the capacity to adapt includes more than the ability to pivot strategies, products, and processes. It also includes the ability to adapt the culture. The idea of cultural adaptation runs counter to the beliefs of some companies. This can be especially true for startups who have begun scaling and outgrown some facets of their startup culture. Sometimes, they want to cling to their existing culture, believing it is what has made them successful. Generally, this belief is justified, and they should probably retain the core beliefs that form their cultural DNA. However, as they grow in size and complexity, there are many aspects of their culture that do require adaptation to enable them to continue scaling.

The need to adapt the culture can also come from an organization experiencing a significant shift in the market, driving a radically new strategy. This new strategy will likely not be fully executable without corresponding adaptation of the culture to maintain strategic alignment. When this happens, unless the company aligns its culture with the new strategy, the culture will eat the strategy for breakfast, and the company will struggle.

Besides evolving your culture to keep up with shifts in strategy, it is also critical to pay attention and adapt to broader changes in the external environment. One recent example of this was the anti-racism movement in 2020. With dramatic increases in support for the Black Lives Matter movement and the mainstreaming of the idea of antiracism, "doing nothing" in response as an organization became widely unacceptable. Because of the increased focus on social justice, leaders began taking a harder look at themselves. They started asking questions they didn't want to ask before about diversity, equity, and inclusion. And when they did this, many found that they needed to make shifts in their culture to align them with who they wanted to be as a company. True Diversity and inclusion are not something a company can merely "respond" to through changes to their website, marketing materials, and internal communication campaigns. As our Diversity strand illustrates, it is grounded in belonging and links individuals through respect and inclusion to celebrate their differences. If you haven't built this into your cultural DNA, you will have to adapt your culture to achieve it.

Ensuring your organization has the capacity to adapt is imperative in today's business environment. With change occurring at blazing speed and sparked by global pandemics, social justice, and new technology, companies must be prepared for anything! Scan the QR below to find out how you can assess your organization's capacity to adapt![100]

Change Only Happens in One Place

Ironically, the same factors that make culture change so critical for success may also be exactly what lead to the change's failure. In fact, despite the overwhelming statistics we presented earlier on  the prevalence and importance of change efforts, they are sadly very unsuccessful. Going back to the Gartner study from earlier, they claimed that two-thirds of transformative initiatives failed. When digging deeper into the numbers, we found that they considered 50 percent of organizational changes clear failures, 16 percent produced mixed results, and only 34 percent were deemed clear successes.

This raises an important question: if these changes are so important and we do them so frequently, why are we so bad at them? Turning again to the research, we find the primary contributors to failed

---

organizational change are management behavior that doesn't support the change (33 percent) and employees resistant to change (39 percent). These two sources combined account for 72 percent of the contribution to failure. Inadequate resources or budget account for a mere 14 percent. [101]

This finding may surprise some, but it makes perfect sense. Change, similar to culture, occurs in only one place—between the ears of individuals. Any meaningful change requires a change in the behavior of individuals, which we've already discussed involves a shift in their underlying beliefs and attitudes to some extent. Therefore, for any change to be successful, there must be a corresponding and lasting change between the ears of the employees affected by that change. This is where the difficulty associated with change comes from and why so many changes fail.

It isn't the difficulty in executing the change, or the absence of resources, or a lack of knowledge or skills that causes change efforts to fail. It is resistance from management and employees who are unwilling to adopt new beliefs and behaviors necessary to support the change. And while this may actually look like outright defiance or even sabotage in extreme cases, the far more common

---

[101] Torben Rick, "Barriers to Organizational Change," Blog Post, September 7, 2016, https://www.torbenrick.eu/blog/change-management/barriers-to-organizational-change.

version of this resistance is merely a withholding of support or engagement. When it comes to making a successful shift associated with an organizational transformation or cultural change, there is a huge difference between *making* it happen and *letting* it happen. Success requires managers and employees to make it happen, or there won't be sufficient energy and alignment in the system to help the change overcome inertia and permanently shift to a fundamentally different system state.

Humans Hate to Lose

To address this universal challenge, it is critical that we understand where this resistance is coming from. Is it true that people just resist change? Well, let me ask you this question: If I told you that at the end of this chapter, we had included all the account information and passwords for a bank account with $1 million and you could have it if you wanted it (don't bother looking, it's not really there), would that represent a change for you? Would you resist that change? For most of us, the answer to those questions would be yes and no, respectively. So, we clearly don't resist all changes!

What we are resisting with change is our perception of loss. With all changes (even the example above), there are losses associated with the change. These may be minor, especially compared to the gain, but they are still present. And the losses can be both logical/tangible such as decreased pay or a smaller office, or they can be emotional/intangible such as less organizational visibility or less enjoyable work.

As humans, we are wired to avoid loss. So much so that we would prefer to avoid losing something more than we want to gain something of far greater value. This is called loss aversion, and studies have suggested that losses are twice as psychologically powerful for us as gains. As an example, since we perceive the impact as being twice as strong, losing $10 would feel twice as bad as being given $10 would feel good. This can lead us to make irrational decisions. A great example of this is the endowment effect, which describes that people place more value on something that they already own than on an identical item that isn't theirs. This comes from psychologist and economist Daniel Kahneman and disproves the theory that humans act in their own best self-interest within economic systems.

Perhaps the most famous example of the e n d o w m e n t effect is Edith Macefield, who refused to sell her home, which was appraised at $100,000 to commercial developers for the incredible sum of $1 million. Ultimately, she forced them to build the mall around her, and she lived in the house until she died in 2008. This behavior isn't just a single story. Kahneman has won a Nobel Prize for his research, and there have been numerous studies that have tested this behavior (although not necessarily to the same extremes). In one such study, participants were given a mug and then could sell or trade it. The study showed that the participants required twice as much to sell or trade the mug than what they said they were willing to give for it before it was theirs. In another study, participants wanted fourteen times as much as their hypothetical buying price to sell NCAA final four tournament tickets.

The Path to the Dark Side

This equation gets even more complex within the organizational setting where we are concerned because organizational and cultural changes aren't merely external changes. They are intricately intertwined with the individuals' environments, relationships, and identity. And as we said earlier, they involve changes to their belief systems and behaviors. Ultimately, organizational changes may become a threat to the individual's self-concept. As you now know, any time there is a threat to our self-concept, there is a high likelihood that it will trigger our defenses. Depending on how self-aware and self-accepting we are, this may not prove to be a huge challenge to our acceptance of the change. However, as we saw earlier, the statistics would indicate that we shouldn't hold our breath.

> **"Fear is the path to the dark side. Fear leads to anger, anger leads to hate, hate leads to suffering."**
>
> **—Yoda**

If employee resistance results from defensiveness, then its root is ultimately fear. As with all defensiveness, this fear will be subconscious, so it will be pointless to ask them directly why they don't like the change. Their self-concept will be threatened in some way which produces fear about their own significance, competence, or likability. They will actually be afraid that they will be ignored, humiliated, or disliked in some way due to the change. Unfortunately, they are also hiding this fact from themselves because it's too painful for them to admit that they are scared about it. So, they will find something (quite possibly something that sounds logical) to dislike or argue about regarding the change. This will become a subconscious smokescreen, and the organization can spend countless time and resources trying to address these issues to no avail. What we are describing here is a part of human psychology and a part of the human condition. We all do it to varying degrees in different circumstances. This is why change is hard.

BEHAVIOR	INCLUSION	CONTROL	OPENNESS
FEELINGS	SIGNIFICANCE	COMPETENCE	LIKABILITY
FEAR	IGNORED ABANDONED	HUMILIATED EMBARRASSED	REJECTED DISLIKED

We shared an example of this from our work supporting a large-scale reorganization following the *Columbia* accident. One challenge we were facing was helping employees to embrace the new organizational structure and reporting pathways. They gave many reasons for why they didn't like the reorganization, and a lot were valid to varying degrees. But by far, the biggest barrier to acceptance of the new organization was the impact it had on employees' identities. Many of these employees had spent their entire careers as part of the shuttle organization. Within NASA, this carried a certain degree of clout. It not only bore the name of the agency's iconic spacecraft, but it was a program that employees considered to be a higher status level than other types of organizations with more budget and authority. To move from "shuttle" to "engineering" felt like a demotion and was a blow to their self-concept. This impacted their feelings of significance and triggered a wide variety of defensive behaviors.

Achieving this organizational change required us to look at many challenges facing the organizations and its members. Converting to a 600-person matrixed engineering organization supporting multiple programs revealed multiple technical and physical issues. We also had to address the psychological and emotional challenges facing employees, including threats to their self-concept. Recognizing this allowed us to work with the employees to help them surface and work through the true source of their resistance while at the same time taking steps to maximize their significance in the design of the new organization. While it wasn't perfect, this transition was amazingly successful, especially given its incredibly ambitious scope and the unforgiving nature of the work performed by the employees involved.

Aligning Change With Self-Concept

Humans have three basic choices for how they can respond to a change. First, they can resist the change. As discussed earlier, this resistance can be either passive or active, and either type will spell doom for the attempted change. The second option that people have is compliance. While this may

---

[102] https://gallaheredge.com/login/

[103] https://gallaheredge.com/themissinglinks

sound like what we want, compliance is actually only a temporary solution because humans only comply in the presence of an external motivator – such as a reward, punishment, or being watched. Once this external motivator is removed, they will likely return to their previous way of doing things. Consequently, compliance isn't truly change. Eventually, the organization will lose focus or energy, and things will return to the status quo.

The third choice that humans have is to internalize the change. This is the true goal we are going for when we initiate an organizational transformation or cultural shift. When a person internalizes a change, they will continue to hold the belief and exhibit the behaviors regardless of external motivators. Change in behavior supported by a change in belief is more sustainable in the long term, but it is not an easy change to achieve. Individuals will only make this choice when the behaviors and beliefs associated with the change align with their self-concept.

In making this statement, we assume those leading the change have presented sufficient logical rationale to substantiate the change. Remember, there are two types of loss: tangible and intangible. While our primary focus here is on the intangible losses, we can't neglect the tangible ones. Clearly, if we ask someone to do something that is not in their self-interest and have failed to make a logical argument for why they should do so, merely addressing the intangible loss will not be enough. Typical change models do a reasonable job at addressing the tangible side of loss, so we will assume that those leading the change have addressed this well enough to take it off the table and allow us to focus on the intangible factors.

The inability to internalize a change results when a conflict arises that challenges how a person sees themselves. This conflict may be between how they currently see themselves (or desire to see themselves) and how they believe the proposed change will cause them to see themselves. At a deeper level, it's not merely that they don't want to do what you are asking them to do; it's that they don't want to be who you are asking them to be. They will push back much harder on this proposed "state of being" than on any single action.

This is why people's resistance to change often seems disproportionately strong compared to the specific task or change itself. Only when we understand the underlying shift or threat in their self-concept can we understand the nature of their resistance. And just as we discussed before, any attempts to engage in logical persuasion around the specific task or change will be ineffective in decreasing resistance because you aren't discussing the real issue. Even if you make concessions around the task or change, it is unclear whether those changes will help the situation unless you get lucky and change it in a way that also shifts it back into alignment with their self-concept.

If you have ever worked as a change practitioner, I'm certain you can recognize here the frustrating and seemingly futile dance often engaged in with stakeholders as you try to gain their buy-in.

Dealing with threats to self-concept overall can be very challenging when working with more than a single individual. Everyone has a unique and complex self-concept, and most of us haven't taken the time to sit down and document exactly what that is in a way that we can easily describe it, much less recognize a threat to it from some proposed change. It is much more useful, especially in the organizational context, to lean on the FIRO framework. This allows us to categorize loss from change in terms of threats to our significance, competence, or likability. These are still absolutely aspects of our self-concept, but rather than asking about specifics of how we want to see ourselves (at least initially), we can instead focus on our feelings about ourselves.

What we want to know is whether a given change will alter how significant, competent, or likable a person will feel. This change can be an increase or a decrease, but this isn't what matters. What we care about is how they feel about this change. For example, when a person feels more or less significant than they want to, that's a warning sign, and we want to explore what is driving that. This can then allow us to uncover a potential conflict with their self-concept.

It's important to note that these feelings can be driven by how individuals see themselves and how they believe others will see them. So, a change in job title due to a reorganization may be meaningless to the individual, but they may have a fear that their significance will decrease in the eyes of their peers or even their in-laws. Consequently, as we are investigating the impact of a change on significance, competence, and likability, we want to view it from the levels of our Inside Out Model: self, team, and organization. We also recommend adding an additional view outside relations to capture potential influences from customers, business associates, family members, etc. We have developed a tool for working with organizations that does exactly this.

Unhooking Buttons

We worked with a promotional marketing agency that was creating a new level within their organization, and they were promoting an existing team member into that new role. This represented a fairly significant shift for a large portion of their company. We used our tool to help them assess their individual and organization resistance to prepare for this change. This exercise helped the leader moving into the new role to surface her subconscious fears about the new position. She was afraid that in moving from being a peer to being in a position of authority, members of the organization would see her as less likable. This new awareness allowed us to address her self-concept issues around her own likability before she ever took on the leadership role. We facilitated open conversations between her and her coworkers about her fears and how they could work effectively together in their new relationship. By doing this, we helped her and the company avoid a rocky transition.

What we have shown in the example above is the key to overcoming this form of resistance. First, we must help the individuals to surface their feelings and fears—both conscious and subconscious—which are producing the resistance. Once these are out in the open, we must work with the individual to understand how they are connected to their self-concept. The final step in the process is to unhook the change from the individual's self-concept, so they no longer see the new behavior or belief as a threat or challenge to who they are.

In the above example, once the leader no longer saw her likability as being linked to her position, the internal resistance went away. In this specific case, the change was in her best interest, so she was not outwardly resisting it. However, the resistance was manifesting itself as stress for her, and she would have managed it in ways that likely would have led to unhealthy team dynamics and organizational issues. The extreme example of this is Michael Scott from *The Office*, who has extreme insecurity about his own likability leading him to compulsively be everyone's best friend. He even buys himself a mug that says "World's Best Boss" on it. She likely wouldn't have become the next Michael Scott, but we're certain it was better for the organization that this resistance surfaced and was dealt with prior to the transition rather than after.

An Attribute Not an Accident

The example above illustrates why it is so critical to build a strong culture within your organization with Maturity as a defining trait. Maturity is a foundational requirement for change because employees must have the self-awareness to recognize the need for themselves to change as part of the cultural shift, the self-accountability to believe that both they and the organization can change and to make it happen, and the self-acceptance to prevent fear from interfering with their acknowledgment and willingness to change. As mentioned previously, this will also provide the much-needed resilience to persevere through the entire change lifecycle. But Maturity isn't the only trait required. Each strand of the Missing Link Culture Model contributes to the capacity to adapt.

Diversity is a critical component for adaptation because the presence of different people, backgrounds, and ideas creates a rich source of data concerning how the environment is changing and creative solutions for how to adapt. Maintaining an inclusive culture where senior decision-makers encourage individuals to flow up innovative ideas and concerns further helps an organization identify and execute adaptation. Ideally, your employees form an early warning system for the need to adapt, similar to the ocean buoys we discussed that provide early warnings for tsunamis. If everyone in the company thinks and looks like you while engaging in the same basic hobbies and interests, the chances of creating an effective early warning system are incredibly low.

Unity and Community also contribute to an organization's capacity to adapt. The ability to identify this need and react depends on employees knowing the company's strategy and understanding how they contribute to it. The company must always be adapting to ensure that its culture, strategy, and market all stay aligned. The control strand offers stability and clear parameters for operating during times of change, which provide a sense of security and keep things from getting too dysfunctional. It also requires openness and trust in teammates to share experiences and maintain focus and morale through the change process. A strong sense of Community can provide a sense of comfort and needed support during uncertain times.

We often talk about organizations having "inertia," and sometimes moving them is compared to turning a ship such as an aircraft carrier. These are great analogies, and the energy and effort required to get an organization to start moving or change directions can be substantial. However, unlike inertia or a ship, it isn't the organization's mass that determines how much energy is required. It is the organization's ability to adapt that matters. Certainly, size influences the ability to adapt due to the sheer logistics involved in executing a change in a multinational or global organization. However, it isn't merely the size that matters. A large organization with an excellent capacity to adapt will be able to change directions faster than a smaller one with a poor capacity to adapt.

If you have taken the time to design your organization according to the Missing Link Model, you have also been designing for low inertia and the capacity to adapt. This is important because companies with these highly effective cultures will enjoy a significant competitive advantage due to their ability to quickly refocus employees and nimbly adapt to their environment. Your organization's capacity to adapt is an attribute, not an accident!

A Simple Formula for Adaptation

To sum this up, adapting to change is complex. It is complex because it involves humans and their response to changes in the environment where they live and work and relationships with other human beings. And most important, it is complex because it involves changes in how they feel about themselves and their role with respect to each. This is why changes fail: Humans resist them, and meaningful changes require active support to overcome organizational inertia. This resistance is often subconscious, which makes breaking down barriers and gaining buy-in exceedingly hard for leaders. Given that one of the primary jobs of leaders is to drive change, this can cause frustration and ultimately burnout.

We use a formula to help leaders consider the choices they make regarding designing and implementing cultural transformation or any other form of organizational change. This formula revolves around the idea that there is a cost associated with any change, and it is important that you assess your various constituencies and stakeholders to ensure you understand what each of them perceives as the cost of change. This understanding will allow you to make better and more intentional decisions to minimize the resistance to change and maximize your chances of success.

Unique to our model for change is the inclusion of fear as a multiplier for the perceived cost of change. As described above, the primary reason people resist change is that it represents a challenge to their self-concept in some meaningful way. This challenge results in fear around their significance, competence, or likability. Understanding how these fears affect stakeholders further enables the organization to facilitate the change by addressing the true issue at its heart rather than spending a lot of time and energy addressing symptoms or "smoke screens" that cover their underlying fears.

The formula is:

CULTURE **x** LEADERSHIP **>** COST OF CHANGE **x** FEAR

Culture—The culture is what determines your organization's capacity to adapt. The extent to which the traits of Maturity, Diversity, Community, and Unity are present within your organization's culture defines how great or small this capacity is. Organizations that are high in all four of these traits possess a high capacity to adapt.

Leadership—The force multiplier behind organizational results is leadership, and the ability to drive organizational evolution is dependent on strong, effective leaders who can communicate the vision and need for change, provide reinforcement and encouragement throughout the process, and maintain the organization's focus on achieving the desired outcomes. This requires inspiring and motivating others by understanding their internal drivers and fears, so they feel heard and understood as you meet their needs.

Cost of Change—For every change, there is some cost associated with it (whether big or small) which makes the change uncomfortable, inconvenient, or disadvantageous. To help people evolve, we want to identify the cost for them and then show them how the benefits outweigh that cost. Related to costs are also the payoffs we get from the way we're currently choosing to behave.

Fear—Just as leadership is the force multiplier on one side of this equation, fear is the force multiplier on the other. The fears of individuals greatly magnify costs. This can be difficult to overcome because often, these fears stem from unconscious feelings about our own self-concept. The greatest barrier to organizational change is its disruption of one's identity.

The formula is primarily used by gaining a deeper understanding of the costs and fears of individuals being asked to change and identifying interventions for mitigating those concerns. The left side of the equation provides insight into how to build change capacity into the organization's culture and assess the fundamental drivers for change. You will want to design your culture and ensure you have strong leadership to increase your organization's change capacity to drive your desired change.

So, the goal is to maximize the change capacity on the left side of the equation by building a strong and healthy organizational culture and developing highly capable leaders while reducing the costs as much as possible on the other side of the equation and helping individuals to surface and address the underlying fears created by the change. The work on the left side of the equation is ongoing, so companies should address this long before undertaking any specific change initiative. If you wait until you need this type of change capacity to start developing it, it's already too late.

The work on the right side of the equation is very specific. It is specific to both the given change event and the particular individual or group of individuals you are focusing on. Consequently, the change equation may look different for different stakeholders based on the unique costs and threats to their self-concept that they perceive. Because we are the ones who decide what value we place on the costs, one of the best ways to reduce the resistance is by helping people to see how they can reassign the value they are placing on the costs. Once again, we do this by bringing these into the conscious and having open conversations about them, incorporating the associated fears. Another way to influence the perception of the costs of change is to invite people to imagine the gains. As humans, our strong loss-aversion draws our attention to the costs by default, but you can choose to override the evolutionary autopilot of your brain by envisioning the future state and the gains that you may experience. This conscious choice to redirect your attention can also help you align your self-concept with the anticipated future state.

By applying the above adaptation formula, leaders can guide their organization through the myriad of challenges associated with cultural and organizational change. This does not absolve them from following the best practices related to change management. There are still a dizzying number of things that must be planned, communicated, managed, and implemented to achieve success. However, the primary barrier leading to failure—the corresponding change in people's beliefs and behaviors—can be diagnosed and addressed. This is the key to success.

OK, now the bank account information and passwords are—psych!! Maybe in our next book...

Chapter 12

How to Create a Safety Culture

"The goal then is to understand why people did not or could not act differently. People acted the way they did for very good reasons; we need to understand why the behavior of the people involved made sense to them at the time."
—Nancy Leveson

 104

Returning the Shuttles to Flight

 Within two hours of losing communication with the space shuttle *Columbia* during its re-entry, NASA established the Columbia Accident Investigation Board (CAIB) to investigate the accident and determine the contributing causes. Almost seven

---

104 https://gallaheredge.com/themissinglinks

months later, they released a 248-page report containing their findings.

NASA took the findings and recommendations within the report seriously and dedicated itself to ensuring that a similar accident didn't occur again. In response to the release of the report, NASA declared the week of November 17–21 as Safety and Mission Success (SMS) Week. During this week, there was a complete standdown from all work activities, and every employee and contractor was asked to read the CAIB report and consider its implications for their work area.

At KSC, we asked individuals to answer three questions:

1. How is the CAIB Report relevant to your work unit?
2. Which area cited in the Organizational Cause Statement in the CAIB Report do you believe impacts mission success in your work unit?
3. What needs to be done to help your organization, KSC, and NASA move forward?

We collected this information from individuals through a survey submission form. We also asked workgroups to meet to discuss the report and the three questions to brainstorm ideas. A scribe was appointed during those meetings to capture suggestions and enter them into the system. By the end of this week, we had managed to collect 2,492 free-form suggestions. Answers ranged from recommendations about training on how to structure PowerPoint charts to the importance of shifting leadership mindset.

As the person responsible for leading the cultural and organizational changes required for return to flight, I (Phillip) wanted to figure out how to sift through the mountain of data and recommendations to effectively focus the limited resources of the center on the highest leverage areas. Like the rest of NASA, I was committed to making meaningful change and not just creating the appearance of change.

Working with a team of twenty-four cross-functional individuals from across the center, we sorted the recommendations into themes and compared those with recommendations from the CAIB report. Since we were attempting to change the culture, I wanted to assess what issues were deeply embedded and presented themselves throughout time. I analyzed data from eight sources (surveys and reports) conducted from 1984 through 2004 and identified seventy-nine different themes. Many of these themes emerged as persistent over the years. For example, listening was identified in seven out of the eight sources, lack of respect for individuals was also identified in seven, while a perceived class system between the engineers and nonengineers was identified in six. I mapped all seventy-nine themes to the CAIB recommendations and SMS Week comments.

Finally, to ensure that we were fully addressing the systemic issues that lay beneath the accident, I created a systems model of the organization and mapped the identified issues to these systems. It could be easy for people to mistakenly believe catchy headlines from the media like the headline from aero-news.net that reads, "*Columbia* disaster comes down to a single conversation." The systems model allowed me to see the systems with the greatest concentration of issues and also ensure that solutions targeted the entire system and didn't overfocus on a single area. Ultimately, I created a relational database to manage this data set which accounted for CAIB recommendations, SMS Week comments, historical trends, organizational systems, and proposed solutions.

Although the Missing Links Model did not exist in its current form at that time, the suite of solutions that we implemented at KSC, which allowed us to return the shuttle fleet to flight, touched every strand.

Maturity: We developed an inventory of critical leadership behaviors that we trained our leaders on. Leaders received coaching around these behaviors, and we trained observers to sit in meetings and provide feedback to leaders on how they exhibited those behaviors, such as inadvertently shutting down conversation through ineffective listening. We also worked with leaders and employees on self-awareness and recognizing cognitive biases that affected their ability to make decisions.

Diversity: We developed training and initiatives around increasing dissenting opinions. We worked to change the perception around dissenting opinions such that someone raising one was a "hero" rather than a "villain" and increasing respect for diverse opinions. "Alternate opinions" were added as a standing agenda item for meetings, and we worked to shift the burden to the system owners to demonstrate safety rather than the dissenter to prove it wasn't safe. We also created a project to improve upward communication and listening for leaders.

Community: We established a comprehensive project around leadership communication. This project focused on increasing transparency and frequency of communication. We developed communication plans within each organization for the leaders to follow and worked with the leaders on their openness. We worked specifically with the Quality Assurance function, which was critical to safety. We helped them to feel a greater sense of respect and value from the rest of the workforce and also to feel a stronger sense of Community both internally as a group as well as with KSC as a whole. How individuals feel about themselves is a significant predictor of how effective they will be, even in challenging situations.

<u>Unity</u>: We worked to help employees internalize the core values and live them. We reorganized the center to create independent Safety and Engineering organizations, reducing conflicts of interest and providing a stronger independent voice to both. We worked across the center to reduce unnecessary overhead that was further contributing to resource challenges.

Obviously, these were just the first steps. Even after the shuttles returned to flight, we continued our focus on organizational culture, and I was asked to establish an Organizational Development group in Human Resources to continue this work. We continued to regularly assess the culture, develop initiatives to manage and evolve it and work with leaders on intentionally designing their organizations. Even today, years after I've moved on, work continues to push back against the forces of complacency and political pressure that would lead to the acceptance of higher risks and make another accident inevitable.

Tailoring for Safety

In the introduction, we said this book wasn't about safety culture. However, given the origins of our model and the nature of our experience, we didn't feel it would be complete without addressing organizational safety. Just as organizational culture, organizational safety is an emergent property of an organization that can only be observed holistically and can't be understood by breaking it down into the component level safety or reliability. Furthermore, the overall safety performance of an organization like NASA must recognize the dynamics affecting the system, the interfaces and relationships, and the human element.

As early as 1968, Jerome Lederer, director of the NASA Manned Flight Safety Program for *Apollo* and one of the founders of system safety, wrote:

"System safety covers the total spectrum of risk management. It goes beyond the hardware and associated procedures of system safety engineering. It involves attitudes and motivation of designers and production people, employee/management rapport, the relation of industrial associations among themselves and with government, human factors in supervision and quality control, documentation on the interfaces of industrial and public safety with design and operations, the interest and attitudes of top management, the effects of the legal system on accident investigations and exchange of information, the certification of critical workers, political considerations, resources, public sentiment and many other nontechnical but vital influences on the attainment of an acceptable level of risk control.

These nontechnical aspects of system safety cannot be ignored."

The goal of system safety is to design the complex system within this expanded environment such that it exists in a stable equilibrium. Rather than trying to assume that mistakes will never be made or that external events will never occur that adversely impact the safety of the system, we want to design the system, so it is forgiving of these events and self-recovering. All states of equilibrium are not equal. The proverbial house of cards is an unstable equilibrium where one tiny push or vibration will cause the whole thing to collapse. Similarly, a marble held against the wall of a bowl is in a state of equilibrium as long as sufficient energy is applied to hold it in place. But as soon as the effort to hold it in place is removed, it will roll down to the bottom of the bowl. Our desire is to have a state of equilibrium that is very stable and requires minimal energy to maintain—like the marble resting at the bottom of the bowl.

We create this stable equilibrium through the design of the technical systems and the organizational system that operates them. The technical systems can be designed with additional margin, redundancies, fail-safes, and human factor considerations. The design of the organizational system includes the structure of the organization, roles and responsibilities, training and skills of the people, resource levels, and of course, the organizational culture.

The organizational culture has a huge impact on how this expanded complex adaptive system behaves and how stable the equilibrium is. The biggest role that culture plays in system safety is to make the system self-healing. A healthy culture that supports safety will continually push back on all of the forces that are incessantly trying to erode the organization's safety margins. Without this pushback, things like schedule or budget pressure will lead the organization to slowly accept more and more risk over time. The safety net that once existed for the inevitable mistakes or external events will be gone, but because it faded away so slowly, everyone will act like it still exists. Without culture standing guard against this slow evolution to an unstable and unsafe state, an accident will be inevitable.

So, while we didn't specifically write this book to address safety, the principles outlined within it can be used to create a very effective safety program. As we mentioned in chapter 9, we wanted to provide a more in-depth example of how to use the missing links to intentionally design your culture. This is just one example of how the model can be tailored to create a culture with specific desired attributes. Organizational safety is merely one type of cultural attribute.

There's No Such Thing as Safety Culture

We always start with a clear picture of the desired culture and how it contributes to your specific strategy and performance goals. Because culture has such a strong effect on safety performance, organizations with a high need for safety provide an excellent example of how you can design your culture for a specific capability. Due to our work experience at NASA, we have a special appreciation for this type of culture and the critical role safety plays.

To start this discussion, it is important to understand what organizational safety is. Safety should not be framed as "never having an accident." Doing so creates a backward-looking mental model. People begin to believe that any action that does not produce an accident is safe. A more effective approach is to view safety as an organizational commitment to identifying and removing the conditions which lead to accidents. In reality, we are concerned with surfacing and consciously managing risk. Safety failures occur because employees fail to do one of two things or both: they fail to take action or fail to appreciate the risk. The goal of safety is safety excellence, not safety perfection. Safety perfection would mean never launching if you're NASA or making no profit if you are a private company. Instead, we want to focus on behaviors that embody safety excellence like openness, compliance, resource provision, and inclusion.

These behaviors arise from an organizational culture and are the typical manifestation that people see and feel. Culture is not the common behaviors; it is the common invisible force that creates those behaviors. Organizational culture is an emergent property of an organization that arises from the interaction of the shared beliefs of the individual employees. This means that culture resides between the ears of human beings. Furthermore, this shared belief system is part of a larger system formed by the organization and, ultimately, society. So, understanding and analyzing culture means seeing it as the emergent product of a complex adaptive system with a dizzying number of variables of widely varying influence on the common beliefs of a group of people.

Given this understanding of organizational culture, there is technically no such thing as a safety culture. Culture is not limited to a specific aspect or goal. By its very nature, it cannot be segmented, targeted, or focused on any single discipline, function, or outcome. However, it is absolutely true that an organization's culture can dramatically impact its safety performance. Some have framed this as the culture's ability to create and sustain the *climate* around safety. Safety climate can change much more rapidly than culture itself, often changing dramatically immediately following an accident or near-miss or even preceding a major inspection or event. However, it is an effective organizational culture that sustains a healthy safety climate over time and ensures it stays at a high level.

Therefore, having a "safety culture " is about what an organization is and not what an organization does. This starts with who the people are at the Self level, then translates into how they behave and interact at the team level, and ultimately culminates with the capabilities the organization possesses at the organizational level. For the organization to succeed, these organizational capabilities must align with the company strategy, and this strategy must obviously be a good fit for the market in which they compete. Defining a small set of truly core values allows the company to intertwine the employees' behaviors with the strategy to ensure a good culture/strategy fit, and if these values also incorporate safety, there is strong alignment throughout the system. Incorporating safety into the values doesn't need to be overt. It works best when it is authentic and fits with the personality and existing or desired culture.

Both organizational culture and safety revolve around behavior, which, as we discussed, stem from a person's belief system. Consequently, we can use the same basic tools and methods to affect safety-specific behaviors that we do to shape

organizational culture. We create the desired culture by designing experiences that foster beliefs in people that then produce the desired behaviors. Again, these beliefs essentially are the culture, so when we create the desired set—which includes both the ones that are wanted as well as excluding the ones that aren't—we have succeeded in creating the desired culture. The proof comes in observing the results, which actually serve to reinforce experiences for employee beliefs.

The Missing Links Model can be used to help organizations design their culture to produce high levels of safety excellence. Each trait contributes to producing this type of culture. It isn't about creating and managing your culture *and* creating a safety culture. The goal is to create and manage your culture in a way that produces safe behaviors and, consequently, safety performance.

[105]

Maturity—Lays the foundation for the chain of action that lies at the heart of a safety culture in

---

practice. A safety organization or program that is silent and takes no action is ineffective. For safety performance to be excellent, employees must act—awareness or knowledge isn't sufficient. The willingness and ability to act on safety issues is rooted in our Self Model and requires employees to move through the following three steps:

1. I must first be willing to accept the existence of a risk and the implications that it has not only on my work but, more importantly, on who I am and the challenge to my self-concept.
2. I must then allow myself to become aware of the safety risk and proactively seek additional information even though doing so may lead to the discovery of additional risks.
3. Finally, I must believe that action is possible, that taking action can and will make a difference, and that my action or inaction will have direct and meaningful consequences. I must act.

CHAIN OF ACTION

Diversity—Ensures that the proper voices are included and heard in decision-making processes, reviews, audits, safety checks, and other processes to avoid groupthink and ensure the proper checks and balances are applied as well as ensuring that the proper mix of technical skills is included.

Community—Creates an environment of trust and openness where employees are honest and upfront about mistakes, problems are found and resolved quickly, and employees are comfortable raising concerns. With Community, there is a genuine sense of responsibility and care for one's fellow workers, which empowers people to do what is right, both aligning their own behaviors to safety and cultivating accountability in others to do so as well.

Unity—Creates an organization with a common sense of purpose and strong unifying values that support and drive the safety culture. These values aren't just words on a poster but are part of how employees live and work at the company. Unity also creates an effective structure for the organization with clearly defined processes and decision mechanisms.

Creating a culture that promotes safety excellence can be a daunting challenge. To help you be successful, we have captured key principles for creating a culture of safety performance. You can download that list by going to The Missing Links book resources page.[106]

Shuttle Accidents and The Missing Links

We have continued to reference the *Columbia* accident, and in part 2, we provided detailed examples of how each trait within NASA's culture contributed to that fateful outcome. While we weren't explicitly discussing safety excellence in those chapters, this is exactly what was being highlighted. Weaknesses in each strand led to a failure to act or a failure to appreciate and manage risk.

Maturity

A great example of an individual breaking the chain of action is the decision not to seek imaging of the orbiter during its flight to ascertain the extent of damage caused by the foam. As discussed in chapter 5, we believe that Linda Hamm couldn't accept that she may not have the ability to fix an in-orbit problem. Because of this, she wouldn't allow herself to become aware of the true problem. The end result is that she failed to listen to the debris assessment team's concerns and never requested imaging support.

---

[106] https://gallaheredge.com/themissinglinks

Essentially, Linda used decreased self-awareness as a defense mechanism to protect against fears stemming from her self-acceptance. This defense mechanism clearly affected her behavior and decisions. This same dynamic was present in the *Challenger* accident and is on clear display in the Netflix documentary, *Challenger: The Final Flight*. In this film, we see a rare perspective of how key individuals involved in the accident responded to the roles they played in contributing to it. Some are clearly remorseful and take accountability for their choices, acknowledging how they could have behaved differently. Others, however, display a shocking lack of accountability, and even with all we know about the accident today, refuse to see how their actions and decisions contribute to it.

William Lucas, who was the director of NASA's Marshall Space Flight Center (MSFC) at the time of the accident, states he wouldn't change any of the decisions he made. He goes even further and justifies the deaths of the crew by comparing them to his forebearers who died when they "came across the Appalachian Mountains in a wagon with horses." Similarly, Lawrence Mulloy, who was the MSFC project manager for the Space Shuttle Solid Rocket Booster Program, says, "I feel I was to blame. But I felt no guilt."

You may be wondering how anyone in a position of influence could look back on a preventable accident like this and state that they wouldn't change anything they did or claim that they feel no guilt. We believe these individuals can't accept what making that mistake would mean about who they are, so they don't allow themselves to even see they made a mistake. Although the statements these men are making sound callous and uncaring, the true driver for these statements is likely just the opposite. Likely, it is because they care so much that they cannot stand the implications of being responsible. This is why they hide that truth from even themselves.

Diversity

We can clearly see the effects of Diversity in the roles that the safety organization and the debris assessment team played in key decision-making meetings. There was a striking lack of Diversity in opinions, thought, function, and even geographic location during key meetings. This was highlighted in our opening story for chapter 6. Without the inclusion of these differing views, it was much easier for bad decisions to be made.

When we look at the *Challenger* accident, we see almost the antithesis of Diversity within the launch decision meetings. Key individuals were applying pressure on engineers to agree to launch, and there was a clear lack of respect for others' technical opinions when they differed. The call for a key individual who was opposing the launch to "take off your engineering hat and put on your management hat" may just as well have been a directive to "think like me." As a result, managers suppressed true inclusion. There is a real difference between being invited to the meeting and meaningful inclusion during the meeting. Decisions involving safety and reliability were made without inviting experts from those communities to be included in the meetings. Consequently, the true risks and inherent limitations of the system weren't adequately included in the decision process. The lack of tolerance for differing opinions combined with the absence of individuals with specialized knowledge created a perfect environment for bad decisions.

Community

We also see the impact that Community had on the *Columbia* accident. A lack of trust led to individuals using nonstandard paths to communicate their concerns. This circumvented some of the procedures NASA had in place to manage risks. There also was a lack of trust between employees and upper management, which led them to soften or bury their concerns during presentations. This lack of openness suppressed both the available information and the full magnitude of the concerns. A lack of true Community between the three centers involved in the analysis and decision-making contributed to poor decisions and a failure to activate NASA's own procedures for assessing and managing risk.

Similar issues contributed to the *Challenger* accident. Although the low level of Community was driven largely by leadership behaviors and the political environment, it still resulted in a lack of trust and openness within the team. As described above, the individuals involved in the launch decision didn't trust one another. This is likely a side effect of the lack of respect and inclusion. There was also a fear of being blamed if something bad happened from launching or not launching. This further deepened the lack of trust between the organizations and individuals and resulted in managers and engineers devoting lots of energy to positioning and self-preservation. Rather than being willing to be open about concerns, individuals instead became "strategic" about what they did or didn't say. Just as in the case of *Columbia*, this lack of openness limited the discussion surrounding the magnitude of the risks and reduced the depth of technical insight possessed by the decision-makers.

Unity

Finally, we can hardly overstate the impact of Unity on these accidents. However, its impact comes primarily from the organizational design and common beliefs rather than from a difference in purpose. In the case of *Columbia*, the organizational structure limited the power and independence of the safety and engineering functions while simultaneously reinforcing the leadership expectations, which heavily influenced Ms. Hamm's self-acceptance. The commonly held belief that failure wasn't an option, along with the beliefs around expectations of competence, further affected how she and other members of the team engaged. The individuals' geographic dispersion, along with decades-old sibling rivalry between the different centers, decreased Community, limited inclusion, and diminished the perception of employees that they truly were one team. Additionally, the impact that the budget and schedule pressures placed on the organization combined with the intense political pressure to complete the International Space Station by an arbitrary fixed date fueled the anxiety of the workforce and introduced numerous cognitive biases into the decision-makers.

The *Challenger* accident ironically suffered from essentially the same challenges. The fact that these organizational design issues were present during the *Challenger* accident almost twenty years earlier demonstrates the complex nature of NASA's existence as a government organization. The competing goals of politicians concerned with the welfare of their constituents and their own political aspirations created a powerful force resisting sustained change. They continued to drive the organization toward delivering the near-impossible on shrinking budgets and politically driven schedules in a way that maximized investment across as many states as possible. NASA's organizational structure wasn't truly optimized to promote the desired behaviors and safety excellence, and the intense pressure employees felt to meet schedules with limited resources greatly exasperated this. We want to be clear that when we discuss the actions and statements from Linda Hamm, William Lucas, or Lawrence Malloy, we don't do so in an attempt to demonize them as individuals. Nor do we seek to excuse them for their decisions. Rather, we wish to point out the complex adaptive system they were a part of and how their Maturity and decisions were created by and helped create this complex system.

Fight Complacency

We could say much more about creating a culture that produces safety; hopefully, this overview demonstrates the holistic application of the model. As you can see, creating a culture that produces safety excellence requires integration across the entire Missing Links Model. It starts with knowing what you are designing for and intentionally identifying the critical behaviors which reduce risk while consciously managing it. The organization must demonstrate true commitment to safety, and the employees must believe this commitment is real. This means that the company must put its money where its mouth is and be willing to pay other nonmonetary costs when necessary in the name of safety.

Pursuing safety excellence is a great example of "progress over perfection" and, like personal growth, is a journey, not a destination. The organization exists within a complex dynamic environment and must constantly resist the pressures to accept more and more risk. In the words of Karen Marais et al., "When a larger view is taken, most accidents in complex systems can be seen to result from a migration to states of increasing risk over time. Once a system has migrated to an unsafe state, accidents are inevitable unless appropriate efforts are made to bring the system to a safe state."[107] Systemic analysis will help to understand when this risk is being unconsciously accepted through local decisions to optimize around short-term performance goals or other environmental adaptations. Safety, like culture, is an emergent property, and your organization's culture is your best defense against devolving safety performance.

---

[107] Karen Marais and Nancy G. Leveson, "Archetypes for Organisational Safety," MIT Department of Aeronautics and Astronautics, Accessed August 9, 2021.

Conclusion

"The world is a complex, interconnected, finite, ecological-social-psychological-economic system. We treat it as if it were not, as if it were divisible, separable, simple, and infinite. Our persistent, intractable global problems arise directly from this mismatch."
—Donella Meadows

108

The Missing Links Revisited

Your organization is a complex adaptive system whose behavior is a function of the system's structure. And because it is comprised of human beings, the system adapts and pushes back when you try to control it. Feedback loops create nonlinear behaviors and result in time delays and persistent patterns of behavior that are difficult to change. Your organization's culture is one of the most powerful influences over its behavior, which ultimately translates into performance and bottom-line results. Culture is an emergent property produced by the interaction of your employees' beliefs and behaviors. It exists between the ears of your people

---

108 https://gallaheredge.com/themissinglinks

and is the key to your success as a leader and as a company.

At the organizational level, we want to produce the traits of Maturity, Diversity, Community, and Unity. These traits define an effective culture; that is, a culture that drives business results, increases employee engagement, and improves lives. To produce these traits, we must first recognize that they are emergent properties of a complex system. It is impossible to work directly on the emergent properties themselves. Additionally, it is impossible to manipulate them by focusing solely on the elements within your organization that produce them (your employees). To intentionally create and manage your organization's culture, you will want to focus on both the elements and the relationships between those elements.

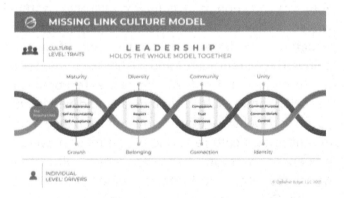

To illustrate this, consider how you manage your health. Your health is an emergent property of your body—another complex adaptive system. As you know, you don't improve your health by working directly on it. Rather you improve your health by focusing on diet, exercise, rest, and a variety of other factors. As you do this, you are not only considering each element on its own. To optimize your health, you want your diet, exercise, and rest to complement each other. The relationships between all three are as important to producing your health as each is on its own. If your volume and type of exercise, for example, isn't supported adequately by your diet and rest, it can actually have a negative impact on your health. When we factor in other variables such as genetics, age, metabolism, injury or illness, lifestyle, and environment, managing health can be fairly challenging.

Similarly, it can be both challenging and frustrating trying to manage the emergent organizational culture of your organization. To help you intentionally manage your organization's culture, we have identified the critical links between humans that you can develop and produce the desired traits. These links primarily support one of the four traits, and you can use them to connect your people together utilizing the individual drivers. Humans have an inherent individual drive for growth, belonging, connection, and identity. By leveraging these drivers, we take advantage of a strong mechanism for linking that already exists within every person. This ensures that you can easily establish the links. We are working within the natural drivers of human psychology.

As a leader, you hold this system together and influence how the links take shape and the culture emerges. Whether by design or accident, you create and shape your organization's culture. You have the ability to intentionally design experiences for your employees that produce the desired beliefs and, ultimately, behaviors that define your culture. You can also work directly on the links to instill the desired knowledge, skills, and beliefs associated with each. In doing so, you can tailor the culture to the unique DNA of your organization while ensuring it fully supports and aligns with your strategy. Designing your culture to perfectly align with and support your strategy is a truly sustainable competitive advantage that will drive your business results.

All Models Are Wrong

To this point, we have presented the model as a series of four strands that connect individual drivers to emergent cultural traits through the missing links. We feel this is an effective way to introduce and visualize how organizational culture is created and managed. However, as British statistician George Box famously said, "All models are approximations. Essentially, all models are wrong, but some are useful." In this case, we believe our model to be very useful, and the real system that it is approximating is exceptionally complex and not nearly as neat and tidy as our model.

While the links we have identified primarily support the emergent trait for their strand, there are also numerous interactions that can occur across strands. True to the nature of emergence in complex systems, we don't want to interpret the model in a reductionist manner. In practice, when applied to an organization, a single strand should not be isolated and analyzed on its own. We want to look at the model holistically and identify patterns and interconnections—not only within strands but across them.

The links work together across the model to produce desirable outcomes like accountability, collaboration, and the organization's capacity for change. Similarly, the organization's ultimate ability to execute effectively comes through a combination of multiple factors, drawing on the full model. So, when analyzing and managing your culture, step back and look at the whole model and how the strands and links are showing up in your organization. Consider how the links may be interacting with each other across the model to produce either desired or undesired organizational behavior. To help you with this and illustrate what this interaction looks like, we will provide a high-level overview of how Maturity supports the other strands.

The Self Is At the Core

We chose Maturity for our example because it is foundational to every aspect of organizational culture, as we have continually emphasized. Our Inside Out Model adeptly illustrates this with the Self at the center. Because everything starts with the self, Maturity is key to growing the capacity for individuals to function at a high level and support the other levels.

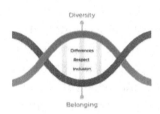

Maturity supports Diversity by allowing individuals to show up and respond to the differences of others in a way that creates space for those differences and produces a sense of belonging for all. The more you develop your Maturity, the less you are threatened by people or ideas that are different from you or who challenge your worldview and belief system. Self-acceptance decreases how you perceive a threat from their differences because you can separate whether you are right or wrong from your self-worth. The greater your ability to accept yourself as you are, the greater your ability to accept someone else as they are. Self-awareness contributes to this by allowing you to recognize when you become defensive and notice how your behavior is affecting others. As always, when you have a high level of self-accountability, you will own your reactions and feelings and take action to manage your behavior. This allows you to be intentional about reducing your defensiveness and choose behaviors that are welcoming and inclusive. A culture of Diversity emerges when people actively invite and include others.

Maturity supports Community by enabling people to build healthy relationships with others, collaborate effectively, and produce high-performing teams. Much of this relies on build-

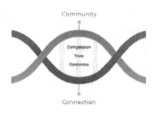

ing trust, which can only be done when people are open and truly know one another. Self-awareness is necessary for you to be open because you can't share more with others than you are aware of yourself. Openness is also supported through a willingness to be vulnerable, which requires self-acceptance. Being clear about your own intent and sharing it with others helps them understand your motivations and establish trust. We also build turst when we follow through on commitments, which requires self-accountability. Both self-acceptance and self-awareness support compassion by enabling ou to see the suffering of others and not become threatened by the reflections of our own weakness that you see in them. Before you can have compassion for others, you must first be capable of having compassion toward yourself.

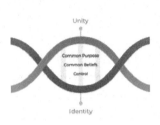

Finally, Maturity supports Unity by enabling humans to simultaneously hold the seemingly contradictory paradigms of individuality and collectivism to support both independence and conformity. To buy into a common purpose and behaviors for the organization, you must first have the self-awareness to know your own purpose and beliefs. Additioanlly, you must possess the self-acceptance to reconcile the purpose and values of the group with your own feelings and beliefs about them. And for control to effectively exist within the organization, individuals must be able to submit to this control and follow its guidance. Submitting to the control of others or taking control when most effective requires self-acceptance when those behaviors differ from. Your preferences. And, of course, self-accountability is the key to following the organization's rules and operating effectively within its structure and policies.

Integrating Across the Missing Links Model

Although Maturity is foundational to organizational culture, it is not the only trait that provides key support to the other strands. As we discussed, the links and strands all support each other. To provide you with further assistance in understanding these connections and integrating the model, we created an N2 diagram. This is a tool from systems engineering that uses a matrix to capture the inputs and outputs between the various subsystems. It is a powerful way to present a lot of information about information flows between multiple elements. A single column of this matrix is shown below, detailing how the other strands return the favor and support Maturity.

⊖ GALLAHER	TO MATURITY
FROM DIVERSITY	When I am around people who are different from me, it helps me to learn more about myself. When I am treated with respect and included, it increases my self-acceptance. Inclusion also increases self-accountability because my opinion was taken into account.
FROM COMMUNITY	When people are more open with me, it supports my self-awareness and enables me to grow. Trust from others increases my self-accountability because I am given the opportunity to contribute. Trusting others can increase self-acceptance by allowing me to be more flexible and acknowledge I can cope with the consequences.
FROM UNITY	When I have a clear understanding of boundaries and what is expected of me, that environment helps me to feel better about myself. This increases my self-acceptance and self-accountability. I understand how I am expected to contribute. This level of clarity also supports self-awareness. Connecting to the company's purpose and beliefs grows my self-awareness.

The full N2 diagram is available for download by going to *The Missing Links* book resources page.[109]

This N2 diagram is just a general overview of how the links support each other. There are almost infinite ways that the links can combine when interacting with the unique values, history, and individuals within an organization to produce specific cultural attributes. This is why there isn't a single prescription or step-by-step procedure for working with organizational culture. It's also why organizational culture is unique to a given organization and can't be easily copied or transferred to another. Your culture is one of your most sustainable forms of competitive advantage. When you do the work to intentionally design your culture to align with your strategy and produce high-performance results, it becomes a competitive advantage that others cannot easily or quickly duplicate.

Your ability to recognize how the links interact within your organizational system to produce your specific culture will grow as you deepen your understanding of the concepts we have presented. True mastery of your culture requires a deep understanding of both your organization and the science of human behavior. This is why you can't outsource culture management. When we work with organizations,

---

[109] https://gallaheredge.com/themissinglinks

we always partner with senior leaders and require their direct involvement in the process. We can provide a deep understanding of the model and its underlying science, but we must rely on you for the organization-specific knowledge. We can never understand an organization as well as the people living in it. This partnership allows us to cocreate the solutions while also ensuring that executives take full ownership of the culture in their organizations.

The End Is the Beginning—Now Is the Time to Act!

This brings us to the end of this part of our journey together. We hope this book has provided great value for you and that you will want to continue on this journey with us. We exist to evolve humanity— to help individuals grow their individual capacity enabling them to contribute to their families, organizations, and society in a greater and more impactful way. We invite you to join us in this quest.

As an individual, you can join us by continuing your journey of growth and constantly striving to increase your self-acceptance, self-awareness, and self-accountability. As a leader, you have great power to serve as a multiplier for this vision of a better world. You have the ability to create a work environment that encourages the growth and development of many others and evolve humanity through evolving your culture.

We can't promise this journey will be easy. In fact, we can probably promise it won't be. But we do feel confident in promising that it will be rewarding. This work is worth it! When you create and sustain an effective culture in your organization, you are truly impacting the lives of others in a very meaningful way. You are increasing the engagement and fulfillment that your employees receive in their jobs which has tremendous physical and psychological benefits. You are improving lives within your organization and even beyond. And bonus: you are driving business results!

So, hopefully, this isn't the end but rather the beginning. We're here to support you on this journey and would love to be a continuing part of your vision for making the world a better place through the mission of your organization. We invite you to continue engaging with our community and us with our Insider Edge platform, reading our blogs, and listening to our podcasts.

Join Insider Edge:[110]

---

[110] https://gallaheredge.com/themissinglinks#register

Blogs:[111]

Podcasts:[112]

If you haven't already, please join our Leader's Journey email list at https://gallaheredge.com/leaders-journey-mailing-list for big ideas, insights into leadership, personal growth, and transforming your company's culture from the Inside Out. And if you have any specific feedback for us regarding this book, we'd love to hear from you! Just send us a note at MissingLinks@gallaheredge.com. We believe in you and know that you can do great things. You, too, can evolve humanity!

---

[111] https://blog.gallaheredge.com/

[112] https://gallaheredge.com/podcasts/the-evolved-leader/

There is no destination, we only have the journey.

Where does your journey go from here?

References

Amen, Daniel, MD. "When You Stop Learning, Your Brain Starts Dying." *LinkedIn*. March 6, 2017. https://www.linkedin.com/pulse/when-you-stop-learning-start-dying-dr-daniel-amen.

Argyris, C. "The Executive Mind and Double-Loop Learning." *Organizational Dynamics*. 11(2) (1982): 5-22.

Ashforth, Blake E. and Mael, Fred A. "Alumni and Their Alma Mater: A Partial Test of the Reformulated Model of Organizational Identification." *Journal of Organizational Behavior* 13(2) (March 1992): 103-123.

Bang, Megan, Lee, Carol D., and Medin, Douglas. "Point of View Affects How Science Is Done." *Scientific American*. October 1, 2014. https://www.scientificamerican.com/article/point-of-view-affects-how-science-is-done.

Brown, Brené. "Shame V. Guilt." Blog Post. January 14, 2013. https://brenebrown.com/blog/2013/01/14/shame-v-guilt/#close-popup.

Burkus, David. "Work Friends Make Us More Productive (Except When They Stress Us Out).

Harvard Business Review. May 26, 2017. https://hbr.org/2017/05/work-friends-make-us-more-productive-except-when-they-stress-us-out.

Career Builder. "Do American Workers Need a Vacation? New CareerBuilder Data Shows Majority Are Burned Out at Work, While Some Are Highly Stressed or Both." May 23, 2017. https://press.careerbuilder.com/2017-05-23-Do-American-Workers-Need-a-Vacation-New-CareerBuilder-Data-Shows-Majority-Are-Burned-Out-at-Work-While-Some-Are-Highly-Stressed-or-Both.

Chowdhury, Madhuleena Roy. "How to Foster Compassion at Work Through Compassionate Leadership." *Positive Psychology*. June 16, 2021. https://positivepsychology.com/compassion-at-work-leadership.

Coca-Cola. "Coca-Cola Bottlers Dedicate Production Capability to Support COVID-19 Test Kits," *GlobeNewswire*. June 1, 2020. https://www.globenewswire.com/news-release/2020/06/01/2041439/0/en/Coca-Cola-Bottlers-Dedicate-Production-Capability-to-Support-COVID-19-Test-Kits.html.

Damasio, Antonio. *Descartes' Error*. New York: Penguin Press: 2005.

Declerck, Carolyn H., Boone, Christophe, Pauwels, Loren, Vogt, Bodo, and Fehr, Ernst. "A Registered

Replication Study on Oxytocin and Trust," Nature Human Behavior 4, (2020): 646-655, https://www.nature.com/articles/s41562-020-0878-x.

Dweck, C.S. *Mindset: The New Psychology of Success* New York: Random House, 2006.

Elmer, Jamie. "What's an Identity Crisis and Could You Be Having One?" *Healthline.* January 22, 2019. https://www.healthline.com/health/mental-health/identity-crisis.

Emplify. "Why People Value Culture More Than Compensation Now." Accessed August 6, 2021. https://emplify.com/blog/value-culture-over-compensation.

Eurich, Tasha. *Insight: Why We're Not as Self-Aware as We Think, and How Seeing Ourselves Clearly Helps Us Succeed at Work and in Life.* 2017.

Fortune Editors. "Activity on Dating Apps Has Surged During the Pandemic." *Fortune.* February 12, 2021. https://fortune.com/2021/02/12/covid-pandemic-online-dating-apps-usage-tinder-okcupid-bumble-meet-group.

Gallup. "A Global Pandemic. And its Impact on Global Engagement, Stress and the Workforce." Accessed August 6, 2021. https://www.gallup.com/workplace/349484/state-of-the-global-workplace.

aspx?g_source=EMPLOYEE_ENGAGEMENT&g_medium=topic&g_campaign=tiles.

Gartner. "Managing Organizational Change: How HR Can Deliver on Complex Organizational Change Management Initiatives." Accessed August 9, 2021, https://www.gartner.com/en/human-resources/insights/organizational-change-management.

Goldberg, Emma. "Personality Tests Are the Astrology of the Office." *New York Times*. September 18, 2019. https://www.nytimes.com/2019/09/17/style/personality-tests-office.html.

Gorman, China. "It's All About: Trust, Honesty, and Transparency." Great Places to Work. August 12, 2014. https://www.greatplacetowork.com/resources/blog/it-s-all-about-trust-honesty-and-transparency.

Hale, Wayne. "After Ten Years: Enduring Lessons." Blog Post. January 31, 2013. https://waynehale.wordpress.com/2013/01/31/after-ten-years-enduring-lessons.

Hardy, Benjamin P. *Personality isn't Permanent: Break Free from Self-Limiting Beliefs and Rewrite Your Story*. 2020.

Housman, Michael and Minor, Dylan. "Toxic Workers." *Harvard Business School*. 2015, https://

www.hbs.edu/ris/Publication%20Files/16-057_
d45c0b4f-fa19-49de-8f1b-4b12fe054fea.pdf.

HR. "The State of Employee Engagement in 2019: Leverage leadership and culture to maximize engagement." May 2019. https://www.hr.com/en/resources/free_research_white_papers/hrcom-employee-engagement-may-2019-research_jwb9ckus.html.

Hunt, Vivian, Prince, Sara, Dixon-Fyle, Sundiatu, and Yee, Lareina. "Delivering Through Diversity." *McKinsey.* January 2018. https://www.mckinsey.com/~/media/McKinsey/Business%20Functions/Organization/Our%20Insights/Delivering%20through%20diversity/Delivering-through-diversity_full-report.ashx.

Kiecolt-Galzser, Janice K., Ricker, Denise, George, Jack, Messick, George, Speicher, Carl E., Garner, Warren, and Glaser, Ronald. "Urinary Cortisol Levels, Cellular Immonocompetency, and Loneliness in Psychiatric Inpatients." *Psychosomatic Medicine* Vol. 46 No. 1 (January/February 1984).

Korn, Ferry. "Korn Ferry Institute Study Shows Link Between Self-Awareness and Company Financial Performance." June 15, 2015. https://www.kornferry.com/about-us/press/korn-ferry-institute-study-shows-link-between-self-awareness-and-company-financial-performance.

Kraaijenbrink, Jeroen. "20 Reasons Why Strategy Execution Fails." *Forbes.* September 10, 2019. https://www.forbes.com/sites/jeroenkraaijen brink/2019/09/10/20-reasons-why-strategy-execution-fails/?sh=644c2edd1ebe.

Magon, Navneet and Kalra, Sanjay. "The Orgasmic History of Oxytocin." Indian Journal of Endocrinology and Metabolism no. 3 (September 2011): 156-161. https://www.ncbi.nlm.nih.gov/pmc/articles/PMC3183515.

Mann, Annamarie. "Why We Need Best Friends at Work." *Gallup.* January 15, 2018. https://www.gallup.com/workplace/236213/why-need-best-friends-work.aspx.

Marais, Karen and Leveson, Nancy G. "Archetypes for Organisational Safety." MIT Department of Aeronautics and Astronautics. Accessed August 9, 2021.

Martino, Jessica, Pegg, Jennifer, and Pegg Frates, Elizabeth, MD. "The Connection Prescription: Using the Power of Social Interactions and the Deep Desire for Connectedness to Empower Health and Wellness." *American Journal of Lifestyle Medicine* 11 (6) (Nov/Dec 2017): 466-475.

Miller, G.E. "The U.S. is the Most Overworked Developed Nation in the World." *20 Something Finance.*

January 13, 2020. https://20somethingfinance.com/
american-hours-worked-productivity-vacation.

Nichols-Whitehead, Penney and Plumert, Jodie M.
"The Influence of Boundaries on Young

Children's Searching and Gathering." *Journal of
Cognition and Development* 2 (4) (2001): 367-388.

Osterhaus, Erin. "Honesty is the Secret to Success."
Blog Post. July 11, 2013. https://cx-journey.
com/2013/07/honesty-is-secret-to-success.html.

Phillips, Katherine W. "How Diversity Makes Us
Smarter." *Scientific American*. October 2014. https://
www.scientificamerican.com/article/how-diversity-
makes-us-smarter.

PricewaterhouseCoopers. "Redefining Business
Success in a Changing World: CEO Survey."
January 2016. https://www.pwc.com/gx/en/ceo-
survey/2016/landing-page/pwc-19th-annual-
global-ceo-survey.pdf.

Rico-Uribe, Laura Alejandra et al. "Association
of Loneliness with All-Cause Mortality: A Meta-
Analysis." *PLoS One* 13 no. 1 (January 2018). https://
www.ncbi.nlm.nih.gov/pmc/articles/PMC5754055.

Rick, Torben. "Barriers to Organizational Change."
Blog Post. September 7, 2016. https://www.

torbenrick.eu/blog/change-management/barriers-to-organizational-change.

Salvagioni, Denise Albieri Jodas, Nessello Melanda, Francine, Eumann Mesas, Arthur, Durán González, Alberto, Lopes Gabani, Flávia, and Maffei de Andrade, Selma. "Physical, Psychological and Occupational Consequences of Job Burnout: A Systematic Review of Prospective Studies." *PLoS One*, 12 (10) (October 2017). https://www.ncbi.nlm.nih.gov/pmc/articles/PMC5627926.

Schutz, Will. *The Human Element: Productivity, Self-Esteem, and the Bottom Line.* Jossey-Bass, 1994.

Silberzahn, R., Uhlmann, E.L., Martin, D.P., Anselmi, P., Aust, F., Awtrey, E., Bahník, Š et al. "Many Analysts: One Data Set: Making Transparent How Variations in Analytic Choices Affect Results." *Association for Psychological Science* 1, no. 3, (2018). https://journals.sagepub.com/doi/10.1177/2515245917747646.

Smith, Sandy. "Presenteeism Costs Business 10 Times More than Absenteeism." *EHS Today.* March 16, 2016. https://www.ehstoday.com/safety-leadership/article/21918281/presenteeism-costs-business-10-times-more-than-absenteeism.

Sorenson, Susan. "How Employee Engagement Drives Growth." *Gallup.* June 30, 2013. https://www.gallup.com/workplace/236927/employee-engagement-drives-growth.aspx.

Sorenson, Susan and Garman, Keri. "How to Tackle U.S. Employees' Stagnating Engagement." *Gallup.* June 11, 2013. https://news.gallup.com/businessjournal/162953/tackle-employees-stagnating-engagement.aspx.

Stone, Michelle. "How Edison's Invention Factory Pioneered Team Collaboration." Autodesk. Accessed August 6, 2021. https://www.autodesk.com/products/eagle/blog/how-edisons-invention-factory-pioneered-team-collaboration.

Szalavitz, Maia. "How Orphanages Kill Babies—and Why No Child Under 5 Should Be in One." *Huffington Post.* November 17, 2011. https://www.huffpost.com/entry/how-orphanages-kill-babie_b_549608.

Tamm, J. W. and Luyet, R., Radical collaboration: Five essential skills to overcome defensiveness and build successful relationships. (Pymble, N.S.W., Australia: HarperCollins, 2004).

Valtorta, Nicole K. et al. "Loneliness and Social Isolation as Risk Factors for Coronary Heart Disease and Stroke: Systematic Review and Meta-Analysis of Longitudinal Observational Studies." *Heart* 102 no. 13 (June 2016). https://heart.bmj.com/content/102/13/1009.

Volini, Erica, Schwartz, Jeff, Mallon, David, Van Durme, Yves, Hauptmann, Maren, Yan, Ramona, Poynton, Shannon. "Belonging: From Comfort to

Connection to Contribution." Deloitte. May 15, 2020. https://www2.deloitte.com/us/en/insights/focus/human-capital-trends/2020/creating-a-culture-of-belonging.html.

Zak, Paul J. "The Neuroscience of Trust: Management Behaviors that Foster Employee Engagement." Harvard Business Review. January-February 2017. https://hbr.org/2017/01/the-neuroscience-of-trust.

Acknowledgements

We are so grateful for the people who have supported our careers, our consultancy, our creation of this culture model, writing this book, and us as humans.

Thank you to Kayla Wonisch, Laura's first employee with Gallaher Edge, for all you have done to help support the growth of the business, the development of our culture models, and the creation of our online platform, Insider Edge. Thank you to Amanda Shields, our marketing manager, whose creativity and input on our book have made it ten times better!

Thank you to the people who have influenced and advanced our thinking as we developed our models: Paul Gustavson, Shane Cragun, Dr. Will Schutz, his son Ethan Schutz, and the work of The Human Element®, Gabriela Buich, and John Sterman. In gratitude to the mentors who have helped us deepen our understanding of humans at work, Judi Bell and Jim Tamm.

Thank you to the people who provided the opportunities that led to the discoveries we wrote about here, Jim Kennedy and Dr. Pat Simpkins. And for the people who worked alongside us as we made the discoveries that we wrote about in the book: the whole workforce at Kennedy Space Center and our clients. We're especially grateful to our earliest clients who took a chance on a young consultancy and have helped spread the word about how we can add value to other organizations: Gregg Pollack at Code School (now Pluralsight), Phil Dumas at UniKey Technologies, and Suneera Madhani and Sal Rehmetullah at Stax by Fattmerchant.

We each want to thank our families. (Phillip) Shelby, Brooklyn, Jared, and Lucas Meade—thank you for believing in what we are doing and your patience with the many weekends spent writing and working to add value to the world. (Laura) Paul and Wendy Gallaher—thank you for all you have done to help shape my self-concept and giving me the borderline delusional sense of self-confidence I have that I can do anything. It has helped me take big steps and make bold moves, including leaving NASA, starting Gallaher Edge, LLC, and writing this book!

About the Authors

Dr. Phillip Meade is a strategist, a public speaker and a leadership expert with a PhD in Industrial Engineering and over twenty professional publications to his name. Following the Space Shuttle *Columbia* accident, he successfully developed a plan to implement the cultural changes necessary for return to flight at Kennedy Space Center.

Dr. Laura Gallaher is an organizational psychologist, executive coach, and speaker with a PhD in Psychology. Dr. Gallaher was recruited by NASA to positively influence culture and strengthen their team leadership capabilities.

Dr. Gallaher and Dr. Meade are the co-owners of Gallaher Edge, a boutique consultancy that applies the science of human behavior to align company cultures from the inside out. Together, they have worked with dozens of organizations across various industries to help leaders develop core characteristics of Maturity, Diversity, Community, and Unity. Their unique combination of organizational psychology and management know-how is a compelling incentive for leaders who want their culture to be their competitive edge. They are best-selling *USA Today* and *Wall Street Journal* authors. Join their Leader's Journey mailing list to receive their free bi-monthly newsletter at gallaheredge.com.